GIRLS IN BLOOM

Coming of Age in the
Mid-20th Century
Women's Novel

francis booth

The words exchanged between the little girls of the band and me were of little interest; they were, moreover, but few, broken by long spells of silence on my part. This did not prevent me from taking as much pleasure in listening to them as in gazing at them when they spoke to me, in discovering in the voice of each one of them a brightly coloured picture. It was with ecstasy that I listened to their pipings. Love helps us to discern things, to discriminate. Standing in the wood, the bird-watcher at once distinguishes the twittering of the different species, which to ordinary people sound the same. The girl-watcher knows that human voices vary even more.

Marcel Proust, *In the Shadow of Young Girls in Bloom*

Do you think that only those who have reached maturity are interesting? You forget that the bud may be sweeter, and often in form is more beautiful, than the full-blown flower.

Sarah Grand, *Babs the Impossible*

There is scarcely a more favourite subject for delineation by poet and artist than the period when childhood is just melting into womanhood.

Lily Watson, *The Girl's Own Paper*, 1887

The change that comes to you when you reach the age of sixteen is very profound. Before that you were a child – now *you are able to have a child*. Before that you were content to be loved by friends and parents, now *you are old enough to love*. In other words, you are a woman – what sort of woman will you be? It's up to you.

Ann Seymour, *The Teen Age Book*, 1953

CONTENTS

GIRLS COMING OF AGE

'Your name, little girl?'

'Jane Eyre, sir.'

In uttering these words I looked up: he seemed to me a tall gentleman; but then I was very little; his features were large, and they and all the lines of his frame were equally harsh and prim.

'Well, Jane Eyre, and are you a good child?'

Impossible to reply to this in the affirmative: my little world held a contrary opinion: I was silent.

Jane Eyre, by Charlotte Brontë and *Agnes Grey* by Anne Brontë, both published in 1847, were the first in-depth, psychological portraits in literature of the transition of a strong-willed but troubled, misfit girl into an adult. They are generally said to be the first female versions of the genre known as the *bildungsroman*: the coming of age novel. They are female in three senses: they were written both by and about a woman and were intended for a female audience. The Brontës may have read Jane Austen's *Mansfield Park*, 1814, in which Fanny Price, like Jane Eyre, is brought up by relatives and her *Northanger Abbey*, which, albeit satirically, shows the coming of age of its young heroine. 'No one who had ever seen Catherine Morland in her infancy, would have supposed her born to be a heroine... But from fifteen to seventeen she was in training for a heroine.' Brontë may also have read two other, earlier eponymous novels of young women growing up: Fanny Burney's *Evelina, or the History of a Young Lady's Entrance into the World*, 1778, and Maria Edgeworth's *Belinda*, 1801. Shortly after *Jane Eyre*, Elizabeth Gaskell published another eponymous novel about an orphan girl growing up and going wrong: *Ruth*, 1853.

There had of course been many male novelists writing about girls coming of age: Samuel Richardson's *Pamela or Virtue Rewarded*, 1740, concerns a fifteen-year-old servant who resists her employer's attempts at seduction and rape and is 'rewarded' by an offer of marriage; his *Clarissa or a Young Lady's Coming of Age*, 1748, is about a girl whose parents, unlike those of Jane Eyre and Fanny Price survive and thrive. In another novel of 1748 written by a man, another Fanny – Fanny Hill – tells of her growing up into a life without virtue, beginning at the age of fourteen when her parents died. *Moll Flanders*, 1722 tells the story of another girl who grows up without a mother – she has not died but has been transported to the colonies after Moll was born in prison – and also fails to choose the path of virtue.

In France, the Marquis de Sade's *Philosophy in the Bedroom*, 1795, is about the sexual coming of age of Eugénie, a 15-year-old girl who also gladly embraces vice; Sade also wrote about two sisters coming of age along diverging paths: *Justine, or The Misfortunes of Virtue*, 1791. and *Juliette*, 1797 – which might have been subtitled *Vice Rewarded*. Back in England, Thackeray also wrote about two girls coming of age in contrasted ways in *Vanity Fair*, 1848, with Becky Sharp and Emmy Sedley, though neither of them exactly succumbs to vice.

Between *Jane Eyre* in 1847 and Carson McCullers' *The Heart is a Lonely Hunter* in 1940, my official starting date for *Girls in Bloom*, there are very few examples of female coming of age novels that were written by women as serious literature for adult readers, though there were many novel series showing girls growing up that were written for a younger female audience: the *Anne Of Green Gables* series; the Emily Starr trilogy; *Little Women* and its successors; the Pollyanna books, *Rebecca of Sunnybrook Farm* and *New Chronicles of Rebeca*, and the *What Katy Did* series, to name just the best known.

But at the beginning of the 1940s, with the decline of modernism – Virginia Woolf and James Joyce both died in 1941 – and the rise of the teenager there was a rise in popularity of the female *bildungsroman* which lasted roughly twenty years. Of the few adult, literary novels written between 1900 and 1940 I will first look at some examples from America and England.

PRECURSORS: AMERICAN PIONEERS

RACHEL GRANT: *DUMPS – A PLAIN GIRL* BY LT MEADE, 1905

LT Meade – Elizabeth Thomasina Meade Smith (1844-1914) – was an Irish author who started writing at seventeen and published at least three hundred novels under her own name, of which around a hundred and fifty were for girls. She also wrote many historical, adventure and mystery novels with a number of male collaborators and was editor of the girls' magazine *Atlanta*. Although her novels are by no means literary, even the ones aimed at a young readership often have a fine sense of literary irony that may have been lost on younger readers. In *A Girl of the People*, 1890, set in working-class Liverpool, the proud Bet, 'a tall girl, made on a large and generous scale,' who loves reading, especially *Jane Eyre*, hates to be called a mammy's girl: 'I ain't tied to nobody's apron-strings – no, not I. Wish I wor, wish I wor.' Bet is suspicious of her mother, rightly so as it turns out: she has done something awful, perhaps the worst thing a mother can do to a girl coming of age with no role models outside of literature. One of the young boys comes up to Bet:

'Oh, yer'll be in such a steaming range! She burnt yer book, yer *Jane Eyre* as yer wor reading – lor, it wor fine – the bit as you read to the Gen'ral and me, but she said as it wor a hell-fire book, and she burnt it...' The boys were right when they said she would be in a rage; her heart beat heavily, her face was white, and for an instant she pressed her forehead against the door of her mother's room and clenched her teeth.

The book burnt! The poor book which had given her pleasure, and which she had saved up her pence to buy – the book which had drawn her out of herself, and made her forget her wretched surroundings, committed to the flames – ignominiously destroyed, and called bad names, too. How dared her mother do it? how did she? The girls were right when they said she was tied to apron-strings – she was, she was! But she would bear it no longer. She would show her mother that she would submit to no leading – that she, Elizabeth Granger, the handsomest newspaper girl in Liverpool, was a woman, and her own mistress.

'She oughtn't to have done it,' half-groaned Bet. 'The poor book! And I'll never know now what's come to Jane and Rochester – I'll never know.'

One of Meade's books that was probably intended for children but is nevertheless a true coming of age story serious enough, literary enough and containing enough psychological insight to make it worth examining here, is *Dumps – A Plain Girl*, 1905, hardly a very attractive title, especially to the audience it was presumably intended for: the plain teenage girl, who would no doubt have much sympathy for the leading character. Her actual name is Rachel, but her older brothers call her Dumps. Like many girls in the female *bildungsroman*, Dumps' father is a learned and widely respected man – a professor who, in the absence of a mother, cannot look after his young family adequately. Rachel lives with her two younger brothers, Alex and Charley in a cavernous but under-furnished and always-cold house next to the London boys' school where their father teaches.

> I am going to tell the story of my life as far as I can; before I begin I must say that I do wonder why girls, as a rule, have a harder time of it than boys, and why they learn quite early in life to be patient and to give up their own will...
>
> Well now, to begin my story.
>
> I was exactly fifteen years and a half. I should not have a birthday, therefore, for six months. I was sorry for that, for birthdays are very nice; on one day at least in the year you are Queen, and you are thought more of than any one else in the house. You are put first instead of last, and you get delicious presents. Some girls get presents every day – at least every week – but my sort of girl only gets presents worth considering on her birthday. Of all my presents I loved flowers best; for we lived in London, where flowers are scarce, and we hardly ever went into the country.
>
> My name is Rachel Grant, and I expect I was a very ordinary sort of girl. Alex said so. Alex said that if I had beautiful, dancing dark eyes, and very red lips, and a good figure, I might Queen it over all the boys, even on the days when it wasn't my birthday; but he said the

true name for me should not to be Rachel, but Dumps, and how could any girl expect to rule over either boys or girls with such a name as Dumps? I suppose I was a little stodgy in my build, but father said I might grow out of that, for my mother was tall.

Ah dear! There was the sting of things; for if I had had a mother on earth I might have been a very different girl, and the boys might have been told to keep their place and not to bully poor Dumps, as they call me, so dreadfully. But I must go on with my story.

Rachel's brothers often invite friends to the house – including one Dutch boy who tells her she is very pretty – but Rachel herself hardly ever dares. When she does, her usually mild, distracted father is angry with her. 'How dare you invite people to my house without my permission?' She replies, 'I am lonely sometimes, father.' She says the words 'in a sad voice; I could not help it; there was a lump in my throat.' Her father does not notice at first but then he asks her, 'why in the world should you be lonely?' Rachel tells him she wants friends, she wants 'some one to love me.' He holds her face, which he tells her is 'nice'. Her father asks her how old she is.

'I'll be sixteen in six months,' I said. 'It is a long way off to have a birthday, but it will come in six months'.

'And then you'll be seventeen, and then eighteen, and, hey presto! you'll be a woman. My goodness, child! put off the evil day as long as you can. Keep a child as long as possible.'

'But, father, most children are happy.'

'And you are not? Good gracious me! what more do you want?'

'I don't know, father; but it seems to me that I want something.'

'Well, look here, you want girls about you do you?'

'Yes, some girls.'

Life in her all-male, dark, grim, cold house is terribly dull for Rachel. She has a 'cracked piano' which is 'not particularly pleasant to play on, and I was not particularly musical.' She likes to read, though her father has put her off learning; he does not see the need to educate girls. Not that Rachel is much bothered about education. 'I hate learning, you know. I never mean to be learned.' Despite her father's enormous academic library, she has very few story-books to read. 'I made up my mind that if the fog did not lighten a bit in the next half-hour I would put the gas on and get the story-book which I have read least often and begin it over again. Oh dear! I did wish there was some sort of mystery or some sort of adventure about to happen.' Rachel has met a couple of girls through her brothers but, 'I had not found on closer acquaintance that those girls were specially attractive to me. They were silly sort of girls; quite amiable, I am sure, but it seemed such a nonsense that they at their age should talk about boys.'

Her father sends Rachel to the country to stay for a while with an older but very sprightly widow named Miss Donnithorne who unexpectedly treats Rachel extremely well, giving her a lovely room to sleep in and buying her gifts and new clothes. The reader realises before Rachel what is going on: Miss Donnithorne is going to marry Rachel's father. Rachel herself only finds out after the marriage has actually happened. But before that, she does wonder if she would have turned out differently if she had had a mother who treated her as Miss Donnithorne does.

Perhaps if I lived always with Miss Donnithorne I should be a different sort of girl; I might even grow up less of a Dumps. But of course not. Nothing could lengthen my nose, shorten my upper lip, or make me big. I must make up my mind to be quite the plainest girl it had ever been my own misfortune to meet. For I had met myself at last in the looking glass in Miss Donnithorne's bedroom; myself and myself had come face-to-face.

In the midst of my pleasure a scolding tear rolled down one of my cheeks at the memory of that poor reflection. I had been proud to be called Rachel, but now I was almost glad that most of my world knew me as Dumps.

Nevertheless, Rachel comes back home a changed person; she has had an early coming of age. Instead of a brown paper parcel containing her clothes she has her very own trunk, with her initials, in the luggage van; it is even carried for her by porters. 'I was wearing the dark-blue dress with the grey fur, so my hands were warm with my little grey muff, and altogether I was a totally different creature from the girl who had travelled down to Chelmsford on the Saturday before.' She hopes her brothers will treat her differently now, 'would begin to see that even Dumps, with her hair neatly arranged and in a pretty costume, could look nearly as nice as other girls.' But, back in her cold, 'comfortless and hideous room,' she thinks about the 'jolly life some girls had, and even a few tears rolled down my cheeks. To be very ugly, to be in no way endowed with any special talent, and to have a great father who simply forgot your existence, was not the most enviable lot in all the world for a girl.'

Rachel takes the news of her father's marriage very badly, out of a strange combination of respect for her dead mother and a fear of change. She takes all the clothes her new stepmother gave her, puts them in the trunk with her initials on the top and, knowing how hurtful this will be, leaves them in the new room intended for her father and his new bride with a card saying, 'Returned with thanks – Rachel Grant.' Regardless, the new lady of the house cleans, brightens and warms the house and makes sure the children have enough to eat – previously the father had always had a hot dinner while the children had cold mutton bones.

> The old order had given way to the new. We were clothed; we were fed; we were considered; we were treated with kindness; our wants were attended to, our little trials sympathised with. In short, love in the true sense of the word had come into the house; the genius of Wonderment had taken to himself the genius of Order and Motherly Kindness, and this latter genius had made the whole house happy.

> But I, at least, was not prepared to take into my heart this good fairy whom the good Queen of all the fairies had sent to us. I stood in my pretty room which my step-mother had arranged for me, and felt as angry and as bitter as girl could feel.

The stepmother's kindness continues however, and Rachel gets the unimaginable sum of ten pounds a quarter as a dress allowance. 'I am quite a proud girl to-day. I am, in fact, almost grown-up; I have taken the first step upwards.' She goes to central London with her two friends and spends all the money, mostly on presents for her family. Rachel does eventually come round to her new stepmother, who introduces her to young society women, including the poised and beautiful, seventeen-year-old Lady Lilian. 'Now, if there was an absolutely radiant-looking creature on this earth, it was Lilian St. Leger. I won't attempt to describe her, for I have no words. I don't suppose if I were to take her features separately I should be able for a single moment to pronounce them perfect; but it was her sweetness and tact, and the way she seemed to envelop me with her bright presence, which was cold water to a thirsty person.'

Rachel even has something of a schoolgirl crush on her. 'I am afraid I was very much enamoured of Lady Lilian; she was the type of girl who would excite the admiration of any one.' But Lilian, to Rachel's astonishment, is unhappy with her looks and social position, and all that those things require of her. She tells Rachel that the one thing she wants is unattainable.

> 'To be very, very plain, to have a free time, to do exactly what I like – to knock over tables, to skim about the country at my own sweet will unchaperoned and unstared at; never to be expected to make a great match; never to have anyone say, "If Lilian doesn't do something wonderful we shall be disappointed."'
>
> 'Oh, well, you never will get those things,' I said. After a time I continued – for she kept looking at me – 'Would you change with me if you could?'

Lilian dodges the question, but turns out to be a true friend to Rachel; Rachel's breathless descriptions of her may well have led the reader into a *Dangerous Liaisons* mindset and we would not have been surprised to find out that the former Miss Donnithorne and Lillian intend to trick and humiliate Dumps in some way. But no. It turns out that the reason Rachel's stepmother has introduced her to Lilian is because she has recently been attending the French boarding school near Paris that Rachel is about to go to and can help smooth her entry into this, literally, foreign environment. 'I was Dumps to her – her darling, plain, practical, jolly Dumps. That was how she spoke of me. She had written to the girls whom she knew at the school, and had told me to be sure to introduce myself as her very dearest friend, as her newest and dearest.' Rachel enters the school along with two existing friends and their joint chaperone. She takes to the school like a duck to water; an ugly duckling at least. She does not turn into a swan but she does bloom and come of age.

The novel ends when she rushes back to London: her father is ill and not expected to survive. She and her step-mother kneel together by her father's bedside; 'I felt that nothing really mattered; and I knew also that the barrier between my step-mother's heart and mine had vanished.' For the first time, she calls her mother. 'For everything that was not love, but was not gratitude towards the new mother who had come into my life, had vanished for ever and ever while I knelt that night by my father's bedside... And so I turned over a new page in life, and my father was spared to us after all.'

CHARITY ROYALL: *SUMMER* BY EDITH WHARTON, 1917

Unusually for Edith Wharton (1862-1937), best known for her novels of patrician Gilded-Age New York like *The House of Mirth* and *The Age of Innocence*, this novella is set in a tiny New England town close to 'the Mountain,' from which Charity has been brought down as a baby by lawyer Royall, as he is universally known, and his wife, who is dead before the story begins; Charity and Mr Royal now live alone together in the 'red house'. 'Charity was not very clear about the Mountain; but she knew it was a bad place, and a shame to have come from;' she knows that she should be grateful to lawyer Royall for saving her. Still, Charity, like many other adolescent girls in fiction, feels trapped in her small and small-minded remote town; 'How I hate everything!' she thinks regularly to herself. She has only once in her life been to even a medium-sized town, and that only for one day.

In the course of that incredible day Charity Royall had, for the first and only time, experienced railway-travel, looked into shops with plate-glass fronts, tasted cocoanut pie, sat in a theatre, and listened to a gentleman saying unintelligible things before pictures that she would have enjoyed looking at if his explanations had not prevented her from understanding them. This initiation had shown her that North Dormer was a small place, and developed in her a thirst for information that her position as custodian of the village library had previously failed to excite.

Two afternoons a week, Charity sits at her desk in the library, 'her prison-house,' which was founded by a long dead author, 'and wondered if he felt any deader in his grave than she did in his library.'
When Mrs Royall had died, there had been talk of sending Charity to a boarding school, initiated by the kindly Miss Hatchard, but lawyer Royall

15

will not let her go. Charity understands that this is because he does not want to let her go and be on his own.

> He was a dreadfully 'lonesome' man; she had made that out because she was so 'lonesome' herself. He and she, face-to-face in that sad house, had sounded the depths of isolation; and though she felt no particular affection for him, and not the slightest gratitude, she pitied him because she was conscious that he was superior to the people about him, and that she was the only being between him and solitude.

Miss Hatchard seems to understand that Royall's feelings for his teenage ward may be other than what they seem. She tells Charity that she is too young to understand; Charity replies, 'Oh no, I ain't,' but in fact she is. It is only later that she realises that her guardian wants to become something like Mr Rochester to her Jane Eyre.

> She was awakened by a rattling at her door and jumped out of bed. She heard Mr Royall's voice, low and peremptory, and opened the door, fearing an accident. No other thought had occurred to her; but when she saw him in the doorway, a ray from the autumn moon falling on his discomposed face, she understood.
>
> For a moment they looked at each other in silence; then, as he put his foot across the threshold, she stretched out her arm and stopped him.
>
> 'You go right back from here,' she said, in a shrill voice that startled her; 'you ain't going to have that key tonight.'
>
> 'Charity, let me in. I don't want the key. I'm a lonesome man,' he began, in the deep voice that sometimes moved her.
>
> Her heart gave a startled plunge, but she continued to hold him back contemptuously. 'Well, I guess you made a mistake, then. This ain't your wife's room any longer.'
>
> She was not frightened, she simply felt a deep disgust; and perhaps he divined it or read it in her face, for after staring at her a moment he drew back and turned slowly away from the door.

In the cold light of day he asks her to marry him. 'As he stood there before her, unwieldy, shabby, disordered, the purple veins distorting the hands he pressed against the desk, and his long orator's jaw trembling with the effort of his avowal, he seemed like a hideous parody of the fatherly old man she had always known.' She mocks him. 'How long is it since you've looked at yourself in the glass?' She tells him she assumes, miser that he is, that he only wants to marry her because 'it would be cheaper to marry me that to keep a hired girl'. Charity insists that if she is to stay in the house there must be another woman; Royall gives in to her and brings in an old woman from the poorhouse as a kind of maid.

> Charity knew that what had happened on that hateful night would not happen again. She understood that, profoundly as she had despised Mr Royall ever since, he despised himself still more profoundly. If she had asked for a woman in the house it was far less for her own defense than for his humiliation. She needed no one to defend her; his humbled pride was her surest protection... Nothing now would ever shake her rule in the red house.

Soon after this, a young man comes to the village: Miss Hatchard's cousin Lucius Harney, an architect come to write a booklet on the local abandoned houses. He comes into the library and dazzles Charity with his knowledge. 'Never had her ignorance of life and literature so weighed on her as in reliving the short scene of her discomfiture.' That night she sees herself marrying him. 'A clumsy band and button fastened her unbleached night-gown about the throat. She undid it, freed her thin shoulders, and saw herself a bride in low-necked satin, walking down an aisle with Lucius Harney. He would kiss her as they left the church.' But Lucius tells Miss Hatchard what a mess the library is in; Charity takes it as a personal insult and is devastated that 'the first creature who had come toward her out of the wilderness had brought her anguish instead of joy'. But soon he makes up with her and they start to spend time together, he seeming genuinely affectionate towards her. Royall is of course jealous and tells Lucius what Charity herself has never known: she is 'the child of a drunken convict and of a mother who wasn't "half human," and was glad to have her go.' This does not seem to put Lucius off and they start to spend most of their time together until suddenly Lucius says he is leaving town. Charity decides she will not beg him, and that if he wants her he must come to her, but the night before he is due to leave she sits outside his bedroom. She does not go in.

In every pulse of her rigid body she was aware of the welcome his eyes and lips would give her; but something kept her from moving. It was not the fear of any sanction, human or heavenly; she had never in her life been afraid. It was simply that she had suddenly understood what would happen if she went in. It was the thing that did happen between young men and girls, and that North Dormer ignored in public and tutted over on the sly. It was what Miss Hatchard was still ignorant of, but every girl of Charity's class knew about before she left school... Since the day before, she had known exactly what she would feel if Harney should take her in his arms: the melting of palm into palm and mouth on mouth, and the long flame burning her from head to foot. But mixed with this feeling was another, the wondering pride in his liking for her, the startled softness that his sympathy had put into her heart. Sometimes, when her youth flushed up in her she had imagined yielding like other girls to furtive caresses in the twilight; but she could not so cheapen herself to Harney. She did not know why he was going; but since he was going she felt she must do nothing to deface the image of her that he carried away. If he wanted her he must seek her.

But Harney does not go at this time and she does eventually give way. 'With sudden vehemence he wound his arms about her, holding her head against his breast while she gave him back his kisses. An unknown Harney had revealed himself, a Harney who dominated her and yet over whom she felt herself possessed of a new mysterious power.' Royall realises what has happened. 'You – damn – whore!' he calls her. But Charity does not see things that way. 'She had always thought of love as something confused and furtive, and he made it as bright and open as the summer air.' But Harney has been deceiving her and soon after, he really does go, leaving her on a very weak pretext; she later finds out that he prefers one of her friends. 'She had given him all she had – but what was it compared to the other gifts life held for him? She understood now the case of girls like herself to whom this kind of thing happened. They gave all they had, but their all was not enough: it could not buy more than a few moments.'

Naturally, Charity is pregnant. 'Charity, till then, had been conscious only of a vague self-disgust and a frightening physical distress; now, all of a sudden, there came to her the grave surprise of motherhood.' Everyone has abandoned her; even the doctor to whom she goes for a pregnancy test tricks her. She journeys by herself up the Mountain and meets her mother who, in a melodramatic twist untypical of Wharton, is dying. Charity thinks for a while that she might go to live there but it turns out to be far too wild for her. When she comes down from the Mountain, the repentant Mr Royall turns out to be an ally and comes to take her home. 'Mr Royall seldom spoke, but his silent presence gave her, for the first time, a sense of peace and security. She knew that where he was there would be warmth rest, silence; and for the moment they were all she wanted.'

ÁNTONIA SHIMERDA: *MY ÁNTONIA* BY WILLA CATHER, 1918

This is the third of Willa Cather's (1873-1947) Midwestern pioneer novels of early twentieth century frontier life which, despite their brevity, manage to encompass the epic sweep of the pioneering move to the West, seeming to hark back to an earlier era of rugged individualism. Despite the title, Ántonia (the Shimerda family have come from Bohemia; all Czech names have the stress on the first syllable, hence the accent over the Á) is not the narrator nor even the central character; she is always slightly off to one side and a little out of focus. Nevertheless, this is a true coming of age story; at the end it fast forwards to Ántonia being a middle-aged woman having had a large number of children, but not with the narrator: despite the title, she is not and never has been 'his' Ántonia. Unusually, a female author uses a male narrator: Jim Burden, ten years old at the start of the novel – Ántonia is two years older – to tell the story of his and other immigrant families, mostly newly arrived from Europe, settling in the virgin territory of Nebraska. The Shimerdas have been tricked by a relative into paying too much for unfit, unusable land, animals and dwellings; at first they live in not much more than a hole in the ground. Ántonia's father cannot reconcile himself to this hard new life; he has been a respected musician in Bohemia but is now reduced to extreme poverty. He kills himself after one misfortune too many.

After their father's death, Ántonia's older brother Ambrosch becomes the head of the family and tries, in his own way, to protect her. When she gets a job as cook for a neighbouring family, the brother fights to stop her from becoming independent.

They had a long argument with Ambrosch about Ántonia's allowance for clothes and pocket-money. It was his plan that every cent of his sister's wages should be paid over to him each month, and he would provide her with such clothing as he thought necessary. When Mrs Harling told him firmly that she would keep fifty dollars a year for Ántonia's own use, he declared they wanted to take his sister to town and dress her up and make a fool of her. Mrs Harling gives a lively account of Ambrosch's behaviour throughout the interview; how he kept jumping up and putting on his As if he were through with the whole business, and how his mother tweaked his coat-tail and prompted him in Bohemian. Mrs Harling finally agreed to pay three dollars a week for Ántonia's services – good wages in those days – and to keep her in shoes. There had been hot dispute about the shoes, Mrs Shimerda finally saying persuasively that she would send Mrs Harling three fat geese every year to 'make even.' Ambrosch was to bring his sister to town next Saturday.

'She'll be awkward and rough at first, like enough,' grandmother said anxiously, 'but unless she's been spoiled by the hard life she's led, she has it in her to be a real helpful girl.'

Mrs Harling laughed her quick, decided laugh. 'Oh, I'm not worrying, Mrs Burden! I can bring something out of that girl. She's barely seventeen, not too old to learn new ways. She's good looking too!' she added warmly.

The narrator, Jim, tells us how good it is 'to have Ántonia near us again; to see her every day and almost every night!' But he does not seem to have, and certainly does not convey to Tony, as he sometimes calls her, any romantic or sexual desires towards her, even though he is 'jealous of Tony's admiration for Charley Harling. Because he was always first in his classes at school, and could mend water-pipes or the door-bell and take the clock to pieces, she seemed to think him a sort of Prince. Nothing that Charley wanted was too much trouble for her.'

Jim's family move from the relative wilderness of the open fields to the relative civilisation of the nearest nearby town, Black Hawk. All this is happening just at the time in American history where the Europeans who had first tamed the wild plains of states like Nebraska were Europeanising the frontier. This is America's *bildungsroman* as much as Ántonia's, the story of the journey from virgin to sophisticate, from wild to tamed, from ingenuous to knowing, innocent to cynical, unstoried to storied. Much is gained, and much is lost in that journey.

> There was a curious social situation in Black Hawk. All the men felt the attraction of the foreign, well-set-up country girls who had come to town to earn a living, and, in nearly every case, to help the father struggle out of debt, or to make it possible for the younger children of the family to go to school.
>
> These girls had grown up in the first bitter-hard times, and had got little schooling themselves. But the younger brothers and sisters, for whom they made such sacrifices and who have had 'advantages,' never seem to me, when I meet them now, half as interesting or as well educated. The older girls, who helped break up the wild sod, learned so much from life, from poverty, from their mothers and grandmothers; they had all, like Ántonia, been early awakened and made observant by coming at a tender age from an old country to a new.

From time to time, travelling entertainers set up a tent in the town where they stage plays and hold dances. 'Ántonia talked and thought of nothing but the tent.' This changes not only Ántonia – formerly a total innocent – but men's attitudes to her. She has come of age from girl to woman in their eyes.

> Ántonia's success at the tent had its consequences. The iceman lingered too long now, when he came into the covered porch to fill the refrigerator. The delivery boys hung about the kitchen when they brought the groceries. Young farmers who were in town for Saturday came tramping through the yard to the back door to engage dancers, or to invite Tony to parties and picnics.

Mr Harling, acting, like her own brother, *in loco parentis*, tells her she must stop. 'This is what I've been expecting, Ántonia. You've been going with girls who have a reputation for being free and easy, and now you've got the same reputation... This is the end of it, to-night. It stops, short. You can quit going to these dances, or you can hunt another place. Think it over.' For him, as for most men, a girl can either be a shy virgin or a seductive siren; there is no middle ground. Ántonia decides to leave, she has been offered work in another house. Mrs Harling tells her something has changed within her. 'I don't know, something has... A girl like me has got to take her good times when she can. Maybe there won't be any tent next year. I guess I want to have my fling, like the other girls.' The narrator himself seems to think that Ántonia is now available: he takes her home after the dance and tells her she must kiss him good night. 'Why, Jim! You know you ain't right to kiss me like that. I'll tell your grandmother on you!' He tells her that her friend Lena let him kiss her, 'and I'm not half as fond of her as I am of you.' Being two years older than Jim, Ántonia is more concerned about his future than he is for hers.

> 'Lena does?' Tony gasped. 'If she's up to any of her nonsense with you, I'll scratch her eyes out!' She took my arm again and we walked out of the gate and up and down the sidewalk. 'Now, don't you go and be a fool like some of these town boys. You're not going to sit around here and whittle store-boxes and tell stories all your life. You are going away to school and make something of yourself. I'm just awful proud of you. You won't go and get mixed up with the Swedes, will you?'
>
> 'I don't care anything about any of them but you,' I said. 'And you'll always treat me like a kid, I suppose.'
>
> She laughed and threw her arms around me. 'I expect I will, but you're a kid I'm awfully fond of anyhow!'

Jim does make good, ending up at Harvard. Ántonia on the other hand is tricked by the man she had been going out with into going away with him; he leaves her, pregnant, before they are married. She returns in shame though she is unbowed. When he comes back from school Jim says to her, 'since I've been away, I think of you more often than of anyone else in this part of the world. I'd have liked to have you for a sweetheart, or a wife, or my mother or my sister – anything that a woman can be to a man.' She looks at him with her 'bright, believing eyes,' glad that he remembers her so fondly when she had disappointed him. 'Ain't it wonderful, Jim, how much people can mean to each other? I'm so glad we had each other when we were little. I can't wait till my little girl's old enough to tell her about all things we used to do.' Jim tells her when he goes away again that he will come back, but he doesn't; 'life intervened, and it was twenty years before I kept my promise.' By this time she is married to a poor but honest man from Bohemia and has a large number of children.

> Before I could sit down in the chair she offered me, the miracle happened; one of those quiet moments that clutch the heart, and take more courage than the noisy, excited passages in life. Ántonia came in and stood before me; a stalwart, brown woman, flat-chested, her curly brown hair a little grizzled. It was a shock, of course. It always is, to meet people after long years, especially if they have lived as much and as hard as this woman had. We stood looking at each other. The eyes that peered anxiously at me were – simply Ántonia's eyes.

MIRANDA GAY: *PALE HORSE, PALE RIDER* BY KATHERINE ANNE PORTER, 1937

Katherine Anne Porter (1890-1980) is most famous now for her only novel, *Ship of Fools*, begun in 1931 but only finished and published in 1962. Apart from this she published only short stories, fewer than thirty, but still has a reputation as one of the century's greatest stylists. She had a fascinating life: having been born in Texas, she married three husbands of various nationalities and lived in several countries, including Mexico, where many of her stories are set, and Bermuda where she began her stories about Miranda Grey, who is usually considered to be her alter ego and spokeswoman. *Pale Horse, Pale Rider* of 1937 consists of three of what Porter called short novels, though they are really long short stories. The first, 'Old Mortality' and the third, which is the title story, concern Miranda; in the first we see her, very briefly, coming of age and in the third she is a young career woman working as a journalist during the First World War, falling in love with a young soldier and getting caught in the Spanish Flu epidemic.

Despite its brevity, 'Old Mortality' is in three parts – in the first Miranda is eight, in the second she is ten and in the third she is eighteen and has eloped from home. Also despite its brevity, the story has more insight into a young woman's coming of age and her relationship to her family and the outside world than many full-length novels. The first part, which finishes in 1902, features Miranda and her older sister.

> Maria and Miranda, aged twelve and eight years, knew they were young, though they felt they had lived a long time. They had lived not only their own years; but their memories, it seemed to them, began years before they were born, in the lives of the grown-ups around them, old people above forty, most of them, who had a way of insisting that they too had been young once. It was hard to believe.

> Miranda persisted through her childhood in believing, in spite of her smallness, thinness, a little snubby nose saddled with freckles, her speckled gray eyes and habitual tantrums, that by some miracle she would grow into a tall, cream-colored brunette, like Cousin Isabel; she decided always to wear a trailing white satin gown. Maria, born sensible, had no such illusions. 'We are going to take after my Mamma's family,' she said. 'It's no use, we are. We'll never be beautiful, we'll always have freckles. And *you*,' she told Miranda, 'haven't even a good disposition.'

Cousin Isabel is a source of romantic wonder and an object of admiration for the two girls as is Aunt Amy, who 'belonged to the world of poetry,' whereas Cousin Eva, 'shy and generous, straining her upper lip over to enormous teeth,' was 'a blot, no doubt about it, but the little girls felt she belonged to the everyday world of dull lessons to be learned, stiff shoes to be limbered up, scratchy flannels to be endured in cold weather, measles and disappointed expectations.' Eva wears her mother's old clothes and teaches Latin in a women's school while she travels around making suffragist speeches, for which she later goes to jail.

Later, the two sisters, 'who read as naturally and constantly as ponies cropped grass, and with much the same kind of pleasure,' discover some 'forbidden reading matter,' gothic novels about 'beautiful but unlucky maidens, who for mysterious reasons had been trapped by nuns and priests in dire collusion; they were then "immured" in convents.' The word immured perfectly describes to them their situation. 'It was the word Maria and Miranda had been needing all along to describe their condition at the Convent of the Rapture of Jesus, in New Orleans, where they spent the long winters trying to avoid an education.' The convent is their home, 'their familiar world of shining bare floors and insipid whole-some food and cold-water washing and regular prayers; their world of poverty, chastity and obedience, of early to bed and early to rise, of sharp little rules and tittle tattle.'

At the age of ten, Miranda decides she is going to be a jockey when she grows up – not that she is going to grow very far up. 'Her father had said one day that she was going to be a little thing all her life, she would never be tall; and this meant, of course, that she would never be a beauty like aunt Amy, or Cousin Isabel. Her hope of being a beauty died hard, until the notion of being a jockey came suddenly and filled all her thoughts.' The father is not sympathetic towards the girls: '"Nest of vi-pers," he boasted, "perfect match of serpents teeth. Can't do anything with 'em." He fluffed up Miranda's hair, pretending to tousle it.'

The next time we see Miranda she is eighteen and has run away to be married, though we are told nothing about either the elopement or the husband. She meets Cousin Eva on a train taking them both to Aunt Amy's funeral; Eva is now fully committed to the suffragist movement for which she has been to jail three times. Miranda has not seen her father since she eloped and he does not welcome her with open arms, in fact he physically pushes her away when he sees her. The end of 'Old Mortality' is one of the best extended descriptions of a girl's coming of age in all of the literature about female adolescence.

'Where are my own people and my own time?' She resented, slowly and deeply and in profound silence, the presence of these aliens who lectured and admonished her, who loved her with bitterness and de-nied her the right to look at the world with her own eyes, who de-manded that she accept their version of life and yet could not tell her the truth, not in the smallest thing. 'I hate them both,' her most inner and secret mind set plainly, '*I will be free of them, I shall not even remember them...*'

She did not want any more ties with this house, she was going to leave it, and she was not going back to her husband's family either. She would have no more bonds that smothered her in love and hatred. She knew now why she had run away to marriage, and she knew that she was going to run away from marriage, and she was not going to stay in any place, with anyone, that threatened to forbid her making her own discoveries, that said 'No' to her...

Oh, what is life, she asked herself in desperate seriousness, in those childish unanswerable words, and what shall I do with it? It is something of my own, she thought in a fury of jealous possessiveness, what shall I make of it?...

Her mind closed stubbornly against remembering, not the past but the legend of the past, other people's memory of the past, at which she had spent her life peering in wonder like a child at a magic-lantern show. Ah, but there is my own life to come yet, she thought, my own life now and beyond. I don't want any promises, I won't have false hopes. I won't be romantic about myself. I can't live in their world any longer, she told herself, listening to the voices back of her. Let them tell stories to each other. Let them go on explaining how things happened. I don't care. At least I can know the truth about what happens to me, she assured herself silently, making a promise to herself, in her hopefulness, her ignorance.

PRECURSORS: ROSAMOND LEHMANN

Most of the adolescent young women in English women's novels from between the two world wars come from privileged, upper-middle-class backgrounds, very much unlike their American counterparts. Like their authors they are often privately educated and only mix within their own social circle, though they may be vaguely aware of the servants. Their concerns are often to do with being a debutante, their coming out ball, finding the right husband. Often these novels are as much comedies of manners as they are coming of age novels, painted with the delicacy of a miniaturist using a very restricted colour palette compared to American novels.

Rosamond Lehmann (1901-1990) was born into privilege and a literary family. The father was the editor of Punch and a Liberal MP; her mother was from Boston, Massachusetts. She and her siblings, together with some of the neighbours' children, were privately educated in a pavilion built specially for the purpose at the end of the garden of their very substantial house, which employed, in addition to the children's' nannies, governesses and tutors, nine servants indoors and four gardeners outdoors.

> My parents didn't approve of girls' schools and we were educated at home... We learned excellent French from our governess, music from a lady in the village, and a charming young woman came from London one week to as drawing. I had the run of my father's library. I was allowed to read anything, and I did.

However, before the First World War, a financial miscalculation reduced the family's circumstances, though hardly to poverty. 'My father was very well off, but he lost half his capital by entrusting it to a friend who speculated with it on the stock market. The poor man shot himself; we became much less rich. We didn't have to leave our home, but it meant the departure of our hated Belgian governess, the loss of our horses and stables, and a much smaller staff'. Lehmann was the second of four children, the great-grandchildren of Robert Chambers who founded Chambers Dictionary. Her sister Beatrix was an actor, stage director and writer, and her brother John a writer and editor.

My grandparents, Frederick and Nina, had a literary and musical sa-lon in mid-Victorian times. Nina was a brilliant pianist and had played with Clara Schumann and Joachim. Writers such as Robert Browning, Charles Dickens, and Wilkie Collins were their close friends. My great-uncle was the painter Henri Lehmann, who did that famous portrait of Liszt. His brother Rudolf painted most of the Vic-torian celebrities of the day. The two brothers' portraits hung in my father's library. I used to sit there and think of them as my ancestors; I feared I could never be worthy of my heritage.

In 1919, Lehmann went as a scholar to Girton College Cambridge, found-ed in 1869 as a women's college, where she gained a degree in English; although she did not believe in girls' schools, Rosamond's mother had herself attended the women's section of Harvard University, after which he lectured in literature to classes of ladies, and became a staunch suffra-gette when she came to England. After the failure in 1940 of her second marriage, Lehmann began a relationship with the poet Cecil Day Lewis which lasted until 1949. During this period published only one novel but had several stories in *New Writing*, a literary magazine committed to anti-fascism, founded in 1936 by her brother John. After her first novel, *Dusty Answer*, 1927 which we will look at shortly, Lehmann published *A Note in Music*, 1930, about two northern women trapped in loveless mar-riages, *Invitation to the Waltz*, 1932, a much lighter work, which we will also look at shortly and a kind of sequel to it, *The Weather in the Streets*, 1936. This was followed after a long gap by *The Ballad and the Source*, 1945 and *The Echoing Grove*, 1953. After the tragic death in 1958 of her young daughter Sally, who was married to the poet JP Cavanagh, she stopped writing but then became interested in spiritualism and published *The Swan in the Evening*, 1967, a kind of fragmentary spiritual autobiog-raphy and in 1976 *A Sea-Grape Tree*, containing more spiritual insights.

In a 1985 interview, Lehmann said that she started writing very early: 'The first time I actually wrote something was at the age of five or six. I was sitting in a walnut tree, eating toffee, and there was a scribbling block on my knees. Suddenly, I started to write a poem. It had three or four stanzas.' Coming from a literary family she found some encourage-ment, though not from her mother; like Maude Hutchins, whom we will examine in detail later, Lehmann had to fight against the family values of stern, patrician New Englanders.

> My mother was from New England. She was very puritanical and upright, and she didn't want us to be conceited. I remember —oh so vividly!—her saying to a guest, 'Rosie writes doggerel,' which pierced me to the heart. But my father was very encouraging, as he was a writer himself and came from a highly literary and artistic family.

In another interview Lehmann said that from an early age her father that no trying to select words for their accuracy and weight, and directed my voracious appetite for reading, and encourage me with unfailing sympathy and patience.'

Lehmann wrote from and mostly about a world that was dying even then: the world of the girl born into the pre-First-World-war English upper-middle class, privileged and set apart from mainstream society, as did some her contemporaries born around the turn of the century: Antonia White, whose *Frost in May*, 1933, is about girls in a convent school, Elizabeth Bowen (1899-1973), whose *The Death of the Heart* we will look at in a later chapter and Elizabeth Taylor (1912-1975), whose *Palladian*, 1946, is a reworking of *Jane Eyre*.

JUDITH EARLE: *DUSTY ANSWER*, 1927

The first lesbian novel is usually said to be *The Well of Loneliness* of 1928 by Radclyffe Hall but *Dusty Answer* by Rosamond Lehmann precedes it by a year. As in Hall's novel there is no explicit lesbianism but there is a strongly implied relationship between two girls at college which was noted by outraged critics of the time, one of whom wrote an article in the London *Evening Standard* titled 'The Perils of Youth,' addressing what he presumed to be the degenerate readers of Lehman's novel: 'To all these sex-ridden young men and women I would counsel, as the best remedy for their troubles, silence and self-control. And I would have them remember that all their discussions will never carry them back beyond the plain unvarnished statement of Genesis, "Male and female created He them"'". Lehmann herself said that the critics regarded her works as 'the ravings of a nymphomaniac.'

It is hard to imagine now why critics were so incensed by *Dusty Answer*: it is a very gentle, bittersweet novel of the manners of the upper-middle-class England of its time, as well as being a *bildungsroman* following Judith's progress through adolescence. Like her author, Judith has been brought up in privilege and privately educated. The first part of the book is a reminiscence of her childhood and her relationship with the cousins who lived next door to her family. By the end of the book she will have had sex – albeit, as it were, offstage – with one of the boys and offered herself – albeit half-heartedly – to the other two. But her main passion is a young woman she meets when she goes to college; for the first she in her life she is meeting people outside her immediate circle and she has a room of her own at last. She is on the way to her coming of age, though she finds that the price of freedom is a separation from the certainties of childhood. 'She sat on a hard chair and said to herself: Independence at last. This is Life. Life at last is beginning; but rather because it seemed so much more like a painful death than because she believed it.'

She is at first out of her depth and lonely in this unfamiliar environment; one of her colleagues asks her if there is anyone she knows from her school. 'I've never been to school. This is the first time I've ever been away from home,' she says. But then she meets Jennifer who, as it turns out, will be the love of her life, even though she loses her in the end. There is never any description of the physical relationship between the two women, though it is strongly implied. At first she does not know the true nature of her feelings, does not dare to confide in Jennifer. Ironically, they first become close over her feelings for Roddy, one of her former neighbours, whom, pre- and post-Jennifer she also thinks is the love of her life and with whom she will make love; her first and only time with a man in the book.

Alone in the dark she stood still and contemplated the appalling image of Roddy risen up again, mockingly asserting that only he was real; that his power to give himself or withhold himself was as the power of life and death.

It was urgent, now, to find Jennifer quickly. She was in her room, lying on the floor, staring at the flicker of firelight over her yellow velvet frock.

'Oh Jennifer!'

Judith sank down beside her, burying her face in her lap.

'Darling.'

'I'm not very happy tonight. It's a mood. I think I don't feel very well. And the night seems so sad and uneasy, with this wind. Don't you feel it?'

Jennifer put out her hands and clasped them round Judith's face, gazing at her sombrely.

'What has he said to you?' she whispered.

'Who?'

'That Martin.'

'Nothing. It's nothing to do with him.'

'You love somebody, I think. Who is it you love?'

'I love nobody.'

Jennifer must never know, suspect, think for a moment...

'You mustn't love anybody,' said Jennifer. I should want to kill him. I should be jealous.' Her brooding eyes fell heavily on Judith's lifted face. 'I love you.'

And at those words, that look, Roddy faded again harmlessly: Jennifer blinded and enfolded her senses once more, and only Jennifer had power.

Judith becomes obsessed with Jennifer. 'Always Jennifer. It was impossible to drink up enough of her; and a day without her was a day with the light gone.' Lehmann's detached authorial voice occasionally shifts into second person to get us closer to Judith. 'Was it that people had the day and the night in them, mixed in varying quantities? Jennifer had the strength of day, and you the strength of night. By day, your little glow was merged in her radiance; but the night was stronger, and overcame her.' The two girls spend as much time as possible together, going swimming together naked; Judith admires Jennifer as if she were a Greek statue. They read and study together, talking with 'excitement, with anxiety, as if tomorrow might part them and leave them for ever burdened with the weight of all they had had to tell each other.' Jennifer becomes 'the part of you which you never had been able to untie and set free, the part that wanted to dance and run and sing, taking strong drafts of wind and sunlight... And yet was checked by a voice that said doubtfully that there were dark ideas behind it all, tangling the web; and turned you inward to grope among the roots of thought and feeling for the threads.'

Of course this intensity cannot last, and it doesn't. By the third year, 'Jennifer was no longer the same. Somewhere she had turned aside without a word, and set her face to a new road. She did not want to be followed. She had given Judith the slip, in the dark.' It turns out that there is another woman in Jennifer's life: the older, more sophisticated and very butch Geraldine, 'so mature and well-dressed; if there was to be a fight, what chance was there for a thin young student in a woollen jumper?' Judith has lost Jennifer but has become almost reconciled; 'how ridiculous, how sad to have made one person into all poetry!' After Jennifer, 'there was nothing in life save work,' as Judith prepares for her exams. 'Three hours. It was over. You could not remember what you have written; but you had never felt more firm and sure of mind. Three hours nearer to life.'

But leaving college these is a great hole in this life, 'a great idleness under whose burden you felt lost and oppressed.' Judith thinks only of the 'single tremendous calamitous significance of Jennifer, how since her going it had been like the muddy bed of the lake whose waters had been sapped day after day in a long drought.' As she leaves the college building for the last time, she leaves behind no real friends: her absorption in Jennifer has prevented her from coming close to anyone else.

Judith returns home and immediately goes off with her society mother – there is no father – to the south of France, travelling around with her, staying in good hotels, dressing elegantly and socialising with equally shallow socialites. But then she meets Roddy again: 'After all, was she going to be obliged to live, to feel, to want to want again?' She is. 'Now the little boy Roddy was this tall man whose shoulder touching hers was more bewildering than the moonrise; whose head above hers was a barrier blocking out the world... The web had broken. Roddy had shaken himself free and come close at last. The whole of their past lives had led them inevitably to this hour.'

He put his hand beneath her chin and turned her face up to his.

'Lovely Judy. Lovely dark eyes . . . Oh your mouth. I wanted to kiss it for years.'

'You can kiss it whenever you want to. I'd love you to kiss me. All of me belongs to you.'

He muttered a brief 'Oh!' beneath his breath, and seized her, clasped her wildly. She could neither move nor breathe; her long hair broke from its last pins and fell down her back, and he lifted her up and carried her beneath the unstirring willow trees.

He had brought her back home. Languorous and bemused she stepped out upon the bank in the breaking dawn, and turned to look at him beneath her heavy lids. She could not see him clearly; he seemed blurred, far away.

'Goodbye,' he said briefly.

'I'll see you before you go,' she said mechanically.

It seems as though Roddy has taken Judith's virginity – or she has given it to him – under the willow trees; it is only implied here but she confirms it later on. Roddy does not love her and does not even want to see her after the incident but still she does not regret it.

After all, it did not seem to have been much: certainly not more than could be borne in secret, without a sign.

It had all been experience, and that was a salutary thing.

You might write a book now, and make him one of the characters; or take up music seriously; or kill yourself.

This is undoubtedly a coming of age moment for her, though not the final one. On the rebound, and only to hurt Roddy, she agrees to marry Martin, another of her childhood neighbours; he is very sweet and charming to her and loves her completely but she cannot really see him as anything other than a childhood friend. 'Poor Martin was not going to be able to save her. Perhaps, instead she was going to destroy him.' Judith quickly relents and tells Martin she cannot marry him; he is devastated and subsequently dies in a boating accident – it is not clear whether or not he has killed himself. Judith continues to travel with her mother and live a shallow life in her mother's shallow international society.

The hours of every day were bubbles lightly gone.

She was Miss Earle, travelling with her elegant and charming mother, staying at the smartest hotel and prominent in the ephemeral

summer society of the health-resort. Her old education sank into dis-
reputable insignificance; best not to refer to it. She was adequately
equipped in other ways. She had a string of pearls, and slim straight
black frocks for the morning, and delicious white and yellow and
green and pink ones for the afternoon; and white jumpers with pleated skirts and little white hats for tennis; and, for the evening, straight
exquisitely-cut sleeveless frocks to dance in...

'If only you were a little more stupid,' said Mamma, 'you might
make a success of the London season even at this late date.'

While travelling she meets Julian, the third of the cousins who used to
live next door to her; he is now a world-weary, experienced and cynical
playboy who offers to make her his mistress, though he makes it clear he
is not interested in marriage. 'Julian must save her this time: surely his
wit and wisdom, surely the unknown world of sexual, emotional and intellectual experience which he held so temptingly, just out of reach –
surely these would, in time, heap an abiding mound upon the past.' But
following the news of Roddy's death, before she has chance to sleep with
him, she changes her mind, implying to him that she is still a virgin. 'Julian – I couldn't give you – what you wanted. I couldn't! It's such a step –
you don't realise – for a woman. She can't ever go back – afterwards, and
be safe in the world. And she might want to.' She does let him kiss her,
however and thinks: 'Now I've been kissed by all three of them.' Julian
later writes Judith a very long letter asking if they can still be friends.
'What a year this has been, and how we grow up!' she answers him. 'I am
all uprooted, and don't know what I shall do. I must begin to make plans.
I suppose I shall never emerge from obscurity in any way. I used to think
it a certainty that I should... Enchantment has vanished from the world.
Perhaps it will never come back, save in memory. Perhaps I shared with
you the last gleam I shall have of it.'

Jennifer also writes to her; she is still with Geraldine and has cut her
hair short in sympathy with her and as a sign of her sexuality. Jennifer
agrees to meet Judith at the cafe in Cambridge that they used to go to
together; Judith goes but Jennifer does not show up. Judith goes home,
perhaps for the last time, finally come of age.

She was going home again to be alone. She smiled, thinking suddenly that she might be considered an object for pity, so complete was her loneliness.

One by one they had all gone from her: Jennifer the last to go. Perhaps Jennifer had never for an instant meant to come back; or perhaps her courage had failed her at the last moment...

We she reached home she would find that the cherry tree in the garden had been cut down. This morning she had seen the gardener start to lay the axe to its dying trunk. Even the cherry tree would be gone. Next door the board would be up: For Sale. None of the children next door had been for her. Yet she, from outside, had broken in among them and taken them one by one for herself. She had been stronger than their combined force, after all.

She was rid at last of the weakness, the futile obsession of dependence on other people. She had nobody now except herself, and that was best.

This was to be happy – this emptiness, this light coloured state, this no-thought and no-feeling.

She was a person who is so past made one great circle, completed now and ready to be discarded.

Soon she must begin to think: What next?

But not quite yet.

OLIVIA CURTIS: INVITATION TO THE WALTZ, 1932

As we saw, Rosamond Lehmann had already written about an adolescent woman in her lyrical first novel *Dusty Answer*; her second novel, *Invitation to the Waltz* is also about an adolescent girl, though it is far lighter in tone than its predecessor and indeed than most of Lehmann's novels. Olivia, who is seventeen on the day the novel opens, lives in a grand country house with her older sister Kate, her parents and a lecherous old uncle. Nothing much happens in the novel except Olivia's preparation for and attendance at her first ball, which does act as a kind of coming of age as well as a coming out for her.

Olivia is typical of the younger sister in fiction, in that she admires and envies her older sister and always feels like the naughty child in the family. The novel opens with Kate waking Olivia in the morning, as she often does; 'regularly one began the day convicted of inferiority, a sluggish voluptuous nature, seriously lacking in will-power. After I'm married I shall stay in bed as long as I want to. Girls often marry at my age. Seventeen today.' Girls of her class are of course often married off to someone suitable, someone who might be at their first ball; Olivia's is imminent and she is aware that she needs to become a woman, even though Kate is not yet married. Both sisters despair of their mother's ability to find them someone worth marrying. 'Mum's standards are so shatteringly low. Always creatures we must be kind to because they're albinos or because they've got hare lips or impediments in their speech.' But Olivia knows she must prepare herself for the inevitable and keeps scrutinising herself to see if she is ready. 'Nowadays a peculiar emotion accompanied the moment of looking in the mirror: fitfully, rarely a stranger might emerge: a new self.'

> In the glass was a rather plain girl with brown hair and eyes, and a figure well grown but neither particularly graceful nor compact . . . But hope had sprung up, half-suppressed, dubious, irrational, as if a dream had left a sense of prophecy . . . Am I not to be ugly after all?
>
> Now I'm seventeen I shall begin to fine down . . . But supposing I'm unable to fine down? There was Kate, who had never had phases. Long lines had acquired light curves with effortless simplicity, and a grace which home-made jumpers might blur but could not conceal. It was unfair that she should have such an easy life; though of course when accused she said she had plenty to worry her: the shortness of her eyelashes, a spot on the chin now and then, a red V at the base of the neck in summer. What were these details compared with a blemished whole?

For Olivia's birthday, Kate has bought her 'a fat leather diary with a lock.' Olivia is genuinely delighted: 'such broad thick paper; room for every kind of private documents; absolute secrecy.' As for most adolescent girls, secrecy is paramount; a diary is somewhere to write one's private thoughts, to converse unheard and unread with the *other* self who is the confidante that the diary represents – to confide in someone who will never betray her. But where to put the key? Olivia's disgusting old uncle Oswald, her father's brother who lives with them, has an idea: he will keep it on his watch chain. Olivia laughs off the suggestion, 'but picturing that key dangling on his paunch, at the disposal of those plump secretive paws, those pages naked at night beneath the opaque scrutiny of those caramel eyes, she felt her blood freeze.' Oswald leers at her. 'A young girl's innermost thoughts, dreams . . . What could be more delightful?' Kate takes her turn at trying to swat him away but he carries on, 'sometimes I wonder if I mightn't – perhaps – be – just a *trifle* – shocked?' He wouldn't be. Olivia keeps the diary in her desk and confides her innermost thoughts to it but none of them are shocking, even to a lecherous, paedophile old uncle.

> My seventeenth birthday. I have decided to keep a record of my inmost real-self thoughts. Perhaps it will help me to find out what I am really like: horrid, I know: selfish, conceited, and material-minded. For instance, lately whenever I tried to concentrate on anything serious or beautiful, I started thinking about the Spencers' dance next week. I am ashamed of my pettiness. I'm going to try to do better this year – develop my character more and not always be thinking about enjoying myself. Always being so happy, I dread disappointment and unhappiness, but they would be good for me. *But I don't want them.*
>
> In this journal I shall write out any poetry that I like – also any poetry I make up. Also perhaps some of my dreams, as they really are so very extraordinary...
>
> *Advice to Young Journal Keepers*. Be lenient with yourself. Conceal your worst faults, leave out your most shameful thoughts, actions and temptations. Give yourself all the good and interesting qualities you want and haven't got. If you should die young, what comfort would it be to your relatives to read the truth and have to say, It is not a pearl we have lost, but a swine?

Good advice indeed, though not followed by most of the young journal keepers in *Girls in Bloom*. The bulk of the novel is taken up with the actual ball itself though nothing significant happens except that Olivia is predictably embarrassed both by the dress that has been made for her by a local dressmaker and her own social ineptitude. Lehmann's patronising view of Olivia is shown by the conversation she has at the ball with Rollo, the son of the Spencers who own the house; his literary taste is obviously far closer to Lehmann's own modernist style than Olivia's predictable and pedestrian schoolgirl taste, which Lehmann, though not Rollo, seems to mock, though very gently. Olivia is fascinated and treats this as a very serious conversation; by her standards it is, though not perhaps by Rollo's.

'What sort of things do you like?'
'Reading mostly. And going for walks by myself. And talking to Kate – that's my sister.'
'What kind of books do you like?'
'Any kind almost. I like poetry especially. The Brontës and Dickens are my favourite novelists, but I like Thackeray too, specially *Vanity Fair* – and George Eliot and Jane Austen. I don't like Scott.'
'Oh, don't you? I rather enjoy a tussle with old Scott.'
'What are *your* favourite authors?'
She hadn't felt so happy all evening. Such an interesting, serious conversation.
'Mine? Oh, I only truly love two books in all the world.'
'What are they?'
'One's called *Tom Jones*. The other's called *Tristram Shandy*. Directly I finish one I start the other, and so on . . . '
'I haven't read them. I must.'

It doesn't seem likely that she will. Despite the lightness of this novel, there is a poignant description of a girl's coming of age which comes, surprisingly, from Uncle Oswald on seeing her coming out of her room in her new dress about to go to the ball.

'*Aha!*' He looked her up and down. She heard his paunchy breathing.
'Oh . . . Do you like it? I –' she put a hand up to her plaits, looked down, feeling the blush begin.
'Charming,' he whispered. '*Siebzehn Jahre alt!* Going to her first ball. Ah!'
She said agitatedly:
'Oh . . . I'm all wrong – I know I am . . . I simply can't get it right. I don't know . . .'
What am I saying – to him of all people? Helplessly she stared into his unknown, his familiar face.
He whispered, nodding rapidly:

'Never mind. You must just wait. Say another ten years.'

'Ten years?'

'About that.'

'Oh . . . But I'll be old. Twenty-seven.'

'Say thirty. You'll be all right then.'

She cried out protestingly.

'Oh, what a long time!'

The shadow of a smile ran over his face.

'You won't find it so. It goes extraordinarily quickly – even the worst of it. And really it can be – very upsetting – very upsetting indeed.' He stopped; then said slowly, in a different voice – a voice with emotion in it, that she had never heard before: 'But it all quiets down. Yes. It gets better. Don't worry. You'll be all right in the end. I should think.'

But as it happens she isn't. In this novel Lehmann does not seem to take Olivia very seriously as a character, but she wrote a much more serious sequel, *The Weather in the Streets*, 1936, following Olivia as a young adult when she is older but no wiser. She has an affair with Rollo, with whom she had the conversation at the ball. He is the brother of her friend Marigold, and is married at the time. The novel was a bestseller, though controversial for its descriptions of divorce, extramarital affairs and backstreet abortions. Her coming of age turns out to be by no means a happy one.

PRECURSORS: THE TOMBOY AS CHARACTER

Before I get onto Carson McCullers' tomboy Mick Kelly, who starts our study proper in 1940, and her sister under the skin Frankie Addams, I want briefly to look at some of their precursors: tomboys in nineteenth and earlier twentieth-century female-authored fiction. Most of the tomboys appearing in earlier coming of age novels appeared in books written for a young rather than an adult audience, going back as far as Jo March in *Little Women*, 1868, the first tomboy in modern fiction.

The word tomboy itself goes back much further, to the sixteenth century in England; it was first recorded in 1553, when it meant a 'boisterous boy,' but it soon changed its meaning and the *Oxford English Dictionary* of 1579 defines it as a 'bold or immodest woman;' perhaps from the word 'tom,' which had the implication of a prostitute for centuries. Shakespeare used tomboy in this sense in *Cymbeline*, 1611, as did Thomas Middleton in *A Game at Chess*, 1624. Tomboy then seems to have gone back to its original meaning and was at one time almost interchangeable with the wonderful word hoyden, of Dutch origin, also originating in the sixteenth century, which will crop up later in Maude Hutchins but which sadly was almost entirely unused in the twentieth century.

George Eliot (a female author using a man's name) has a hoyden in *Middlemarch* (1872): 'Mary was a little hoyden, and Fred at six years old thought her the nicest girl in the world.' In *Agnes Grey*, 1847, Anne Brontë (who published under the male name Acton Bell) has 'Miss Matilda, a strapping hoyden of about fourteen, with a short frock and trousers.'

Miss Matilda Murray was a veritable hoyden, of whom little need be said. She was about two years and a half younger than her sister; her features were larger, her complexion much darker. She might possibly make a handsome woman; but she was far too big-boned and awkward ever to be called a pretty girl, and at present she cared little about it... still less did she care about the cultivation of her mind, and the acquisition of ornamental accomplishments... As an animal, Matilda was all right, full of life, vigour, and activity; as an intelligent being, she was barbarously ignorant, indocile, careless and irrational; and, consequently, very distressing to one who had the task of cultivating her understanding, reforming her manners, and aiding her to acquire those ornamental attainments which, unlike her sister, she despised as much as the rest... As a moral agent, Matilda was reckless, headstrong, violent, and unamenable to reason. One proof of the deplorable state of her mind was, that from her father's example she had learned to swear like a trooper.

Louisa May Alcott's *Eight Cousins*, (1875) has 'Mrs. Jessie, who had been a pretty hoyden years ago herself,' but who worries about the tomboyishness of young Rose. The doctor tells her not to. 'Let the girl run and shout as much as she will, it is a sure sign of health, and as natural to a happy child as frisking is to any young animal full of life. Tomboys make strong women usually, and I had far rather find Rose playing football with Mac than puttering over bead-work.' Mrs Jessie objects that 'she cannot go on playing football very long, and we must not forget that she has a woman's work to do by and by.'

In Carol Ryrie Brink's popular 1936 children's novel *Caddie Woodlawn*, the eponymous heroine is the classic young tomboy, more like her brothers than her sister. 'In 1864 Caddie Woodlawn was eleven, and as wild a little tomboy as ever ran the woods of western Wisconsin. She was the despair of her mother and of her elder sister, Clara. But her father watched her with a little shine of pride in his eyes, and her brothers accepted her as one of themselves without a question.' Also a frontier tomboy was young Laura from Laura Ingalls Wilder's *Little House on the Prairie*, a series of nine novels set in the 1870s and running from 1934 to 1943 which became two different TV series and a planned movie, which at the time of writing had run into difficulties. The casting team for the movie, inviting girls aged from ten to fourteen to audition for the part of Laura, described her as the classic Midwestern tomboy who also has brothers and a more 'feminine' older sister:

The smart and spirited middle child of Charles and Caroline Ingalls, Laura is a tomboy and adventure-seeker living in the Prairie Lands in 1870. Laura is the type of girl who marches to the beat of her own drum and prefers the outdoors to reading and homework. She has a close relationship with her family and dearly loves her 'Pa' and older sister Mary. When her family moves from their home in the Big Woods of Wisconsin to Independence, Kansas, she embraces the adventures she encounters on their journey. Life is not easy, but Laura rises to the challenge.

Staying in the Midwest, in Willa Cather's *My Ántonia*, another frontier novel, which we looked at earlier, the narrator has a similar character for a neighbour, 'Sally, the tomboy with short hair,' who is fourteen. 'She was nearly as strong as I, and uncannily clever at all boys' sports. Sally was a wild thing, sunburned yellow hair, bobbed about her ears, and a brown skin, for she never wore a hat. She raced all over town on one roller skate, often cheated at "keeps," but was such a quick shot one couldn't catch her at it.' This description contains many of the elements of the tomboy in women's fiction: bobbed hair, dark skin, frenzied behaviour and skill at traditionally male sports. So how do these tomboys come of age? In most cases they don't: the children in children's novels never grow up so we never find out whether they become 'normal' women as they mature. There is never the slightest hint in any of the following novels that a girl with short hair, a boy's name and boyish interests might come of age as lesbians; we will however look in a later chapter at a number of books from the 1950s about girls who do.

JO MARCH: *LITTLE WOMEN* BY LOUISA MAY ALCOTT, 1868/69

The most well-known and well-loved tomboy in the novel is also the earliest fully-realised example: Jo March. Although she is only one of the sisters, she is undoubtedly the best loved. We will see later how several of the heroines in *Girls in Bloom* love *Little Women* and idolise Jo. Of all the March sisters, Jo is deliberately the strongest and most sympathetic as a literary character; as with other novels we will look at, her author clearly loves her. With her gender-neutral name, she embodies many of the elements of the heroines of later female coming of age novels. Like many of Jo's successors, she finds that, as she is growing older, and changing from a girl into a 'little woman,' it is becoming hard to hold on to her tomboy ways, which seem to come from her physical as much as her mental attributes. 'Fifteen-year-old Jo was very tall, thin and brown, and reminded one of a colt; for she never seemed to know what to do with her long limbs, which were very much in her way... Round shoulders had Jo, big hands and feet, a fly-away look to her clothes, and the uncomfortable appearance of a girl who was rapidly shooting up into a woman, and didn't like it.' In her case the pressure to become more feminine is not so much from the adults around her as from her sisters.

'Jo does use such slang words,' observed Amy, with a reproving look at the long figure stretched on the rug. Jo immediately sat up, put her hands in her apron pockets, and began to whistle.

'Don't, Jo; it's so boyish.'

'That's why I do it.'

'I detest rude unlady-like girls.'

'I hate affected, niminy, piminy chits.'

'Birds in the little nests agree,' sang Beth, the peace-maker, with such a funny face that both sharp voices softened to a laugh and the 'pecking' ended for that time.

'Really, girls, you are both to be blamed,' said Meg, beginning to lecture in her elder sisterly fashion. 'You are old enough to leave off boyish tricks, and behave better, Josephine. It didn't matter so much when you were a little girl; but now you are so tall, and turn up your hair, you should remember that you are a young lady.'

'I ain't! and if turning up my hair makes me one, I'll wear it in two tails till I'm twenty,' cried Jo, pulling off her net, and shaking down her chestnut mane. 'I hate to think I've got to grow up and be Miss March, and wear long gowns, and look as prim as a China-aster. It's bad enough to be a girl, anyway, when I like boys' games, and work, and Mellors. I can't get over my disappointment in not being a boy, and it's worse than ever now, for I'm dying to go and fight with papa, and I can only stay at home and knit like a pokey old woman.

CHARLIE LABORDE: *CHARLIE* BY KATE CHOPIN, 1900

Girls in coming of age novels often keep diaries: it is a very good device for an author to let us in on the girl's feelings, and in this case for the author to enjoy herself playing with ideas of fiction, style and truth. The authors themselves had in many cases kept diaries as a teenager: as a fourteen-year-old, Jo March's author Louisa May Alcott wrote in hers: 'I have made a plan for my life, as I am in my teens, and no more a child. I have not told anyone about my plan; but I'm going to be good.' New Orleans-based novelist and short-story writer Kate Chopin (1859-1904; Chopin was her married name) also kept a diary throughout her childhood and adolescence. 'You are the only one, my book, with whom I take the liberty of talking about myself.' Something of a tomboy herself when she was younger, Chopin resented the social life of the debutante that she was forced into. At the age of eighteen she wrote in her diary: 'What a nuisance all this is – I wish it were over. I write in my book for the first time in months; parties, operas, concerts, skating and amusements *ad infinitum* have so taken up my time that my dear reading and writing that I love so well have suffered much neglect.'

Chopin's work was in its day considered immoral and dangerous: she was almost a proto-feminist and anti-racist; something of a literary godmother to later Southern women writers, especially Catholics like Flannery O'Connor. Chopin's late novel *The Awakening*, 1899, is indeed about the awakening – sexual and emotional – of its married protagonist , Edna Pontellier, who, dissatisfied with her marriage, finds freedom and falls in love with another man, Robert. They do everything together except sleep with each other, including going swimming, which Edna regards as the height of freedom. To avoid consummating their relationship, he moves away and Edna leaves her husband and sets herself up in her own house, a free woman. She has an affair with the town lothario, though it is purely physical for her. Robert refuses to live with her and, free but alone she swims off into the sea, never to be seen again.

With her gender-neutral name, her masculine interests and her many sisters, Chopin's Charlie Laborde is in many respects Jo March's immediate successor (*Charlie* was written in 1900 but unpublished until 1969). And in her fondness for and friendliness with the black servants on her father's estate in New Orleans, she is a precursor to Carson McCullers' Frankie Addams. And, like many of her successors, she loves her father above anyone else in the world. In turn, her father is proud of her, in her role as his only – substitute – son. 'Charlie could ride and shoot and fish; she was untiring and fearless. In many ways she filled the place of that ideal son he had always hope for and that had never come.'

In the space of this short story/novella, Charlie, who is seventeen at the beginning, does come of age, moving from tomboy to lady to mistress of her father's estate. We first see her, late for the school lesson at which all her sisters are already present, 'galloping along the green levee summit on a big black horse, as if pursued by demons.' She is 'robust and pretty well grown for her age,' with short hair and wearing 'a costume of her own devising, something between bloomers and a divided skirt which she called her "trouserlets." Canvas leggings, dusty boots and a single spur completed her costume.' Charlie does not do well at her lessons and does not even understand the need for them; like many tomboys she does not want her free thinking and creativity to be squashed into the metaphorical corsets of academic study any more than she wants her body squashed into the actual corsets of a fine lady. 'What was the use of learning tasks one week only to forget them the next? What was the use of hammering a lot of dates and figures into her head beclouding her intelligence and imagination?'

Unusually for a tomboy, though quite normally for the heroine of a coming of age novel, Charlie writes poetry. 'She was greatly celebrated for two notable achievements in her life. One was the writing of a lengthy ode upon the occasion of her Grandmother's seventieth birthday; but she was perhaps more distinguished for having once saved the levee during a time of perilous overflow when her father was away.' Nevertheless, Charlie is considered to have many shortcomings and 'never seemed to do anything that anyone except her father approved of. Yet she was popularly described as not having a mean bone in her body.'

Charlie seems more at ease in the shacks of the black plantation workers and their families than in her own home. 'Charlie seemed not to have many ideas above corn bread and molasses herself when she sat down to dine with the Bichous. She shared the children's *couche couché* in the homely little yellow bowl like the rest of them.' Charlie likes to tell the children tall tales of how she goes into the woods killing tigers and bears and a story about a magic ring which, when she turns it three times and repeats a Latin verse enables her to disappear. She takes one of the children out shooting with her, although her father does not approve of her taking out the gun. She accidentally shoots a stranger coming to the estate, though he is not seriously wounded and takes it in good part. Nevertheless, it is decided that Charlie has gone too far this time and has to be sent away to school.

Surprisingly, Charlie very quickly begins to act and dress like a young lady; the diamond ring that had belonged to her late mother becomes not just a memento but 'an adornment,' and other items of family jewellery which previously only had sentimental associations become objects to help 'proclaim the gentle quality of sex.' Charlie grows her hair and wants 'lace and embroideries upon her garments; and she longed to be deck herself with ribbons and *passementeries* which the shops displayed in such tempting array.' When she enters the Seminary, 'no fault could have been found with her appearance which was in every way consistent with that of a well-mannered girl of seventeen.' She is determined to 'transform herself from a hoyden to a fascinating young lady, if persistence and hard work could do it.'

Charlie takes up poetry again, with great success. 'Equipped with a very fine pen point and the filmiest sheet filmy writing paper, Charlie wrote some lines of poetry in the smallest possible cramped hand.' Soon afterwards she wins a competition to write an address to the founder of the Seminary. All goes well until her father nearly dies in an accident back at their estate, Les Palmiers, and Charlie goes home. While there she and her other sisters gets a letter from their eldest sister saying she is to marry the man whom Charlie shot, and for whom Charlie herself had had feelings and aspirations. Charlie is appalled, and briefly reverts to her hoydenish ways, riding wildly off on her horse like did when she was younger; it is as if the devil had taken hold of her, according to one of the black estate workers. But this ride is cathartic.

> In her mad ride Charlie had thrown off the savage impulse which had betrayed itself in such bitter denunciation of her sister. Shame and regret had followed and now she was steeped in humiliation such as she had never felt before. She did not feel worthy to approach a her father or her sisters. The girlish infatuation which had blinded her was swept away in the torrents of a deeper emotion, and left her a woman.

Charlie literally comes of age. In the end, she seems to resign herself to the attentions of Mr Gus, a very shy family friend and neighbour who helps out on the estate while the father is ill and who has always had feelings for Charlie.

> There is no telling what would have become of Les Palmiers that summer if it had not been for Charlie and Mister Gus. It was precisely a year since Charlie had been hustled away to the boarding school in a

state of semi-disgrace. Now, with all the dignity and grace which the term implied, she was mistress of Les Palmiers.

PEGGY VAUGHAN: *A TERRIBLE TOMBOY* BY ANGELA BRAZIL, 1904

Between 1904 in 1946 the British writer Angela Brazil (1868-1947, pronounced Brazzle) published fifty novels for girls, the great majority set in girls' boarding schools, as well as publishing many short stories in girls' magazines; it is no exaggeration to say that she invented the girls boarding school story. Brazil herself went to a girls boarding school in Lancashire, where she became head girl, having previously attended Manchester high school. She worked for a time as a governess, but after the death of her father, a cotton merchant, she, her mother and her sister went travelling around Europe and the Middle East; quite bold at the time. She later settled in Wales and began writing professionally at the age of thirty-six, though she had previously written many stories.

Brazil was highly successful and appealed to a very big audience: her original publishers sold over three million copies of her books. Influenced herself by LT Meade, whom we looked at earlier, Brazil influenced practically all subsequent authors of girls' books, and books set in boarding schools, from Elinor Brent-Dyer, through Enid Blyton to JK Rowling; apart from the practice of magic and the presence of boys, Hogwarts could be straight out of Angela Brazil. (Brazil's *The Madcap of the School* even has a sixth-former called Hermione Graveson, a name not totally unlike Rowling's Hermione Grainger. She even speaks like Rowling's character: "'Look here!" said Hermione briefly. "What prompted you to make such an utter exhibition of yourself just now? I never saw anything more sickening in my life!"')

Brazil's first published novel, *A Terrible Tomboy* is not strictly a boarding school story, but does concern relationships between teenage girls. Fifteen-year-old tomboy Peggy is always getting into trouble, walking along the beam in the barn fifteen feet from the ground, 'her brown curls flying in wild disorder, and her arms stretched out on either side to balance herself as she went on her perilous journey.' Her friend Lillian is horrified but the narrator is clearly smitten with her, as presumably were her teenage readers.

The worst of it was who Peggy really did not mean to be naughty; she was so eager, so active, so full of overflowing and impetuous life, with such restless daring and abounding energy, but in the excitement of the moment her wild spirits were apt to carry her away, simply because she never stopped to think of consequences. She had always a hundred projects on hand, each one of which she was ready to pursue with unflagging zeal and that absorbing interest which is the secret of true enjoyment.

Unlike polite, well behaved girls who do what is expected of them, the implication is that the tomboy is the one who gets the most out of life. Brazil's celebration of the tomboy must have gladdened the hearts of any young reader who did not like to, or was unable to conform the image of the pretty but obedient, smart but modest, well-schooled, well-dressed, marriage-oriented teenage girl, though neither the word nor the concept of the teenager existed at the time.

Brazil's appeal probably extended to girls who were unsure about their own sexuality: there is of course no explicit lesbianism, everything is very chaste, but girls do kiss girls, and occasionally schoolteachers, in the closeted society of the girls' boarding school. There are in fact characters called Lesbia in two of her novels, though this reference would almost certainly have been lost on her readers at the time, and may well have been lost on Brazil herself; certainly, even insofar as her novels are coming of age novels at all, none of the relationships between girls ever extends into anything outside of school or outside of girlish playfulness. Brazil ends chapter one of *A Terrible Tomboy* with a fervent encomium to tomboys everywhere.

Such natures as Peggy's taste life to the full; for them it is never a stale or worthless draught. Each moment is so keenly lived that time flies by eager wings, and though there may be stormy troubles sometimes, as a rule the spirit dwells, like the swallows, in an upper region of joy, which is scarcely dreamt of by those who cannot soar so high.

IRENE ASHLEIGH: *A MODERN TOMBOY: A STORY FOR GIRLS* BY LT MEADE, 1904

Although this novel was written several years after Angela Brazil's *A Terrible Tomboy*, it was quite late in the career of LT Meade, the Anglo Irish writer whose Rachel Grant we looked at earlier. Meade had already published a long list of novels and was an influence on Brazil as well as many others. Like Brazil's novels it concerns the relationship between girls in a private school, one of whom, Irene, is the 'modern' tomboy of the title. As with Brazil's tomboy novel, the author is clearly enamoured of her tomboy creation.

> I was made in a sort of fashion that I really cannot keep indoors. No rain that ever was heard of could keep me in, and no frost, either. And I have lain sometimes on the snow for an hour at a time and enjoyed it. And there's scarcely a night and I spend in bed. I get out, whatever poor old Frosty may do to keep me within bounds. I can climb up anything, and I can climb down anything, and I like to have a boat on the lake; and when they are very bad to me I spent the night there in the very centre of the lake, and they can't get at me, shout as they may. No, I never take cold.
>
> The only thing I am keen about is to be allowed to wear colours that I like. I love gay colours – red one day, yellow the next, the brightest blue the next. I hate art shades. I am not a bit aesthetic. Once they took me to London, but I ran away home. Oh, what a time I had! I am a wild sort of thing. Now, do you suppose that any mother, of her own free-will, would have a daughter like me? Of course I am a changeling. I suppose I belong to the fairies, and my greatest wish on earth is to see them someday. Sometimes I think they will meet me in the meadows or in the forest, which is two miles away, or even in the lake, for I suppose fairies can swim. But they have never come yet. If they came I'd ask them to let me go back to them, for I do so hate indoor life and civilisation and refinement.

PETROVA FOSSIL: *BALLET SHOES*, BY NOEL STREATFIELD, 1932

Noel Streatfield (1895-1986; note that she was a female author with a male name), was born in Sussex, England and was the daughter of the Bishop of Lewes. She wrote several children's books, of which *Ballet Shoes* – beautifully illustrated by her older sister – was the first and most well-known and well-loved by more than one generation of girls; her subsequent books were renamed by the publishers to have the word Shoes in the title, though in fact they are not a series. Like Jo March, Petrova in *Ballet Shoes* by is one of a group of sisters but very unlike the others. She is a different kind of tomboy to outdoorsy, sporty girls like Charlie Laborde: she does not charge around on a horse or play boys' games but loves staying in the house and tinkering with mechanical things, unlike her more conventionally feminine, artistic sisters Posy and Pauline. Petrova is said to be 'very stupid with her needle, but very neat with her fingers; she was working at a model made in Meccano. It was a difficult model of an aeroplane, meant for much older children to make.' Like a conventional boy, Petrova 'knows heaps about aeroplanes and motorcars,' and, like Carson McCullers' Frankie Addams, wants to be a pilot when she grows up (the author Maude Hutchins, whom we will look at in depth later, actually was). When it is suggested that the sisters, who want to be famous for something artistic, learn ballet, Petrova does not seem to be ballet material. 'Well, she won't be good at it to my way of thinking, but it might be just the thing for her – turn her more like a little lady; always messing about with the works of clocks and that just like a boy; never plays with dolls, and takes no more interest in her clothes than a scarecrow.' Predictably, Petrova is bored by the dancing but finds something interesting to do at the weekends.

> Petrova had a thin, pale face and high cheekbones, very different to Pauline's pink-and-white oval and Posy's round, dimpled look; she was naturally more serious than the others, and so, being bored for eight hours in each week did not show on her, as it would on them. It was Sundays that saved her. After morning church she went straight to the garage, put on her jeans, and though only emergency work was really done on Sundays, the foreman always had something ready for her. Very dirty and happy, she would work until they had to dash home for lunch. Afterwards, occasionally, they came back until tea-

time; then they washed and popped across the road to Lyons, but usually they went on expeditions in the car.

Those expeditions were their secret; Petrova never even told the other two about them. The best of them were to the civil flying-grounds, where they watched the planes take off and alight, and often went up themselves. Sometimes they saw some motor-car or dirt-track races; but Petrova like the flying Sundays best. Although, of course, she was years too young to fly, in bed, and at her very few odd moments, she studied for a ground license; she knew that when she did, an aeroplane would obey her, just as certainly as Posy knew that her feet and body would obey her.

GEORGE FAYNE: *THE SECRET OF RED GATE FARM* BY 'CAROLINE KEENE', 1931

There are two famous Georges in youth detective fiction: George Fayne in the Nancy Drew series and George Kirrin of the Famous Five (Perhaps significantly, there were also two famous female writers who called themselves George: Sand and Eliot.) Like many other tomboys, these two Georges are not the sole or even the central character in the novels. The fantastically popular Nancy Drew series, which extended to sixty-four books in the original format and many subsequent spin-offs, was written by a team of writers working for the insanely prolific writer and publisher Edward Stratemeyer, who started hiring writers in a syndicate as early as 1905 to flesh out his draft stories for young people. The syndicate produced, among others, the Bobbsey Twins, Hardy Boys, Rover Boys, and Tom Swift series for boys as well as the Dana Girls and Kay Tracey detective series that were written about girl detectives for girl readers. The Kay Tracey and Nancy Drew series were credited to Carolyn Keene, an entirely fictitious author: the books were in fact written by a series of writers, some of whom were men.

Nancy Drew's friend George Fayne is first introduced in book six, *The Secret of Red Gate Farm*; as is often the case in fiction, the dark-skinned, dark-haired tomboy is contrasted with a more conventional literary beauty, with more feminine tastes, in this case the 'blond, pretty Bess, who had a love for feminine luxuries.' George on the other hand is 'dark-haired... Her boyish name fitted her slim build and straightforward, breezy manner.' Nancy Drew herself is 'the attractive, titian-haired sleuth.' In the next book in the series, *The Clue in the Diary*, blond Bess is described as a 'slightly plump, pretty girl,' whereas George is introduced as 'Bess's slim, shorthaired cousin, who enjoyed her boy's name.'

GEORGE KIRRIN: FIVE ON A TREASURE ISLAND BY ENID BLYTON, 1942

Like most fictional tomboys, the other George in a children's detective series, George Kirrin, has short hair and a dark complexion from being outdoors all day. We first meet her when her three cousins do; their father (who is a writer, like many fathers in *Girls in Bloom*) tells them, 'it will be awfully good for Georgina to have company, because she is such a lonely little girl, always going off by herself.' They are a bit apprehensive about meeting her for the first time; Julian says, 'I wonder what Georgina's like. Funny name isn't it? More like a boy's than a girl's. So she's eleven – a year younger than I am – same age as you, Dick – and a year older than you, Anne.' Georgina's mother warns them, 'you may find George a bit difficult at first – she's always been one on her own, you know... George hates being a girl, and we have to call her George, as if she were a boy. The naughty girl won't answer if we call her Georgina.' This turns out to be true; Anne is the first to speak to her.

> 'I say! Are you Georgina?'
> The child in the opposite bed sat up and looked across at Anne. She had very short curly hair, almost as short as a boy's. Her face was burnt a dark-brown with the sun, and her very blue eyes looked as bright as forget-me-nots in her face. But her mouth was rather sulky, and she had a frown like her father's.
> 'No,' she said. 'I'm not Georgina.'
> 'Oh!' said Anne, in surprise. 'Then who are you?'
> 'I'm George,' said the girl. 'I shall only answer you if you call me George. I hate being a girl. I won't be. I like doing the things that boys do. I can climb better than any boy, and swim faster too. I can sail a

boat as well as any fisher-boy on this coast. You're to call me George. Then I'll speak to you. But I shan't if you don't'.

'Oh!' said Anne, thinking that her new cousin was most extraordinary. 'All right! I don't care what I call you. George is a nice name, I think. I don't much like Georgina. Anyway, you look like a boy.'

'Do I really?' said George, the frown leaving her face for a moment. 'Mother was awfully cross with me when I cut my hair short. I had hair all around my neck; it was awful.'

The two girls stared at one another for a moment. 'Don't you simply hate being a girl? asked George.

'No, of course not,' said Anne. 'You see – I do like pretty frocks – and I love my dolls – and you can't do that if you're a boy.'

CARSON MCCULLERS: THE TOMBOY AS AUTHOR

The great generation of writers that emerged in the 20s, poets such as Elliott, Crane, Cummings and Wallace Stevens, prose-writers such as Faulkner, Hemingway, Fitzgerald and Katherine Anne Porter, has not been succeeded or supplemented by any new figures of corresponding stature with the sole exception of this prodigious young talent that first appeared in 1940 with the publication of her first novel, *The Heart Is a Lonely Hunter*. She was at that time a girl of twenty-two who had come to New York from Columbus, Georgia, to study music.
Tennessee Williams, 'Praise to Assenting Angels'

Carson McCullers (1917-1967) was born Lula Carson Smith but chose to use the gender-neutral Carson; she was the epitome of the literary tomboy: as tall as a man, with long, lanky limbs, short, bobbed hair, boyish dress and elfin face – the ideal author to create fictional tomboys and she did, in two of literature's greatest tomboys, indeed greatest characters: Mick Kelly and Frankie Addams, with their equally gender-neutral names. McCullers told the poet Louis Untermeyer: 'By the time I was six I was sure that I was more of a man,' though she was not the strong, rugged type like Mick Kelly: McCullers was always quite sickly, having had three devastating strokes before the age of thirty and being regularly hospitalised for a variety of illnesses; she died before she was fifty but in her late photographs she looks nearer to seventy.

McCullers had intended to be a musician rather than a writer, and at one time thought she might become a professional pianist. She was never academic and did not enjoy school; she was beaten up during her first week in high school and, as she says in her autobiography, although 'nothing else that dramatic ever happened to me, the dullness of school was a dreadful experience. When I graduated at seventeen, I didn't even attend all the ceremonies, but asked the principal to keep my diploma, as my brother would pick it up the next day.

I still wanted to be a concert pianist so my parents did not make me go every day. I just went enough to keep up with the classes. Now, years later, the high school teachers who taught me are extremely puzzled that anyone as negligent as I was could be a successful author.

The truth is I don't believe in school, whereas I believe very strongly in a thorough musical education. My parents agreed with me. I'm sure I missed certain social advantages by being such a loner but it never bothered me.

But, although her piano teacher encouraged her, McCullers 'realised that Daddy would not be able to send me to Juilliard or any other great school of music to study.' So she told him that she had 'switched "Professions," and was going to be a writer. That was something I could do at home, and I wrote every morning.'

Although McCullers was physically attracted to other women, she rarely had physical relationships with them; but then she probably only ever had a physical relationship with one man: her husband Reeves McCullers, whom she married twice. Reeves was bisexual and, like Carson, chose to use his gender-neutral middle name. He seems to have been attracted to male soldiers and he probably gave McCullers the idea for her second novel, *Reflections in a Golden Eye*, which is about homosexuality on an army base. It was nowhere as well received as her first novel, *The Heart is a Lonely Hunter*, where Mick Kelly appears. *Reflections* was made into a film directed by John Huston and starring Marlon Brando and Elizabeth Taylor – very much the dream team at the time – but like the novel it was a failure critically and commercially.

A lot of people thought that McCullers was already burnt out even at that early age, though she later proved them wrong with *The Member of the Wedding* and *The Ballad of the Sad Café*. Other writers treated her with a mixture of awe and suspicion. The English novelist Elizabeth Bowen, whom we will look at later, although close to some southern American writers, especially Eudora Welty, was wary of McCullers.

I always felt Carson was a destroyer; for which reason I chose never to be closely involved with her. Affection for her I did feel, and she also gave off an aura of genius – unmistakable – which one had to respect. Possibly, some of the company she kept did her no good... Carson remains in my mind as a child genius, though her art, as we know, was great, sombre, and above all, extremely mature.

An important part of the company McCullers kept was her close friend, the homosexual playwright Tennessee Williams, a lifelong advocate and supporter. In his unpublished essay 'Praise to Assenting Angels,' Williams recounted how he first met her when she paid him a visit on the island of Nantucket, 'in response to the first fan-letter that I had ever written to a writer, written after I had read her latest book, *The Member of the Wedding*.' Williams at the time was seriously ill and thought he was going to die; to make things worse, the weather had been appalling with heavy winds and gales. But the weather changed the moment McCullers arrived and, 'almost immediately after Carson and the sun appeared on the island, I relinquished the romantic notion that I was a dying artist.' The two writers talked over 'hot rum and tea,' read poetry and rode bicycles together. One night they saw 'a marvellous display of the Aurora Borealis, great quivering sheets of white radiance sweeping over the island and the ghostly white fishermen's houses and fences. That night and that mysterious phenomenon of the sky will always be associated in my mind with the discovery of our friendship, or rather, more precisely, with the spirit of this newfound friend, who seemed as curiously and beautifully unworldly as that night itself.'

Although she created two of the greatest fictional tomboys, not all McCullers' teenage girls are tomboys: in several of her short stories she gives us sensitive and touching pencil portraits of a variety of adolescents on the verge of coming of age. In 'Like That,' written in 1935/36 but not published until much later, the unnamed thirteen-year-old narrator, who is a bit tomboyish, watches as her eighteen-year-old sister grows away from her and towards her boyfriend, Tuck, with whom the sister apparently has her first sex one night. Her sister's coming of age and her older brothers' leaving home make her feel isolated and nostalgic; like many teenage girls she does not want to become a woman with all that entails.

> I never have been so lonesome as I was that night. If ever I think about being sad I just remember how it was then – sitting there looking at the long bluish shadows across the lawn and feeling like I was the only child left in the family and that Sis and Dan were dead or gone for good... But I'm as hardboiled as the next person. I can get along by myself if Sis or anybody else wants to. I'm glad I'm thirteen and still wear socks and can do what I please. I don't want to be any older if I get like Sis has. But I wouldn't. I wouldn't like any boy in the world as much as she does Tuck. I'd never let any boy or any thing make me act like she does. I'm not going to waste my time and try to

make Sis be like she used to be. I get lonesome – sure – but I don't care. I know there's no way I can make myself stay thirteen all my life, but I know I'd never let anything really change me at all – no matter what it is.

I skate and ride my bike and go to the school football games every Friday. But when one afternoon the kids all got quiet in the gym basement and then started telling certain things – about being married and all – I got up quick so I wouldn't hear and went up and played basketball. And when some of the kids said they were going to start wearing lipstick and stockings I said I wouldn't for a hundred dollars.

In 'Wunderkind', McCullers' first published story from 1936 when she was only nineteen years old, the teenage Frances (we will encounter many characters with variations on the name Frances) is a precocious piano student, as McCullers herself was before she turned instead to writing; we will see shortly how for Mick Kelly in *The Heart is a Lonely Hunter*, having a piano would be the most wonderful thing in the world. In 'Wunderkind' Frances has a negative kind of coming of age when she is suddenly unable to face the piano. 'She felt that the marrows of her bones were hollow and there was no blood left in her. Her heart that had been springing against her chest all afternoon felt suddenly dead. She saw it gray and limp and shriveled at the edges like an oyster.' McCullers herself was considered something of a wunderkind when *Lonely Hunter*, her first novel, was published in 1940 and she took the serious literary world's breath away at the age of twenty-two; in the publicity photo she looks even younger, like an eager, doe-eyed, chipmunk-faced teenager, though she is holding a cigarette in a very adult manner, as she nearly always is in photos.

On a much lighter note, the story 'Correspondence,' published in the *New Yorker* in 1942, contains four letters written by a schoolgirl, Henky Evans, to a putative pen pal in Brazil whose name she has got from a list on the blackboard at school. He apparently does not reply to her letters; she tries four times and eventually gives up in disgust. In the first letter she includes a nice, succinct description of herself; several of the girls in *Girls in Bloom* try to describe themselves but this is one of the best examples of a girl opening herself up to a stranger, navigating the fine line between modesty and boasting, swinging between the poles of self-assurance and self-doubt that all teenagers feel, not knowing which details are key and which are unimportant. She uses the first letter to consider her own future; how she may come of age. As for all teenage girls her future self is a different person, the future is another country; writing to a foreign pen friend is like putting a message in a bottle for herself to find when she is older. (We will see later how Shirley Jackson's Harriet Merriam and her friend write descriptions of what their life will be like in ten years' time and bury them in the ground.)

> Maybe I ought to tell you something about myself. I am a girl going on fourteen years of age and this is my first year at High School. It is hard to describe myself exactly. I am tall and my figure is not very good on account of I have grown too rapidly. My eyes are blue and I don't know exactly what colour you would call my hair unless it would be a light brown. I like to play baseball and make scientific experiments (like with a chemical set) and read all kinds of books...
>
> I have not decided just exactly what I am going to be and it worries me. Sometimes I think I want to be an Arctic explorer and other times I plan on being a newspaper reporter and working in to being a writer. For years I wished to be an actress, especially a tragic actress taking sad roles like Greta Garbo. This summer however when I got up a performance of Camille and I played Camille it was a terrible failure. The show was given in our garage and I can't explain to you what a terrible failure it was. So now I think mostly about newspaper reporting, especially foreign corresponding.
>
> I do not feel exactly like the other Freshmen at High School. I feel like I am different from them. When I have a girl to spend the night with me on Friday night all they want to do is meet people down at the drug store near here and so forth and at night when we lie in the bed if I bring up serious subjects they are likely to go to sleep. They don't care anything much about foreign countries. It is not that I am terribly unpopular or anything like that but I am just not so crazy about the other Freshmen and they are not so crazy about me.

She signs the first letter, 'Your affectionate friend, Henky Evans,' as she does the second, but by the third letter she is getting very impatient: 'I cannot possibly understand why I have not heard from you. Didn't you receive my two letters?' She signs this one Henrietta Evans, and the final one, in which she is truly a woman spurned, she signs, 'Yrs. truly, Miss Henrietta Hill Evans. P.S. I cannot waste any more of my valuable time writing to you.'

MICK KELLY: THE HEART IS A LONELY HUNTER, 1940

A gangling, towheaded youngster, a girl of about twelve, stood looking in the doorway. She was dressed in khaki shorts, a blue shirt, and tennis shoes – so that at first glance she was like a very young boy.

This is very much in line with the descriptions of the tomboys we have looked at so far, as well as contemporary descriptions of McCullers herself. Mick – we are not told her birth name – is part of a large cast of strange characters, including two deaf mutes, in a poor, isolated southern town that could easily be a setting for a Eudora Welty or Flannery O'Connor story but could also be Columbus, Georgia where McCullers was born. One of the characters is Biff Brannon, the owner of the New York Cafe, with 'two fists and a quick tongue,' who has 'a special friendly feeling for sick people and cripples,' including Mick – especially Mick, who is certainly an outsider even though she is not sick or crippled. 'He thought of the way Mick narrowed her eyes and pushed back the bangs of her hair with the palm of her hand. He thought of her hoarse, boyish voice and her habit of hitching up her khaki shorts and swaggering like a cowboy in the picture show. A feeling of tenderness came in him. He was uneasy.'

Another of the characters who is fond of Mick is Portia, the daughter of the town's black doctor, a wise and almost saintly figure; McCullers' sympathetic portrayal of African-Americans and the way her Southern characters show no prejudice was quite shocking for 1940, though probably helped with her critical reception by the East Coast literary elite. Portia's Shakespearean name and the fact that her father is a doctor imply her parents had an education way beyond what would be expected of Southern black families of the time, though she does talk in a kind of dialect. Portia works as a maid in the Kelly household but complains to her father that she is not being paid properly.

'There ought to be some other job you can get.'

'I know. But the Kelly's is really grand white peoples to work for. I really fond of them as I can be. Them three little children is just like some of my own kinfolks. I feel like I done really raised Bubber and the baby. And although Mick and me is always getting into some kind of quarrel together, I has a real close fondness for her, too.'

'But you must think of yourself,' said Doctor Copeland.

'Mick now –' said Portia. 'She a real case. Not a soul know how to manage that child. She just as biggity and headstrong as she can be. Something going on in her all the time. I has a funny feeling about that child. It seem to me that one of these days she going to really surprise somebody. But whether that going to be a good surprise or a bad surprise I just don't know. Mick puzzles me sometimes. But still I really fond of her.'

Although Mick is described as being like a young boy, she is in fact extremely tall for her age, as was McCullers herself, and completely fearless, as McCullers wasn't. 'Five feet six inches tall and a hundred and three pounds, and she was only thirteen. Every kid at the party was a runt beside her.' Sometimes Mick climbs the ladder to the top of an unfinished building. 'She spread out her arms like wings. This was the place where everybody wanted to stand. The very top. But not many kids could do it. Most of them were scared, for if you lost your grip and rolled off the edge it would kill you.' And despite her tomboyishness and rough clothes, she has the pretensions and dreams of any teenager – any teenage boy, anyway.

M.K. – that was what she would have written on everything when she was seventeen years old and very famous. She would ride back home in a red-and-white Packard automobile with her initials on the doors. She would have M.K. written in red on her handkerchiefs and underclothes. Maybe she would be a great inventor. She would invent little tiny radios the size of a green pea that people could carry around and stick in their ears. Also flying machines people could fasten on their backs like knapsacks and go zipping all over the world. After that she would be the first one to make a large tunnel through the world to China, and people could go down in big balloons. Those were the first things she would invent. There were already planned.

But the biggest thing in Mick's life in music, especially classical music; she walks around the streets of the town in the evenings listening to the radios in the houses playing different stations. 'There was one special fellow's music that made her heart shrink up every time she heard it. Sometimes this fellow's music was like little colored pieces of crystal candy, and other times it was the softest, saddest thing she had ever imagined about.' The composer turns out to be Mozart, though she cannot at first spell his name and has no idea who he is. She also listens to music by someone who turns out to be Beethoven; it makes her face her own littleness – big as she is she does not contain multitudes. 'Wonderful music like this was the worst hurt there could be. The whole world was this symphony, and there was not enough of her to listen.'

The thing Mick wants most in the world is a piano: 'If we had a piano I'd practice every single night and learn every piece in the world.' She also wants to write music, and notes down snatches of songs, 'but she didn't feel satisfied with them. If you could write a symphony!' In the private box that, like most teenage girls, she has under her bed, Mick has a notebook; she draws five lines across a test page. 'At the top of the page she wrote SYMPHONY in large letters. And under that MICK KELLY. And she couldn't go any further.' Mick is trying, with no success at all, to build a violin out of the scraps of wood that she finds around the house; unlike most of the girls in *Girls in Bloom*, her poor family cannot afford to buy her any kind of musical instrument and would presumably have no sympathy for the music she loves, nor her musical ambitions, even if she were to tell them. But she has no one to confide in, and this is her private world amid her chaotic house full of parents, a raft of siblings and several paying guests.

> Some kind of music was too private to sing in a house cram full of people. It was funny, too, how lonesome a person could be in a crowded house. Mick tried to think of some good private place where she could go and be by herself and studying about this music. But though she thought about this a long time she knew in the beginning that there was no good place.

As in most of McCullers' fiction the mother is all but invisible; the only other female character drawn in any detail is Portia, but Mick is fond of her father and seems to be the one out of all of his children that he talks to the most openly, but she still cannot tell him about her secret thoughts and her night-time wanderings listening to music – 'the hot, dark nights.'

> These nights were secret, and of the whole summer they were the most important time. In the dark she walked by herself and it was like she was the only person in the town. Almost every street came to be as plain to her in the night time as her own home block. Some kids were afraid to walk through strange places in the dark, but she wasn't. Girls were scared a man would come out from somewhere and put his tea-pot in them like they was married. Most girls were nuts. If a person the size of Joe Louis or Mountain Man Dean would jump out at her and want to fight she would run. But if it was somebody within twenty pounds of her weight she would give him a good sock and go right on... She learned a lot about music during these free nights in the summer-time. When she walked out in the rich parts of town every house had a radio. All the windows were open and she could hear the music very marvellous. After a while she knew which houses tuned in for the programmes she wanted to hear.

Mick is in the middle of her family: her eldest sibling is Bill and she also has younger brothers, including Bubber; there is also a neighbour's daughter, known just as the baby, and she acts almost as a nanny to them both. Mick also has two older sisters, Hazel and Etta, with whom she shares a room and who are 'O.K. as far as sisters went. But Etta was like she was full of worms. All she thought about was movie stars and getting in the movies,' though Etta is not 'naturally pretty like Hazel.' But eighteen-year-old Hazel is 'plain lazy. She was good-looking but thick in the head.' Like the March sisters, the older girls complain about Mick's 'silly boys clothes,' but it is exactly because she has older sisters that she wears them. 'I wear shorts because I don't want to wear your old hand-me-downs. I don't want to be like either of you and I don't want to look like either of you. And I won't. That's why I wear shorts. I'd rather be a boy any day, and I wish I could move in with Bill.'

Mick's coming of age, such as it is, begins with a party she decides to hold at her house and the clothes he decides to wear for it.

The dress she would wear was laying out on the bed. Hazel and Etta had both been good about lending their best clothes – considering that they weren't supposed to come to the party. There was Etta's long blue crêpe de chine evening dress and some white pumps and a rhinestone tiara for her hair. These clothes were really gorgeous. It was hard to imagine how she would look in them... She stood in front of the mirror a long time, and finally decided she either looked like a sap or else she looked very beautiful. One way or the other... she stuck the rhinestones in her hair and put on plenty of lipstick and paint. When she finished she lifted up her chin and half-closed her eyes like a movie star. Slowly she turned her face from one side to the other. It was beautiful she looked – just beautiful.

She didn't feel like herself at all. She was somebody different from Mick Kelly entirely.

The party gets out of hand and many people come uninvited; 'it was the wildest night she had ever seen,' though nothing especially bad happens to her or anyone else. It ends with her and the others running around playing in ditches outdoors like children, but Mick is no longer a child by the time she gets home. 'Her old shorts and shirt were lying on the floor just where she had left them. She put them on. She was too big to wear shorts any more after this. No more after this night. Not any more.' Contemplating Mick maturing, McCullers uses the character of Biff to rehearse a rather bizarre but obviously highly personal and deeply heartfelt meditation on intersexuality.

Mick had grown so much in the past year that she would be taller than he was. She dressed in the red sweater and blue pleated skirt she had worn every day since school started. Now the pleats had come out and the hem dragged loose around her sharp, jutting knees. She was at the age when she looked as much like an overgrown boy as a girl. And on that subject why was it that the smartest people mostly missed that point? By nature all people are of both sexes. So that marriage and the bed is not all by any means. The proof? Real youth and old age. Because often old men's voices grow high and reedy and they take on a mincing walk. And old women sometimes grow fat and their voices get rough and deep and they grew dark little moustaches. And he even proved it himself – the part of him that sometimes almost wished he was a mother and that Mick and Bay were his kids.

Mick never seems to have any feelings for other girls, and there aren't any in the novel. But she does get quite close to the boy Harry, who is very passionate about fascism and world events. They take a trip out to the lake to have a picnic one day; taking off their bathing suits, 'they turned towards each other. Maybe it was half an hour they stood there – maybe not more than a minute,' before Harry says they ought to get dressed. But then *it* happens, or at least it seems to: McCullers draws an impressionistic veil over it but shows how Mick's coming of age is advanced by it.

They both turned at the same time. There were close against each other. She felt him trembling and her fists were tight enough to crack. 'Oh, God,' he kept saying over and over. It was like her head was broke off from her body and thrown away. And her eyes looked straight into the blinding sun while she counted something in mind. And then this was the way.

This was how it was...

'It's this way,' he said. 'I never had even kissed a girl before.'

'Me neither. I never kissed any boy. Out of the family...'

'It was all my fault. Adultery is a terrible sin anywhere you look at it. And you were two years younger than me and just a kid.'

'No, I wasn't. I wasn't any kid. But now I wish I was, though.'

'Listen here. If you think we ought to we can get married – secretly or any other way.'

Mick shook her head. 'I didn't like that. I never will marry with any boy.'

'I never will marry either. I know that. And I'm not just saying so – it's true'.

His face scared her. His nose quivered and his bottom lip was mottled and bloody where he had bitten it. His eyes were bright and wet and scowling. His face was whiter than any face she could remember...

'I'm leaving town. I'm a good mechanic and I can get a job some other place. If I stayed home mother could read this in my eyes.'

'Tell me. Can you look at me and see the difference?'

Harry watched her face a long time and nodded that he could. Then he said:

'There's just one more thing. In a month or two I'll send you my address and you write and tell me for sure whether you're all right.'

'How you mean?' she asked slowly.

He explained to her. 'All you need to write is "O.K." And then I'll know...'

She felt very old, and it was like something was heavy inside her. She was a grown person now, whether she wanted to be not.

But Mick's coming of age does not turn out the way she hoped: she goes directly from tomboy schoolgirl to overworked, overtired and defeated mature woman when, to help the family's disastrous finances, Mick leaves school to work in a shop, her dreams and ambitions unrealised. 'What good was it? That was the question she would like to know. What the hell good it was. All the plans she had made, and the music. When all that came of it was this trap – the store, then home to sleep, and back at the store again.' While she was still at school, when she came home 'she felt good and was ready to start working on the music. But now she was always too tired.' Then things get even worse: John Singer dies; he is the deaf mute who was originally the main focus of *Lonely Hunter* – it was originally titled *The Mute*. Singer has been a lodger at the Kelly house and been very sympathetic to Mick, who has become quite obsessed with him, though not in a sexual way.

There were these two things she could never believe. That Mister Singer had killed himself and was dead. And that she was grown and had to work at Woolworth's.

She was the one found him. They had thought the noise was a backfire from a car, and it was not until the next day that they knew. She went in to play the radio. The blood was all over his neck and when her dad came he pushed her out the room. She had run from the house. The shock wouldn't let her be still. She had run into the dark and hit herself with her fists. And then the next night he was in a coffin in the living-room.

All this changes Mick irrevocably. Biff notices the changes more perhaps than Mick herself.

And Mick. The one who in the last months had lived so strangely in his heart. Was that love done with too? Yes. It was finished. Early in the evening Mick came in for a cold drink or a sundae. She had grown older. Her rough and childish ways were almost gone. And instead there was something ladylike and delicate about her that was hard to point out. The ear-rings, the dangle of her bracelets, and the new way she crossed her legs and pulled the hem of her skirt down past her knees. He watched her and felt only a sort of gentleness. In him the old feeling was gone. For a year this love had blossomed strangely. He had questioned it a hundred times and found no answer. And now, as a summer flower shatters in September, it was finished. There was no one.

But Mick has never had any idea of Biff's feelings for her, which in any case have evaporated with her coming of age. Biff preferred Mick as a tomboy to Mick as a grown woman. At the end of the novel Mick is philosophical about her new womanhood.

Mick frowned and rubbed her fist hard across her forehead. That was the way things were. It was like she was mad all the time. Not how a kid gets mad quick so that soon it is all over – but in another way. Only there was nothing to be mad at. Unless the store. But the store hadn't asked her to take the job. So there was nothing to be mad at. It was like she was cheated. Only nobody had cheated her. So there was nobody to take it out on. However, just the same she had that feeling. Cheated.

But maybe it would be true about the piano and turn out O.K. Maybe she would get a chance soon. Else what the hell good had it all been – the way she felt about music and the plans she has made in the inside room? It had to be some good if anything made sense. And it was too and it was to and it was too and it was too. It was some good.

All right!

O.K.!

Some good.

FRANKIE ADDAMS: THE MEMBER OF THE WEDDING, 1946

It happened that green and crazy summer when Frankie was twelve years old. This was the summer when for a long time she had not been a member. She belonged to no club and was a member of nothing in the world. Frankie had become an unjoined person who hung around in doorways, and she was afraid.

Like Mick Kelly and her author, Frankie Addams is a tall, gangling tomboy – 'she was almost a big freak, and her shoulders were narrow, the legs too long... Her hair had been cut like a boy's, but it had not been cut for a long time and was now not even parted.' At the age of 'twelve and five-sixths' Frankie is five feet five and three-quarter inches tall and wears size seven shoes. 'In the past year she had grown four inches, or at least that was what she judged. Already the hateful little summer children hollered to her: 'Is it cold up there?' Frankie calculates that 'unless she could somehow stop herself, she would grow to be over nine feet tall.'

Unlike Mick however, Frankie does not feel part of any community or family. She has no mother – again, there is an absence of a mother figure – a distant father who is always at work and a much older brother who is away in the army (the highly successful play that McCullers made from the novel specifies the setting as August 1945, at the end of the Second World War). Frankie is not a member of the club of thirteen and fourteen-year-old girls at school who have 'parties with boys on Saturday night. Frankie knew all of the club members, and until this summer she had been like a younger member of the crowd, but now they had this club and she was not a member. They said she was too young and mean.'

The only people with whom Frankie has close contact are Berenice Sadie Brown, who has been 'the cook since Frankie could remember,' and Frankie's six-year-old cousin John Henry; much of the novel and the play, which both take place in a very short timescale, are spent with the three of them around the kitchen table. Like Portia in *Lonely Hunter*, Berenice is a very sympathetically-drawn black, female character from a time when white authors largely avoided them; she was played to great acclaim in the first production of the stage version of *Member of the Wedding*, which opened on December 22, 1949 in Philadelphia, by local actress and jazz/blues singer Ethel Waters, who ten years earlier had been the first African-American to star in her own television show.

Frankie was played by a very young-looking, twenty-three-year-old Julie Harris, whose hair was cropped to make her look younger and more tomboyish; the day before the opening night the director asked to cut it even shorter and to do it herself, as Frankie had done. Harris went on to be nominated for an Academy Award for playing the same role in the 1952 film of the play, in which Ethel Waters also starred.

McCullers was very concerned about racial balance in her work and Berenice Sadie Brown may be based partly on the maid, Lucille, her family had when she was young. In her autobiography, McCullers tells the story of how Lucille, when 'she was only fourteen and a marvellous cook, had called a cab to go home.' When the taxi driver arrived he shouted, 'I'm not driving no damn nigger.'

> People, kind, sweet people who had nursed us so tenderly, humiliated because of their color... We were exposed so much to the sight of humiliation and brutality, not physical brutality, but the brutal humiliation of human dignity which is even worse. Lucille comes back to me over and over; gay, charming Lucille.

Reviewing *Lonely Hunter* in 1940, the black writer Richard Wright had remarked upon 'the astonishing humanity that enables a white writer, for the first time in southern fiction, to handle Negro characters with as much ease and justice as those of her own race.' And in 1948 McCullers had written a letter to the editor of the local newspaper in Columbus, where she was born, protesting the library's refusal to allow black readers.

> I believe that no one owes a greater debt to the Columbus Public Library that I. During my childhood and the formative years of my youth, our library was my spiritual base.
>
> I understand there has been some altercation about allowing all citizens, white and Negro, the use of the new Columbus Public Library. I do not understand the concrete issues involved but I understand too well the abstract ones. Always it has been an intolerable shame to me to know that Negroes are not accorded the same intellectual privileges as white citizens. As an author, represented in the library, I feel it is my duty to speak not only for myself but for the august dead who are represented on the shelves.

The wedding of which Frankie wants to be a member is happening in a few days in Winter Hill and Frankie cannot wait to go – unlike Mick, who is firmly anchored in her community, Frankie cannot wait to go anywhere away from where she is.

'I wish tomorrow was Sunday instead of Friday. I wish I had already left town.'

'Sunday will come,' said Berenice.

'I doubt it,' said Frankie. 'I've been ready to leave this town so long. I wish I didn't have to come back here after the wedding. I wish I was going somewhere for good. I wish I had hundred dollars and could just light out and never see this town again.'

'It seems to me you wish for a lot of things,' said Berenice.

'I wish I was somebody else except me.'

This was the summer that 'Frankie was sick and tired of being Frankie. She hated herself, and had become a loafer and a big no-good who hung around the summer kitchen: dirty and greedy and mean and sad.' Frankie has become aware of the outside world, not like 'a round school globe,' but as 'huge and cracked and loose and turning a thousand miles an hour.' She is aware of the war, of Patton 'chasing the Germans across France,' though it is 'happening so fast that sometimes she did not understand'. Frankie wants to join something, anything but she cannot join the war. She wants to donate blood to the Red Cross so that the army doctors would say that 'the blood of Frankie Addams was the reddest and strongest blood that they had ever known,' but the Red Cross say she is too young. Frankie feels 'left out of everything... She was afraid because in the war they would not include her, and because the world seemed somehow separate from herself.' All these things made her 'suddenly wonder who she was, and what she was going to be in the world;' who is this 'great big long-legged twelve-year-old blunderbuss who still wants to sleep with her old Papa.' But she is now too old to sleep with her father and sleeps alone in her room, a member of nothing. Her best friend has moved away to Florida and 'Frankie did not play with anybody any more.'

It was also this summer that Frankie had become a criminal, at least in her own mind. She had taken her father's gun from the drawer and gone out shooting with it on a vacant lot. She had also stolen a knife from the Sears and Roebuck store, but one sin had been worse than any of them.

> One Saturday afternoon in May she committed a secret and unknown sin. In the MacKeans' garage, with Barney MacKean, they committed a queer sin, and how bad it was she did not know. The sin made a shrivelling sickness in her stomach, and she dreaded the eyes of everyone. She hated Barney and wanted to kill him. Sometimes alone in the bed at night she planned to shoot him with the pistol or throw a knife between his eyes.

Like Mick Kelly, after she has committed what we assume is the same sin, Frankie is afraid that people will see the difference in her, afraid of 'the eyes of everyone.' After a while though this unspecified sin 'became far from her and was remembered only in her dreams.'

The imminent wedding makes Frankie even more aware of her separateness. Her brother and his bride are hundred miles away: 'They were them and in Winter Hill, together, while she was her and in the same old town all by herself.' This is when Frankie has the revelation: she can be a member of something, a member of the wedding. McCullers comes up with one of the greatest sentences in coming of age literature:

> *They are the we of me.* Yesterday, and all the twelve years of her life, she had only been Frankie. She was an *I* person who had to walk around and do things by herself. All the other people had a *we* to claim, all other except her. When Berenice said *we*, she meant Honey and Big Mama, her lodge, or her church. The *we* of her father was the store. All members of clubs have a *we* to belong to and talk about. The soldiers in the army can say *we*, and even the criminals on chain-gangs. But the old Frankie had no *we* to claim, unless it could be the terrible summer *we* of her and John Henry and Berenice – and that was the last *we* in the world she wanted. Now all this was suddenly over with and changed. There was her brother and the bride, and it was as though when first she saw them something she had known inside of her: *They are the we of me.*

For a moment Frankie believes she has come of age: 'it was just at that moment that Frankie understood. She knew who she was and how she was going into the world.' But of course Frankie does not understand. She cannot be a member of the wedding, she cannot be the third person in a couple. 'I'm going off with the two of them to whatever place that they will ever go. I'm going with them... It's like I've known it all my life, that I belong to be with them. I love the two of them so much.' Noting that her brother's name is Jarvis and his fiancée is Janice she has already decided to change her name to F. Jasmine Addams. 'Jarvis and Janice and Jasmine. See?' she says to Berenice, but Berenice does not understand. Berenice asks what she will do if the couple don't accept her. 'If they don't, I will kill myself,' she says, with 'the pistol that Papa keeps under his handkerchief along with Mother's picture.'

F. Jasmine does not even discuss any of this with her brother, whom she has not seen for two years – we never see him at all: neither he nor his fiancée appear first-hand in the novel. But still she walks around the town 'as a sudden member... entitled as a Queen... It was the day when, from the beginning, the world seemed no longer separate from herself and when all at once she felt included.' Frankie is now so bold that she goes to a hotel room with a soldier – McCullers does not make explicit the fact that her brother is also a soldier and perhaps her desire to be a 'member' of her brother and his new wife extends, if only subliminally, to the physical. Frankie has never met the soldier before and does not even find out his name. He seems not to realise how young she is and assumes she is a prostitute. Having got herself into a difficult situation, she does not know how to get out of it.

F. Jasmine did not want to go upstairs, but she did not know how to refuse. It was like going into a fair booth, or fair ride, that once having entered you cannot leave until the exhibition or the ride is finished. Now it was the same with the soldier, this date. She could not leave until it ended. The soldier was waiting at the foot of the stairs and, unable to refuse, she followed after him.

Once upstairs, neither of them seems at first to know what to do next.

Already F. Jasmine had started for the door, for she could no longer stand the silence. But as she passed the soldier, grasped her skirt and limpened by fright, she was pulled down beside him on the bed. The next minute happened, but it was too crazy to be realised. She felt his arms around her and smelled his sweaty shirt. He was not rough, but it was crazier than if he had been rough – and in a second she was paralysed by horror. She could not push away, but she bit down with all her might upon what must have been the crazy soldier's tongue – so that he screamed out and she was free. Then he was coming towards her with an amazed pained face, and her hand reached the glass pitcher and brought it down upon his head... He lay there still, with the amazed expression on his freckled face that was now pale, and a froth of blood showed on his mouth. But his head was not broken, or even cracked, and whether he was dead or not she did not know.

Fortunately for F. Jasmine the soldier is not dead. She goes to the wedding as she had planned but nothing else goes according to plan. She cannot explain to them about the we of me and can only say: 'Take me! And they pleaded and begged with her, but she was already in the car. At the last she clung to the steering wheel until her father and somebody else had hauled and dragged her from the car.' The wedding party drives off without her and she is left 'in the dust of the empty road,' still calling out: 'Take me! Take me!'

In the third part of the narration she is now called Frances; she had started as the tomboy Frankie, then briefly became the delusional F. Jasmine, but Frances seems to be her coming of age name, her woman's name. Berenice talks to her kindly.

The kind tone Frances could not stand. 'I never meant to go with them!' she said. 'It was all just a joke. They said they were going to invite me to visit when they get settled, but I wouldn't go. Not for a million dollars.'

But although her delusion has been shattered and she has come of age Frances still returns the next day to the feeling of separateness. 'There had been a time, only yesterday, when she felt that every person she saw was somehow connected with herself,' but now she sees the world again as something separate from her. Having left her father a note saying she is leaving, Frances ends up back in the sleazy hotel where she had been with the soldier, but now a policeman is there; it turns out that her father has asked the police to try to find her. The Law, as she thinks of him, asks her what he is doing there.

'What am I doing in here? she repeated. For all at once she had forgotten, and she told the truth when she said finally, 'I don't know.'

The voice of the Law seemed to come from a distance like a question asked through a long corridor. 'Where were you heading for?'

The world was now so far away that Frances could no longer think of it. She did not see the earth as in the old days, cracked and loose and turning a thousand miles an hour; the earth was enormous and still and flat. Between herself and all the places there was a space like an enormous canyon she could not hope to bridge or cross.

The novel ends quite suddenly with a flash forward: we are told that she has met a new friend, Mary Littlejohn, and that John Henry has died of meningitis. 'She remembered John Henry more as he used to be, and it was seldom now that she felt his presence – solemn, suffering, and ghost-grey.' At the very end her father has had a letter from her brother, who is now stationed in Luxembourg.

'Luxembourg. Don't you think that's a lovely name?'

Berenice roused herself. 'Well, Baby – it brings to my mind soapy water. But it's a kind of pretty name.'

'There is a basement in the new house. And a laundry room.' She added, after a minute, 'We will most likely pass through Luxembourg when we go around the world together.'

Frances turned back to the window. It was almost five o'clock and the geranium glow had faded from the sky. The last pale colours were crushed and cold on the horizon. Dark, when it came, would come on quickly, as it does in wintertime. 'I am simply mad about –' But the sentence was left unfinished for the hush was shattered when, with an instant shock of happiness, she heard the ringing of the bell.

Life magazine, December 1944:

TEEN-AGE GIRLS: THEY LIVE IN A WONDERFUL WORLD OF THEIR OWN

There is a time in the life of every American girl when the most important thing in the world is to be one of a crowd of other girls and to act and speak and dress exactly as they do. This is the teen age.

Some 6,000,000 US teen-age girls live in a world all their own – a lovely, gay, enthusiastic, funny and blissful society almost untouched by the war. It is a world of sweaters and skirts and bobby sox and loafers, of hair worn long, of eye-glass rims painted red with nail polish, of high school boys not yet gone to war. It is a world still devoted to parents who are pals even if they use the telephone too much. It is a world of Virgil's Aeneid, second-year French and plane geometry, of class place, field hockey, 'moron' jokes and put-on accents. It is a world of slumber parties and the hit parade, of peanut butter and popcorn and the endless collecting of menus and match covers and little stuffed animals.

American businessmen, many of whom have teen-age daughters, have only recently begun to realise that teen-agers make up a big and special market... The movies and the theatre make money by turning a sometimes superficial and sometimes social-minded eye on teen-agers.

Their new importance means little to the teen-age millions. By their energy, originality and good looks they have brought public attention down from debutantes and college girls to themselves. Moving through the awkward age, the troubles of growing up, their welter of facts and taboos, they eventually become – in the judgement of almost every Western nation – the most attractive women in the world.

The idea of the teenager began somewhere shortly after 1940 and was already well established by the end of the Second World War. In *The March of Time*, a Time-Life newsreel of 1945, the voice-over said: 'Of all the phenomena of wartime life in the United States, one of the most fascinating and mysterious, and one of the most completely irrelevant, has been the emergence of the teen-age girl as an American institution in her own right.' But not everyone considered the teenage girl to be completely irrelevant; in the early to mid-1940s a whole new range of magazines, and sections in magazines were launched to appeal to this new audience, as advertisers realised their commercial value. Possibly the first of these was *Calling All Girls*, which began in September 1941, three months before America entered the Second World War.

Although it did not use the word teen-age the cover of the first issue described itself as 'A BRAND-NEW MAGAZINE FOR GIRLS AND SUB- DEBS,' the term that had been used since the 1920s to describe sub-debutantes, girls who were not yet quite old enough to, in the English sense, 'come out;' the term was later replaced by the word teen-ager, the two terms coincided for many years. The editorial in the first issue of *Calling All Girls*, clearly not written by a teenage girl, rather patronisingly described its intentions.

Well, girls, at last we have a magazine of comics and stories and things but it is published just for us! I wonder why nobody ever thought of this before. Most of the comic magazines are filled largely with comics that boys like better than girls, but CALLING ALL GIRLS is going to have what we want and nothing else.

Look through this first issue and you will see what I mean. Thirty-two pages of fascinating comics . . . our kind of comics. And then there are thirty-two pages of stories and articles that tell many things of special interest and help to us girls.

Calling All Girls was published by Parents' Magazine Press, and was certainly intended not to offend any parents; the stories were very bland, with no hint of romance, let alone sex, the advice columns were about etiquette and grooming, and there was no mention of boyfriends, though as the 40s went on it did acknowledge the issue of dating. The January/February 1945 issue had an article called 'How to Get Your Man.'

This is the story of how to chase a boy which tells mostly how not to. Not that we mean to hand down a lecture on how to be stand-offish. This is not the place for extremes. But the fact stands that a straight line – including a beeline – is not always the shortest distance between two points, when the two points are girl and boy.

Calling All Girls had had to move with the times. In September 1944 a new kind of magazine, *Seventeen*, far more youth-oriented, had appeared. It read as if it had been written by, not just for, the teenage girl. The editorial in the first issue said, breathlessly:

> It isn't everyone who can be born at the age of Seventeen . . . but here we are, brand-new, and yet – we're Seventeen in spirit.
>
> SEVENTEEN is your magazine, High School Girls of America – all yours! It is interested only in you – and in everything that concerns, excites, annoys, pleases or perplexes you...
>
> SEVENTEEN is interested in *what you do*. Are you a music fiend, a bookworm, a movie fan? Do you like art, history, poetry or humor? Do you squander your leisure, or do you consider time a precious commodity?
>
> We are keenly interested in *what you think*. Are you so baffled by the confusions of reality that you take refuge in a world of your own? Or do you feel that the world is your oyster – just waiting to be opened and produce its pearl?
>
> But – most important of all – SEVENTEEN is interested in *what you are* . . . the kind of human being you are. Are you tense and ill-at-ease or comfortable and relaxed? Have you a chip on your shoulder or a smile on your lips? Are you interested only in yourself and your closest family and friends, or do you care what happens to people you will never see?

These and other questions were exactly the issues that the new generation of teenage novels, which we will look at shortly, were addressing. The first issue of *Seventeen* sold out its 400,000 copies in the first six days. By September 1948 it had a circulation of 1 million and by July 1949 it had 2.5 million subscribers. The magazine's marketing team claimed that it was actually read by 6 million teenage girls, the number that *Life* magazine had claimed was the total of teenage girls in America. This was a market that no advertiser could ignore; in 1948 *Seventeen* claimed that 1,738 advertisers had spent $11,690,499 on the magazine since its founding.

Before these teen-specific magazines appeared in the 1940s and early 1950s, teenage girls had had to make do with their own section in their mother's magazine. The large, glossy aspirational adult woman's magazine *Ladies' Home Journal* had had a regular forum for teenage girls: the *Sub-Deb* column, which had first appeared in July 1928. In its early days, the column had given serious, formal advice on balls, college and marriage but as early as 1931 it had become breezy and more informal and by the 1940s was addressed to teenage girls in general. However, the advice in the column was still aimed at the daughter of the kind of woman who was assumed to be a subscriber to the magazine: of a certain social and financial standing, or at least aspiring to it; the ideal consumer and the ideal target for advertising. The magazine was at that time full of advertisements for the latest fashions in clothes and domestic furnishings, as well as in beauty products, baby items and labour-saving kitchen appliances. From the beginning it was made clear that the *Sub-Deb* column was intended to attract advertising. The *Journal* ran a full page colour ad in the Saturday Evening post titled 'The Sub-Deb: A New Purchasing Director.'

Until July 1928, the neglected age of girls was from 10 to 18. But in that month the Sub-Deb, a page for girls, made its first appearance in the *Ladies' Home Journal*. It was a spontaneous success! Here at last were the smart, new ideas for which girls had been seeking – new parties for summer and winter and special holidays; new accessories of dress, sent especially from Paris; new haircuts; new books; new thoughts on beauty... So here, ready-made, is a new audience of wide-awake youngsters, who today are a very real influence in whatever purchases the whole family may contemplate.

By the 1940s the *Sub-Deb* column was full of advice on boys and dating, obviously encouraging teenage girls to date, go steady and eventually marry so that they could aspire to the same branded goods as their mothers. In its April 2, 1945 edition, *Life* Magazine had a cover article on the new phenomenon of Sub-Deb clubs, members of the National Sub-Deb Federation, directed at that time by Elizabeth Woodward of the *Ladies' Home Journal*.

High-school girls are the most violently gregarious people in the world and Sub-Deb clubs are one way they get together. Sub-Deb Clubs are particularly popular in the Middle West. In Indianapolis they are an epidemic... There are some 700 Sub-Deb Clubs in Indianapolis with 6000 members and all kinds of strange and wonderful names. The members refer to the hapless minority outside the clubs as 'squares' and 'droops,' but the clubs are not snobbish. Anyone with a friend can start one... The regular monthly meetings of the clubs produce some remarkably energetic things. In the meeting shown at the left, members of boys' clubs have set up an *Information Please*-type board to answer girls' questions about men. Sample exchanges: Q: 'Do boys expect to neck after a date?' A: 'Depends on the mood a fellow's in.' Q: 'what do boys think of flirts?' A: 'They're kind of fun if there aren't too many people around.'

By 1948 the *Sub-Deb* column of *Ladies Home Journal*, now edited by Maureen Daly, author of the seminal 1942 teenage novel *Seventeenth Summer*, which we will discuss later, was also talking openly about dating: 'Even the most casual steady dating is fundamental preparation for a more permanent home-and-hearth-side relationship later on.' In the June 1950 edition some of the clubs responded to the magazine's question about their plans for the summer.

Last year we had a vacant lot where we grew everything from onions to flowers. We divided up and everyone had a few rows of her own and we gave prizes for appearance, cultivation and taste (but not the flowers, of course!) At the end of the summer the club gave a garden party in honour of the winners. This year we hope to go on hikes either in the country or into the mountains and have the Sub-Debs sketch the scenery. We might even give prizes for the best work and the work that shows the most promise.

SUB-EAGLETTE DEBS, *Denver, Colorado*

Every summer we form a softball team and challenge other clubs from our school. Often we arrange (this is our favourite fun) and buy several large watermelons. Then we ride down to the Potomac River where there are plots of grass to sit on and have a watermelon picnic!

SUB-DEB CLUB, Washington, DC

One of our club member's folks own a beautiful cabin near the river. We spend a week or two each some of the. We swim, hike, boat, sunbathe, play tennis, softball and even croquet. We do all our cooking and have loads of fun.

JINX COAXERS CLUB, *Oxford, Nebraska*

All these girls are obviously 'joiners', whereas almost all of the protagonists of the novels in *Girls in Bloom* are shy loners who would die of embarrassment before joining anything. They are also obviously from a class of girls whose parents can afford cabins by the river and boats: normal, well-adjusted, middle-class parents with normal, well-adjusted, middle-class teenage children; very unlike the girls in most coming of age novels.

The *Sub-Deb* column regularly conducted surveys and printed letters from its readers: the most common topic from the mid-1940s onwards seems to be boyfriends and dating. The column for March, 1951 includes advice on how old a girl should be before she starts dating (fourteen in the big cities and sixteen or seventeen in the country), what to do when you have been stood up, what to do if you are taller than the boy you like, and whether it is okay to call a boy on the telephone (yes if the call is 'necessary' but otherwise the girl should 'resist the impulse! Find yourself a good book, call your best *girl* friend or, better yet, tonight's algebra assignment').

The *Sub-Deb* column in the May 1951 issue is titled *Notes on Necking*; it starts by distinguishing between 'necking' (acceptable in certain circumstances) and 'petting' (to be avoided). 'Necking is kissing a boy a few times, holding his hand, letting him put his arm around you. Petting means no holds barred.' The article assumes that 'no smart girl pets,' and that kissing should be restricted to one special boy; it includes advice on how to avoid having to kiss a boy good night and how to avoid 'parking' – it is assumed that all the boys a girl might want to date have a car – where the boy wants to park the car in a quiet spot at the end of the date; it is not made explicit why a boy might want to do this, nor why a girl might want to avoid it. The July 1952 issue contained a summary of answers to the question: at what age is a girl old enough...

... to wear make-up: 'Thirteen or fourteen is fine for light lipstick, with maybe a touch of face powder for dates, but a girl looks silly if she tries heavier stuff like rouge and eye make-up before she's out of high school.'

. . . to wear high heels: 'A smart girl always wears low heels for school, but high heels are okay for dress-up occasions by the time she's sixteen — if she knows how to walk in them. Best idea is to lead up to them gradually through a Cuban or college heel.'

... to pick out her own clothes: 'Thirteen is usually the time when a girl's taste collides with her mother's. The girl should have complete say in small items like blouses and skirts, but pay attention to her mother's taste in expensive items like coats and suits. The girl should okay all purchases because she knows best what's a fad with her crowd.'

... to go with boys in crowds: 'Thirteen or fourteen is usually right, although the girls have to wait until the boys get interested. Group get-togethers for things like movies, parties and school games are a good beginning and help prepare a girl for real dates to come.'

... to go with boys on dates: 'Fifteen or sixteen is average — and it's better to start with double dates because they're more fun at first and make it easier on the girl's conversation.'

By the mid-1950s the *Sub-Deb* column was starting to take a hard line on teenage girls who did *not* date. The column for August 1953, now edited by the playwright Ruth Imler, has the subheading 'What date? I'm still wishing and waiting...' Imler warns her young readers not to be too intellectual or inward-looking, exactly the problem – assuming, like Imler, you think it is a problem – that most of the teenagers in *Girls in Bloom* share.

If you're sixteen or over, attractive – or so you've been told by at least one other person than your father – and you've never had a date, or date very rarely, ask yourself:

- *Do I get along better with adults than with girls and boys my own age?*
- *Do I spend so much time on my music (or art or Latin) that I haven't any left for anything else?*

A girl who chats easily with Aunt Harriet but just silently twists straws while the rest of the gang exchange school gossip over malts often scorns the efforts of the girls make to improve their appearance and personality. 'I want a boy to like me for myself,' she insists, yet never gives a boy a chance to know her real self. Because she's a little afraid to compete with girls her own age, she avoids most teen-age activities. Besides, she is absolutely certain she'd make a mess of them anyway. (How can she possibly know this if she never even *tries*?)

Or if she does try and doesn't succeed dramatically, she's convinced she's just too thin, too serious, too stupid, etc. etc. etc. anyway. (Actually, she gives up when she discovers she can't be *perfect*!) If she stopped to study other girls (a good idea), she'd realise that no girl is completely satisfied with her figure, personality and IQ. And that the girl who develops her own special abilities first and who ignores or works on her flaws second has the most fun.

Another 'late dater' is the girl who is unusually interested in her studies, hobbies or talent... If she'd be her intelligent, interesting self more openly and in more places where boys are too (interest clubs at school, or church groups) *and* she'd also cultivate a dating knowledge of dancing, tennis, swimming and grooming, she'd meet those very boys who think most girls are dopey. They're pushovers for a discriminating girl; they find her fun. And she is.

Dancing, tennis, swimming and grooming are among the things the adolescents in *Girls in Bloom* strenuously avoid; they are mostly outsiders who are not generally interested in popularity, spending more time on 'music (or art or Latin)' than on their image, their friends and boys.

In this same year, 1953, the young model Betty Cornell published her *Popularity Guide* for teenage girls who *did* want to increase their popularity. Cornell says that she herself was overweight, mousy and unattractive until she turned herself around; 'if I can do it so can you,' is the theme of the book, which contains advice on clothes, make-up, diet and dating.

First of all let me say that I don't consider myself any great shakes as far as being an author goes. I'm not a writer. I'm a model. But the truth of the matter is that because I am a model I decided to write this book.

I wrote this book to set down for you the things I learned about beauty and popularity from being a model.

Cornell wants her young teenage reader to be 'polished' and 'poised'. 'The girl with poise is the girl who knows about good personal care and good conduct. She may not be the prettiest girl, but she's certainly one of the most popular. She gets the dates, the class offices, the bids to college proms'. By 1953 the idea of the teenage girl as being someone other than simply a smaller version of her mother was widespread; Cornell makes it explicit that her advice is aimed straight at the shy, uncertain teenager whose mother does not have the answers to all the questions. 'I hope that you as teenagers will find my suggestions helpful, they are specifically designed for you, not for your mothers or your grandmothers... The purpose of my book, then, is to help you teen-agers make the most of yourselves'. Here is Betty's checklist for the girl setting out for school in the morning.

1. Underwear – Is it clean? Does it fit?
2. Blouse or sweater – Is it clean? Does it smell fresh?
3. Skirt – Any wrinkles, any spots or stray dirt?
4. Shoes – Are they polished and are they trim at the heels?
5. Stockings or socks – Are they clean? Is the seam straight?
6. A last look, to straighten out a lock of hair, check on the nose, chin, and lipstick, and you're off.

Betty does not ask 'you' to check if your homework has been done, whether you are ready to take today's test and get an A, whether the essay, story or poem you have written for class is fit to stand against the great literature you love reading so much. She does not seem to appreciate that some girls, including most of the girls in *Girls in Bloom*, are genuinely more interested in self-expression and intellectual growth than in popularity: 'every girl, I don't care who she may be, wants to be attractive and popular... If you put real elbow grease into acquiring beauty, poise and polish, you will find it pays off with more dates, more fun, more good times. Gee, what more could anyone ask?' Quite a lot, as we will find out later.

In the same year as Betty Cornell's book appeared, 1953, an English publisher released *The Teen Age Book*: 'the first book produced in this

country specially for girls of seventeen to nineteen,' edited and introduced by Ann Seymour, the editor of *Woman and Beauty*.'

TO THE YOUNG WOMEN
OF SEVENTEEN
EIGHTEEN
NINETEEN

THIS IS YOUR BOOK *and it is long overdue. During the war you won the
right to be considered as young people, not grown-up children. The
Teen Age Book has been compiled with this fact in mind.*

*In it, we discuss the things you consider important. We try to help
you to dress well, look as you would like to look, think clearly and
talk so that you are worth listening to. We hope the result will not
only entertain but encourage you to clarify your ideas, aims and
ambitions and to develop so that people are pleasantly aware of you
as a charming person.*

The book is an odd mixture of advice, fiction, non-fiction, dressmaking,
theatre and art, no doubt hastily put together to satisfy a perceived new
audience. Some of the advice is as patronising as one might expect. In an
introductory article by Seymour, titled 'Youth is not Beauty,' the author
defers, as the reader would be expected, to the wisdom of men.

A famous educationalist once said to me, 'I would rather a girl go out
into the world knowing how to comb her hair becomingly than carrying a degree.

'There's no place in my office,' said a successful business man to
me another time, 'for the girl who isn't intelligent enough to know
how much appearance counts.'

'I don't give a damn about the colour of her eyes,' a nice young
man told me, 'but I do want my girl to look slick.'

Seymour advises that, 'if you have youth all that is needed for beauty is
plain food, plenty of drinking water, fresh air, baths and proper elimina-
tion of the bowels.' If only it were that simple. She also advises, 'if you are
to be a success in work, marriage and attaining all that is dear to a woman, you must learn to be the kind of person who is neither unpleasant to

look at or listen to, nor hard to get along with.' To be fair to this anthology, Seymour and others do assume that a girl will have a job, maybe even a career, as well as, perhaps even instead of, a husband. One article, entitled 'Growing Pains,' directly addresses the coming of age from schoolgirl to worker, though not career woman; the editor's introduction to the article does everything it can to lower the expectations of any girl excited to be leaving school and starting work.

> A vast number of you will soon be starting work. You are going to earn your living, and to your amazement it will be a very small living! Suddenly from a secure and simple world you step into a large and confusing scene. You find it matters to no one that you were a House Prefect, or that the School Magazine hailed you as a genius. You are now merely the newest run-about in the office. It is all very deflating; so Rita Bull, of 'teen age herself and working at her first job, wrote this to help other girls make an easy transition.

An article by Frank Owen, Liberal MP and journalist, takes women rather more seriously. It is titled, worryingly, 'Petticoat Power.' But in fact it urges young women in the post-war European environment of a shortage of men to take a full part in the political process.

> The first thing for the Intelligent Young Woman to realise about the politics of Britain is that she is going to be the person who has the power to decide them.
> Why? Because there are already nearly two million more women voters in this country than there are men. At twenty-one years of age every woman, along with every man, gets the right to vote at parliamentary elections.

At the back of the book there are a series of colour advertisements for products aimed at the target demographic, who are assumed to be far less interested in politics than in beauty products. They include an ad for bras and corsets: 'Seventeen – the age when feminine loveliness is being formed and when the delicate line, soon to reach a firmer mould, needs the gentle aid of the Gossard Line of Beauty.' And in the end, there is no doubt of the kind of woman the teenage girl is being advised to become. An article about overcoming shyness includes this advice: 'Make a list of your special knacks and polish them up so that people will know that when it comes to sewing, cooking, dancing, drawing, music, letter-writing or dozens of other accomplishments, you just can't be beaten.' Politics and climbing the career ladder are not included as worthy accomplishments.

The advice to teenagers in *Ladies' Home Journal* remained focused on that elusive popularity throughout the 1950s, even after the *Sub-Deb* column ceased. In its last issue of the 1950s, the *Journal* began an advice column for teenagers – ostensibly aimed at both boys and girls, though it is hard to imagine any teenage boys risking being caught reading *Ladies' Home Journal* – which was written by teenage heart-throb singer, the wholesome and parent-friendly Pat Boone for 'my good friends 'twixt twelve and twenty.' Boone (or his ghost writer) advises his teenage fans: 'A truly attractive person is all-round attractive,' and that with girls who are only popular with boys and vice versa, 'there's something out of balance in his or her popularity make up, believe me!' Boone tells a story about Jinny, 'the kid sister of a friend of mine when she was in junior high school. In eighth grade she went through what her older brother called "the dreadful age."' Naturally, he does not discuss issues like the onset of menstruation and female hormones, just saying, 'it's possible, when you're making the transition from childhood to that adolescent paradise we call the teens, to hit a point where you are neither fish nor fowl, neither boy nor man, a little girl or a grown woman, and it can be temporarily confusing!' It certainly can. In Jinny's case things got to the point where she liked 'nuthin' or nobody,' until the summer when everything changed for her.

During the summer Jinny went away to camp and had a terrific time. She also had a nineteen-year-old girl councillor who she admired. Jinny of the thundercloud countenance returned Jinny of the smiling face. When she went back to the same school for the ninth-grade that fall she began to come home with different reports: 'I don't know what's happened to Miss T. this summer, she must have inherited money or something. She's *sure* changed.'... 'Lydia's my best friend. She's so different!'... 'Carl's teaching me to play tennis. Has *he* changed!'... 'Jim has asked me to Halloween party. He's so different!'

It got to where her brother and her mother and I couldn't keep straight faces. In fact, we really broke up when one day she finally asked thoughtfully, 'Mom is it possible that I've changed too?'

Boone does not of course consider the possibility that Jinny might have changed because of an experience with the nineteen-year-old female councillor that her parents would absolutely not approve of. (We will look at 1950s lesbian coming of age stories in a later chapter.)

Pat Boone, born in 1934, was already one of the last of a generation of singers whom teenage girls could listen to with their parents: the same year Boone released his first record, 1954, Elvis Presley – born just seven months later than Boone but seeming to be from an entirely different generation – was already recording; in 1956 Presley released *Heartbreak Hotel* and the era of parent-friendly music was over. Mothers, and especially fathers, of teenage girls would never again sit round their teenage daughter's record player singing along with her. Or watch their daughter's idols on TV: Elvis's suggestive gyrations were first seen on the Ed Sullivan show on September 9, 1956, with him provocatively performing *Ready Teddy* and *Hound Dog* to the horror of parents all across America. Elvis was paid an astonishing $50,000 for three appearances on the show; the first reached 82.6% of the American TV audience. By his third appearance protests from concerned parents ensured that he was filmed only from the waist up. But it was too late; teenage rebellion had begun and teenage girls began to stop wanting to listen to music with their mothers, let alone become them.

By the mid 1950s teenage girls were quickly becoming far more knowing and independent and were demanding a much more adult openness about relationships and romance. There were less interested in Sub-Deb summer camps and school softball and more interested in sex. They didn't want to read their mother's magazine, they wanted magazines that they would have to hide from their mother. The market responded. The beginning of the 1950s in America saw the first wave of teenage pulp, comic book-style magazines: hand drawn, colour illustrated love stories, sometimes quite steamy and featuring characters and storylines that seem rather risqué for the time; they certainly seem designed to attract the disapproval of any teen girl's parents. Not only are the stories almost identical to those in adult romance magazines but the characters in the drawings do not look like teenagers, they look like women in their twenties: the beautiful, sophisticated women the teenage reader no doubt aspired to be.

The steamy *Teen-Age Diary Secrets* which ran for just a few issues in 1949 and 1950 would have given any girl's mother a heart attack: story titles from one typical issue are: 'I Was Torn Between Two Loves', 'Confessions of a Hat-Check Girl', 'Hijacker of Hearts', and 'Second Hand Sweetheart'. The same publisher, St John, also issued *Teen-Age Romances*, which ran from January 1949 all the way to December 1955, *Going Steady* from February 1954 to October 1955 and the even steamier *Teen-Age Temptations* from October 1952 to August 1954. The sidebar on the front of issue one reads: 'I'd watched other girls make pickups on street corners so I tried. But I wasn't very lucky . . . My limelight trail ended in court and even worse, the story was in all the papers!' Some of the stories in these magazines however are poignant, miniature coming of age stories. *Teen-Age Romances* issue one has the story 'Was I Too Young for Love?'

> What pitfalls lie in the path of a girl who falls madly in love with her first date? I had to learn the hard way because nobody could tell me that love-at-first-site is blind – terribly blind, and those who pursue it are doomed to mocking disappointment and despair!

Eileen is in her senior year but has never taken boys seriously; then she meets Ted, an older boy who has left school and enlisted in the Armed Forces. Eileen now feels she has a real boyfriend and takes down all the pictures of movie stars from her wall. Her older sister tries to give her some advice. 'Don't take him to seriously. They are all alike, men, that is. They make a lot of big promises but never keep even the little ones.' Eileen replies, 'you don't understand sis! Ted is different.' But he isn't. While he is away on duty he writes to Eileen infrequently and rather distantly. In his absence, she realises that he is not *the one* after all. When Ted comes back, they go to a dance together but things are not the same; 'something happened to me since you've been away.' Eileen runs away from Ted. 'Suddenly a fierce pain ripped my heart and a lump rose in my throat. With tears streaming down my cheeks, I turned and fled! For a full minute I cried like a baby – cried until I wrung the last tear from my eyes – until my heart no longer ached.' Eileen has changed: she realises that Ted was simply the first of what may be many. 'It was wonderful

while it lasted! I'll – I'll never forget it as long as I live! My first love!'
This is Eileen's first coming of age moment. 'Yes, I had learned my first
lesson about love – the hard way. But I did not regret it. In spite of the
tears and heartaches, it had been fun!'

Another of the early pulp teen magazines was *Popular Teen-Agers*,
from Star Publications, which ran from September 1950 to November
1954. It ran letter and advice columns for confused teenagers; the target
audience seem to have been far more innocent and inexperienced than
the characters in the stories, who seem to have come of age, whereas the
girls reading them don't. Issue twenty-one, from April 1954, had a column on 'How to Get A Second Date'.

> Be sweet from the moment he enters your home. Let him talk to your
> parents and add to the conversation. Don't argue with Mother, Dad,
> or the kids. Your boy friend will like you better if you don't. Remem-
> ber, he has a family too.
>
> To keep the evening lively and to keep your boy friend happy and
> comfortable, it's up to you to get the conversation started. The best
> way is to start with a question. When you're alone, tell him when you
> noticed him first. If possible remark about what he was wearing at the
> time. This will flatter him. Your follow-up is, 'When was the first time
> you notice me?' Now he'll talk and before long you will be reminiscing
> happily.

For the teenage girl who got the second date, and many subsequent ones,
there was *Teen-Age Brides* which had a brief run between August 1953
and August 1954. On the front cover of the first issue, above the title, the
strapline ran: 'HOW YOUNG SHOULD A YOUNG GIRL MARRY? READ "I WAS A
CHILD BRIDE" the revealing, unexpected story of our times...' This was obviously intended to produce a heart attack in the parents of any girl who
found a copy in her room. *Teen-Age Brides* was strongly pro-marriage,
though hardly in a parent-friendly way; the introduction to the first issue
ran:

> Dear Readers:
>
> Welcome to the very first issue of a brand-new kind of romance
> magazine! Never before have you thrilled to a book like TEEN-AGE
> BRIDES! With its all-true stories ripped right from the heart of real life,

it tears aside the curtain of false modesty surrounding young, passionate marriage in a way that no other magazine has ever dared to do!

TEEN-AGE BRIDES faithfully follows the marriage road and desire's path . . . revealing with uncensored honesty the ecstasies, the passions, the furies and, yes even the hidden heartaches of the young, newlywed life!

From beginning to end, this and every future issue of TEEN-AGE BRIDES is a song to marriage, and nothing is held back! It is heartbreak's lament . . . or a ballad sung in rapture's hushed whispers . . . a torch song aflame with the fires of youth!

Phew! This sounds like the blurb for a pulp version of *Madam Bovary*; it is not at all the view of marriage to be found in magazines like *Ladies Home Journal*. Any passion the girl might have had as a teenager is expected to have been left behind at the altar. In issue two of *Teen Age Brides*, October 1953, the story 'Too Young to Know,' about a teen marriage that went horribly wrong, is both a salutary tale and a kind of dark coming of age story. 'Headlong, I rushed to meet life . . . blindly I rushed into marriage . . . breathless, eager, hungry to live and love . . . And painfully unaware that I was . . . too young to know.' Laura is seventeen but her boyfriend Matt is older and she has to hide her relationship from her parents. Matt asks Laura to marry him immediately; they elope and marry in secret. But right from the start the marriages and successful.

> We had lied about our ages – we had lied about *everything*! But Matt managed to find a modest apartment and a modest job, and at first we were in heaven! All too soon, however, there were problems . . . bitter words, terrible arguments.

Among other things, Matt is upset if his dinner is not on the table when he comes home. 'We were both frightened of responsibility, frightened of reality, disillusioned about marriage – and gradually drifted further and further apart.' Laura wishes she could ask her parents for help, but it is too late for that. 'I had no right to go to them. After the shock of our elopement, my folks told us we had to work out our own problems – like true adults.' Then Laura tells Matt she is pregnant. 'You can't be serious! A baby would ruin everything! We are not ready for a baby yet! Are you listening?' Matt runs out of the house and is run over by a car. 'He died instantly – and my youth died with him! Matt had been my girlish dream of happiness – and now the dream is over.' Laura has come of age in the worst possible way. 'Left alone now to care for my son, I grew up fast – out of necessity!' But Laura's parents take her back and look after her son while she goes out to work as a secretary. There she meets Tim, who turns out to be unfaithful and finally she marries Dick. 'I was through searching for happiness! It had been waiting for me all along – and now I intended keeping it – forever!'

At the end of the 1950s and the very beginning of the 1960s, a new wave of teenage pulp magazines began to appear. The comic publisher Charlton, who had previously published pulp science fiction, horror, crime and war comics moved into the teenage romance market with a series of illustrated magazines containing short stories in which usually a teenage girl has a problem with a boy – sometimes with an older man – but, within the space of a few hundred words and five pages of illustrations, things turn out okay. *Teen-Age Love* began in July 1958, *Teen Confessions* in August 1959, *Teen Secret Diary* in October 1959 and *Teen-Age Confidential Confessions* in July 1960; its first issue was subtitled YOUNG EMOTIONS EXPOSED and at the bottom of the front cover promised: EXTRA! AS TIMELY AS TODAY'S NEWS: 'TOO YOUNG FOR LOVE.'

Teen-Age Confidential Confessions had an advice column, called *Teen Age Trouble*, written by 'one of the country's leading authorities in the field,' Dr Harold Gluck, who 'has had many years of experiences with boys and girls of your age. He knows what bothers them and the sensible help and advice they need.' His advice is very much the same as that given to Sub-Debs years earlier. In one letter, Doris T writes:

I am just fourteen though everyone says that I look as if I am at least seventeen or eighteen. I know that I am very mature for my age. There is a boy in our neighbourhood. He quit school and works as a clerk in a fruit market. I met him two months ago.

He wants me to go steady with him and says that if we like each other we can get married in a year or so. In fact he even said he would start saving up money now in a bank account in case we get it off good.

My mother still thinks I am a kid and can't see that I am grown-up. All she wants to tell me is what to do, and also what I shouldn't do. A friend of mine gave me this comic magazine and I read your column. You help other people. So please help me. My boyfriend Bill knows I am writing this letter to you.

Doctor Gluck takes Doris' mother's side. 'So you think you are already intellectually mature?' In that case, he says, think like a grown-up woman: you want to grow up, but 'you can't Harriet. The child of fourteen is not the young girl of nineteen. And the girl of nineteen isn't the woman of twenty-five.' Doris' mother 'knows you are only a child – and you ARE!' Doris, according to Doctor Gluck, has not yet come of age.

In the UK, the emergence of the teenager was acknowledged by the end of the 1940s, but the British teen magazine was far more staid than its American equivalent. In November 1947, *Girl's Own Paper*, which had been running since 1880, had an illustrated feature called 'Teen-age Bar.'

It's here! Of course, it had to happen. British teenagers had to be recognised as definite personalities with styles and clothes of their own. And so a Teen-age Bar has been opened by Harrods of Knightsbridge, London. Based on the American idea, the Bar is complete with high stools, chromium and shining plate glass. Better still, the clothes themselves have an air of casual sophistication that will go straight to the heart of any girl. Most of the clothes are in American teen-age sizes. Hats follow the adult fashions, but are mainly selected for the simplicity and prettiness that will appeal to the younger set.

The next month, December 1947, *Girl's Own Paper* renamed itself *Girl's Own Paper and Heiress*, acknowledging the importance of the teenage market and specifically addressing itself to the new phenomenon of the teenage girl. The editorial in the first issue under the new title briefly explained its intent and its title: Heiress is meant as a British version of Sub-Deb.

It is appropriate that the Christmas number of GIRL'S OWN Paper should introduce you to our new title HEIRESS, because we feel that in this teen-age magazine – planned from cover to cover to suit your tastes and interests – has been added to the present title because it so aptly describes YOU – heiress to all the good and lovely things in life and at the age when you are about to enter into your possessions.

The format did not change under the new *Heiress* title, remaining paper-back-sized with around seventy pages, mostly containing fashion, make-up, cookery, career advice and short fiction with a large number of advertisements for clothes, cosmetics, food and household products; very much not a pulp magazine and quite suitable to be read by any teenage girl's mother. There is none of the steamy passion of the American illustrated pulps; the most risqué it gets is an advertisement for Slix: 'For the teen-agers' especial delight. Gay, delicate Petti-Panti set in sheer Sea-Island cotton, consisting of camisole bra and petticoat with panties combined.'

The October 1949 issue has a short story concerning a girl's coming of age, called 'Slow Boat to Growing Up', that is worth quoting from. Teenage Janie is going to a party where she knows that 'heart-throb' Austen will be. He 'wore beautiful clothes, he tanned like a film hero and he was dazzling.' She borrows her older sister's dress to wear; nothing she owns could be considered 'adult.' 'Now she was a beautiful young lady, now she had grown up with magical swiftness.' She also borrows her sister's make-up and shoes, which are rather too small – the Cinderella reference will return in a couple of paragraphs. Janie's regular date, Marcus, comes to pick her up. 'Oh, my, look at you!' he gasps. 'I thought I'd grow up,' she replies. They arrive at the party. Janie sees Austen, standing in the story for the handsome Prince.

> For the moment she avoided Austen, feeling embarrassed. Growing-up had come suddenly; it made her feel different and a shade gauche. She would rather he got to know that she was there, than that she should direct his attention to her. But he saw her at once.
> 'Hallo, hallo, hallo! Half a minute, Janie. Whatever have you been doing to yourself?'
> 'Cinderella grows up,' she said pertly.
> 'It's shattering. And you were such a sweet kid!'
> There was no answer that she could make. Janie felt the pertness ebbing; there ought to be a slick reply, and there wasn't one. Just emptiness when she wanted most to be clever.

Marcus whisks her away just in time but the shoes are too tight and she cannot dance in them. Reliable old Marcus runs her home so that she can change her dress and her shoes; 'she changed quickly, into her own frock, and came back with her hair shining, and her eyes like stars... Suddenly she knew that there is no quick boat to maturity. Growing-up takes time, but it's a lovely time, really.'

Girl's Own Paper and Heiress magazine sometimes included career advice for its teenage readers; even in the UK the economy was improving by the end of the 1940s and kept growing throughout the 50s. The very first issue of the combined magazine, December 1947, had advice on how to become a model, what they call a mannequin.

Too many girls want to do become mannequins because they think it is a highly-paid glamour job. It is neither. It is very precarious, tiring work, and though at times a mannequin may earn over £10 per week, most of her pay goes on new clothes, make-up, etc.

However there *is* a demand in London for new mannequins of the right type; and if you do succeed the reward is a very pleasant life. The first year is the most difficult, and a girl with a home in London or a private income behind her stands the best chance of success.

The first thing you learn at a good training school is that glamour jobs are not wanted. The mannequins who obtain work most frequently are the pleasant girls whose good temper shows in their faces. The gorgeous creatures who indulge in sulks or temperament are soon 'through'. Dress designers and photographers might naturally have no time to deal with them.

Some things *do* change. Just under a year later, the October 1948 issue has an article written by a young woman who has successfully become a mannequin and describes the job very matter of factly; 'the average hours worked are usually from 9 or 10 am until 5 or 6 pm, and the salaries vary from £5 to £8 or more a week, according to the experience of the model'. This is less than the £10 a week promised in the earlier issue, but still a very good wage at the time, especially for a young woman. Other issues have advice on how to become a freelance writer, a social worker or an office worker. The typical heroine in an *Heiress* short story is a seventeen-year-old office worker; the October 1949 issue has an article called 'So You're No Career Girl?' by someone who is 'a successful businesswoman who started at the bottom. Today she is a Director of two companies and Director and Company Secretary of a third.' It describes in detail the different jobs a young woman can do in an office, with the wages they would be likely to attract. According to the article, young women are essential to the smooth running of any office, which of course will be run by men. 'Any busy business man knows he would have a rough time if it were not for those efficient girls who take over his office every morning, handle the details, and see that the wheels keep moving'. The author advises women to take a commercial course at college and get help from home. 'Perhaps your father can give you some of his business typing.' Any experience the young woman can get will be useful in the future. 'You never know how handy it will be, even when you marry!' So the lucky teenage girl can look forward to a life of office drudgery to add to her life of domestic drudgery as a housewife.

Tellingly, the articles and fiction in *Heiress* magazine were all written by women whereas the stories and illustrations in the American pulp magazines were mostly written by, or at least credited to, men. Men were also credited for all the articles in another British magazine for teenagers which started in July 1950: *The Teen-Age Magazine*, a black and white monthly concentrating heavily on film and music with a lot of black and white photos of singers and movie stars and a small amount of fiction. The editor in the first issue acknowledges that the idea of the teenager is already well accepted: looking for a suitable picture of a teenager for the front cover of the first issue, 'I searched through thousands of photographs of women of all shapes and sizes until one assistant at an agency remarked: "Teen-agers are not news."'

The cover picture he went with was of the eighteen-year-old Elizabeth Taylor (the actress not the author), drinking a glass of milk and looking very prim. The subheading is 'Elizabeth Taylor becomes president of the Teen-Age Club.' Taylor was at that time a good role model for and the envy of all teenage girls: at age eleven she had played Velvet Brown in *National Velvet*, 1944, after which she played the beautiful young out-of-towner for whom the young man falls in *Life With Father*, 1947, then the title role in coming of age movie *Cynthia*, 1947, Amy March (the youngest sister) in *Little Women*, 1949, the teenage bride in *Father of the Bride*, 1950. She was then an actual bride at eighteen, marrying wealthy playboy Conrad Hilton in 1950, looking impossibly beautiful in a spectacular white dress, starring in a fairy tale ceremony watched by millions: the dream life for any teenage girl. However the dream quickly turned sour and the couple divorced 205 days later, a month before Taylor's nineteenth birthday. Hilton's alleged 'mental cruelty' was no doubt a coming of age moment for her and for many other teenage girls.

But this was after the first issue of *The Teen-Age Magazine* and, since teenagers had become old news and the cover picture was so chaste, the editor has obviously decided to spice things up: the first 'Teen-Age Digest' page starts with a rather racy feature.

STUDENT SUSPENDED . . . 'Do you believe in free love?'

There was a terrific rumpus at the Regent Street Polytechnic in London when student-editor Ian Kerr of the college magazine *Forum* prepared a twenty-point quiz on morals, love and sex for the polytechnic's 3,000 students.

Asked Ian Kerr in the questionnaire which was banned by the authorities: 'Do you believe in free love? Do you favour pre-marital sexual intercourse? Do you believe in marriage? Have you had sexual relationship (*a*, frequently; *b*, occasionally)? Do you believe moral behaviour is impaired by student life?'

Ian submitted his questionnaire to the committee of the student's Council. They threw it out.

Mr John Jones, director of education at the Polytechnic said: 'His questionnaire represents an attitude of mind. If I were a parent I should resent my child being asked such questions.'

Miss Lyn Houghton, fellow-student at the college, was also suspended for posing for a picture showing her dancing cheek to cheek with a man.

But the idea of teenagers as children who need protecting was dying out fast; teenagers were beginning to be treated like young adults not big kids – Kerr's question about sexual experiences did not think to add '*c*, never'. Teenagers were beginning to be seen as both consumer and worker, as an important driver of the economy with their own needs and their own spending power, not just younger versions of their parents. Ten years after its wartime article on the teenage girl, *Life* magazine's June 1954 issue had an article that talked about high school teenagers not only driving their own cars but often buying them with their own money. Whereas Europe had been devastated and bankrupted by the war, America came out of it into a period of rapid economic growth; the American teenager – both male and female – had gone straight from being at school to being an affluent consumer, buying up all the clothes and cars the country could produce.

> These are the children who were called 'Depression babies.' They have grown up to become, materially at least, America's luckiest generation.
>
> Young people 16 to 20 are the beneficiaries of the very economic collapse that brought chaos almost a generation ago. The Depression tumbled the nation's birth rate to an all-time low in 1933, and today's teenage group is proportionately a smaller part of the total population than in more than seventy years. Since there are few of them, each – in the most prosperous time in US history – gets a bigger piece of the nation's economic pie than any previous generation ever got. This means they can almost have their pick of the jobs that are around... To them working has a double attraction: the pay is good and, since their parents are earning more too, they are often able to keep the money for themselves.

The teenager had triumphed.

SHIRLEY JACKSON: MOTHER OF THE TEEN

An academic critic, Jeanette H Foster, in a book called *Sex Variant Women in Literature*, 1956, referred to Shirley Jackson's *Hangsaman*, which we will look at in detail in a later chapter, as 'an eerie novel about lesbians.' To be fair to Jackson, this is a bizarre reading of the novel but she was incensed. Her biographer, Judy Oppenheimer, quoted her as saying, 'I happen to know what *Hangsaman* is about. I wrote it. And dammit it is about what I say it is about and not some dirty old lady at Oxford. Because (let me whisper) I don't really know anything about stuff like that. And I don't want to know... I am writing about ambivalence but it is an ambivalence of the spirit or the mind, not the sex. My poor devils have enough to contend with without being sex deviates along with being moral and romantic deviates.' There is in fact no lesbianism in the work of Shirley Jackson (1916-1965), or indeed sex of any kind, though it is implied that Natalie Waite in *Hangsaman* has had a sexual experience that she does not remember and which is not described in the novel; either way, it is certainly not a lesbian experience.

One reason for this lack of sex among her teenage protagonists might be that Jackson had daughters of her own who might read her work. She might not have known much about lesbianism but she did know a lot about the adolescent girl; she wrote several of them into her novels and stories and we will later be considering three of them in depth: Natalie Waite; Harriet Merriam and Merricat Blackwood. Jackson's style might be called Northern Gothic, in contrast to Flannery O'Connor's Southern Gothic – we will also be looking at O'Connor's Sabbath Lily Hawks later. Jackson's Gothic is much cooler and less febrile than O'Connor's, the horror is more subtle and told with a flat, deadpan manner. The work which first made Jackson (in)famous was the short story 'The Lottery,' first published in the *New Yorker* in 1948, in which we slowly come to realise that the apparently very normal inhabitants of the apparently very normal village annually select by lottery one of their neighbours to stone to death; it is the banality, the ordinariness of the people and their environment – what Hannah Arendt later called the banality of evil – that makes it so shocking; Jackson was deluged with hate mail of a very vicious and personal nature. Her most famous novel, *The Haunting of Hill House* is an equally subtle and slow-revealing story but this time a full-length novel, that Stephen King praised as one of the greatest of American ghost stories and that has been compared with *The Turn of the Screw* for its pervasive atmosphere of ambivalent menace. King especially praised the book's first line: 'No live organism can continue for long to exist sanely under conditions of absolute reality.' King said, 'there are few if any descriptive passages in the English language that are finer.'

One of Jackson's most Gothic novels is *The Sundial*, which Jackson herself called 'a nasty little novel full of mean people who hate each other.' As in *We Have Always Lived in the Castle* and *The Haunting of Hill House*, a grand old house is at the centre of the story and a character in its own right. This was a key trope in Gothic novels with malign settings like the Castle of Otranto, Castle Udolpho and Northanger Abbey, though the latter turns out not to be malign at all. In Jackson's version of the Gothic castle lives one of her most memorable creations, the appalling ten-year-old well Fancy Halloran (another version of the name Frances), not yet a teenager and nowhere near to coming of age but fully realised in wickedness; a kind of literary version of Wednesday Addams. (*The Addams Family*, with their own spooky, Gothic house, had started appearing in *The New Yorker* in 1938.)

> Young Mrs Halloran, looking after her mother-in-law, said without hope, 'maybe she will drop dead on the doorstep. Fancy, dear, would you like to see Granny drop dead on the doorstep?'
>
> 'Yes, Mother.' Fancy pulled at the long black dress her grandmother had put on her...
>
> 'I am going to pray for it as long as I live,' said young Mrs Halloran, folding her hands together devoutly.
>
> 'Shall I push her,' Fancy asked. 'Like she pushed my daddy?'
>
> 'Fancy!' said Mrs Ogilvie.
>
> 'Let her say it if she wants,' young Mrs Halloran said. 'I want her to remember it, anyway. Say it again, Fancy baby.'
>
> 'Granny killed my daddy,' said Fancy obediently. 'She pushed him down the stairs and killed him. Granny did it. Didn't she?'

Later, Fancy is talking to her Aunt Fanny, after whom she is named (another Frances). They are talking about who is going to inherit the house; Aunt Fanny points out that Fancy has plenty of toys and does not want for anything. Here Jackson perfectly captures how scary children can be:

'I have my dollhouse,' Fancy said suddenly, looking for the first time squarely at Aunt Fanny. 'I have my beautiful little doll's house with real doorknobs and electric lights and the little stove that really works and the running water in the bathtubs.'

'You are a fortunate child,' Miss Ogilvie said.

'And all the little dolls. One of them,' Fancy giggled, 'is lying in the little bathtub with the water really running. They're little doll house dolls. They fit exactly into the chairs and the beds. They have little dishes. When I put them to bed they have to go to bed. When my grandmother dies all *this* is going to belong to me.'

'And where would we be then?' Essex asked softly. 'Fancy?'

Fancy smiled at him. 'When my grandmother dies,' she said, 'I am going to smash my dolls house. I won't need it any more.'

By the time her later novels were being published, Jackson had teenagers of her own and knew how to write them. As well as publishing her serious work, both novels and stories, she regularly contributed frothy vignettes of her own family life to women's magazines, which were collected as *Life Among the Savages*, 1953 and *Raising Demons*, 1957; the demons of course being her own children: Laurence; Joanne; Sally and Barry, in that order. Joanne, known in the family as Jannie, is a keen reader, unlike her older brother – in this they are very much like many of the brother/sister pairs in *Girls in Bloom*. Jannie is also like many of her fictional counterparts in that she is obsessed with *Little Women* to an extent that even her writer mother finds worrying. In one scene Jackson calls to her from the foot of the stairs.

> There was a pause and then Jannie said, sniffling, 'Yes?'
>
> 'Good heavens,' I said, 'are you reading *Little Women* again?'
>
> Jannie sniffled. 'Just the part where Beth dies.'
>
> 'Look,' I said, 'the sun is shining and the sky is blue and –'

Later they have a full-blown mother/daughter bonding session over that book and writing in general; again like many of her fictional counterparts, Jannie wants to be a writer, as does Jackson's daughter Sally: Jackson's late essay 'Notes for a Young Writer' was 'originally written as a stimulus to my daughter Sally, who wants to be a writer.' Although not obviously a tomboy herself, Jannie, like most girls, identifies most closely with Jo.

> I was sitting at the kitchen table grating potatoes for potato pancakes and was thus a wholly captive audience when Jannie came in from school with her arithmetic and spelling books, and, of course, *Little Women*. She put the books down, took off her jacket and hat, took an apple, and sat down at the table across from me. 'I've been meaning to ask you for a long time,' she said. 'Suppose I wanted to write a book. Where would I begin?'
> 'At the beginning,' I said smartly; I had just grated my knuckle.
> 'I wish Laurie and Barry were girls,' she said.
> 'Why on earth?'
> 'And Sally's name was Beth.'
> 'Why put the whammy on Sally? Why don't *you* be Beth?'
> 'I'm Jo.'
> 'And Laurie is Meg? And poor Barry has to be Amy?'
> 'If they were only *girls*.'
> 'And does that make me Marmee? Or can I be the old cook?'
> 'Hannah? When *I* write *my* book –'
> 'I'd rather be crazy old Aunt March, come to think of it. Who do you like for Professor Bhaer?'
> Jannie turned pink. 'I didn't really think about that yet,' she said.
> Charitably, I changed the subject. 'Don't you have any homework to do?' I asked.
> She sighed. 'I've got to write a book report, she said. 'That's why I'd like to write a book, so then I could write a book report on *that*, and save all that time.'

As well as contributing these domestic scenes to various magazines, Jackson also wrote and published several essays about the joys and perils of being the mother of an adolescent girl. In 'Mother, Honestly!' She talks about being the mother of a twelve-year-old girl and captures perfectly the sudden transition from girl to about-to-be woman.

> Those mothers who have lasted till a child has reached twelve have themselves pretty well in hand... now that the girl is twelve she is

practically grown-up and can take care of herself and begin to be responsible.

I know mothers who keep telling themselves and telling themselves it is like that, their voices getting more and more shrill, wringing their hands and grinding their teeth. Now the girl is twelve, they say, she's practically grown-up. She is. She is. She *is*.

That's me.

Last year I sent my daughter, an agreeable child who liked to play baseball and thought boys were silly, off to camp. I got back – and it only took two months – a creature who slept with curlers in her hair, bought perfume from the five-and-ten, and addressed me as nothing but 'Mother, *honestly!*...'

She has learned from her Home Ec teacher and her Scout leader how to manage perfectly well in the kitchen, but if her mother is around she drops cups of flour and burns eggs and steps on the cat. She can shut herself in the bathroom combing her hair until her mother beats feverishly and hysterically on the door, yet she is never late for school because that is where the boys are...

She is growing up and pretty soon now she will start being responsible and neat and sensible. I must be more tolerant... One thing really bothers me. I recently met a mother whose daughter is sixteen. When I remarked casually that I would be happy when my daughter outgrew her present stage and became more sensible and responsible, she just looked at me for one long minute and then began to laugh. She laughed and laughed and laughed. As I say, that bothers me a little.

Jackson later wrote an article called 'On Girls of Thirteen' where she talks about the mythical girl to whom her daughter always refers when she is forbidden to do something. This girl is 'thirteen years old. She is allowed to cut her own hair. She is also allowed to wear lipstick all the time; she uses bright red nail polish and heavily scented bath salts, and stays up as late at night as she pleases.' This imaginary girl goes to any dance she likes and stays out as late as she likes afterwards, goes to the movies on school nights and is allowed to walk out with a boy without having to introduce into her parents first. 'I don't know her name or where she lives, but I'd like to get my hands on her. Just for about five minutes. She is the lowest common denominator, the altogether anonymous "everyone else" who rules the lives of thirteen-year-old girls and their miserable mothers.'

Jackson points out that 'a bevy of thirteen-year-olds has only one mind, and it is the mind of everyone else.' These girls have obviously been reading *Sub-Deb* columns. 'The group has firm opinions (second-hand, of course, and not infrequently handed down by some teenage idol) on such momentous subjects as drinking and smoking (bad), learning to drive (good), showing off in public (bad, particularly if there are boys around), acting on a stage (very good indeed), and going steady (all right if everyone else is doing it and if someone asks you).'

I hunch myself over the wheel of the car, teeth clenched, when I am driving a pack of them to town so Patty can buy herself a blouse (it takes six of them to buy Patty a blouse, six giggling girls and three hours of shopping) and I hear the conversation going on behind me. I know by now that if I am putting six girls into my car the front seat beside me will always be left empty, but I can still hear them. What Ricky did, and what the teacher said, and oh, it was so *funny*, and does anyone remember what Johnny said to Cheryl when she dropped her pencil and oh, it was so *funny*, and one thing about Sandy, even though she is terribly pretty, and all the boys go for her, it's that fellow in college she really likes, even if he is almost 18, and Cheryl knows for a fact they're going steady. Linda heard this from Carole and Carole heard it from her big sister and her big sister says Sandy's not the one he *really* likes, and when Patty came right out and said so to her face, oh, it was so *funny*. Then Carole said that Cheryl liked Tommy, and oh, it was so...

There is a thirteen-year-old girl, Betsy, in Jackson's story *The Missing Girl*, set in the Phillips Education Camp for Girls Twelve to Sixteen; both the story and the setting are rather reminiscent of Eudora Welty's story *Moon Lake*. She is as awkward and as uncommunicative with adults as Jackson's non-fictional thirteen-year-olds. Betsy, who has roomed with the eponymous missing girl, is being questioned by the chief of police. She tells him the missing girl 'said she had something to do.' The chief asks Betsy how she said it; perhaps she was lying? '"She just *said* it", said Betsy, who had reached that point of stubbornness most thirteen-year-old girls have, when it seems that adult obscurity has passed beyond necessity. "I *told* you eight times."' Later in the same story, the librarian tells the chief, 'one girl is much like another, at this age. Their unformed minds, unformed bodies, their little mistakes.'

Finally, in Jackson's essay 'All I Can Remember' which was printed as the preface to the story collection *Just an Ordinary Day*, she talks about her memories of herself as a teenager. She begins: 'all I can remember clearly about being sixteen is that it was a particularly agonising age.' Like some of her characters, and many others in *Girls in Bloom*, she is a voracious reader and this is the age at which she decides to become a writer. Again, Jackson perfectly captures the awkwardness of the teenager and the difficulty of communication between herself and her parents; the teenage Jackson in this description very closely matches Harriet Merriam in *The Road Through the* Wall, whom we will meet later.

> I also remember such a tremendous and frustrated irritation with whatever I was reading at the time – heaven knows what it could have been, considering some of the things I put away about that time – that I decided one evening that since there were no books in the world fit to read, I would write one.
>
> After dismissing the poetic drama as outmoded and poetry as far too difficult, I finally settled on a mystery story as easiest to write and probably easiest to read...
>
> After the first two or three murders, the story got rather sketchy, because I had not enough patience to waste all that time with investigation, so I put the names of my characters together and took my manuscript downstairs to read to my family.
>
> My mother was knitting, my father was reading a newspaper, and my brother was doing something – probably carving his initials in the coffee table – and I persuaded them all to listen to me; I read them the entire manuscript, and when I had finished, the conversation went approximately like this:
>
> BROTHER: Whaddyou call *that*?
> MOTHER: It's very nice, dear.
> FATHER: Very nice, very nice, (*to my mother*) You call them about the furnace?
> BROTHER: Only thing is, you ought to get *all* those people killed. (raucous laughter)

MOTHER: Shirley, in all that time upstairs I hope you remembered to make your bed.

I do not remember what character eventually came out of the hat with blood on his hands, but I do remember that I decided never to read another mystery story and never to write another mystery story; never, as a matter of fact, to write anything ever again. I had already decided finally that I was never going to be married and certainly would never have any children.

This is almost exactly what fourteen-year-old Harriet Merriam in *The Road Through the Wall*, which we will look at later, says in the note describing where she will be in ten years' time that she buries in the ground, though by the time Jackson wrote that she was very much married and very much had children.

> *In ten years I will be a beautiful charming lovely lady writer without any husband or children but lots of lovers and everyone will read the books I write and want to marry me but I will never marry any of them. I will have lots of money and jewels too.*

In Jackson's *Hangsaman*, which we will also look at in more detail later, seventeen-year-old Natalie Waite has a very similar thought:

> Seventeen years was a very long time to have been alive, if you took it into proportion by the thought that in seventeen years more – or as long as she had wasted being a child, and a small girl, silly and probably playing – she would be thirty-four, and old. Married, probably. Perhaps – and the thought was nauseating – senselessly afflicted with children of her own. Worn, and tired.

SEVENTEENTH SUMMER: TEEN NOVELS OF THE 1940S

The rise of the teenager in the 1940s was accompanied by the rise of the teenage novel: novels written for and about teenage girls. As well as the adult, literary novels we will be looking at, the 1940s and 50s saw several books and series of books by female authors about girls in their 'seventeenth summer,' intended to be read by girls of around that age or younger; the demographic for the *Sub-Deb* columns and Betty Cornell's advice. But unlike the Sub-Debs, these 'practically seventeens' are generally not obsessed with their looks, their figure or dating boys; they are mostly bookish and shy – like, presumably, the girls who read them – though they often have more glamorous and more extroverted older sisters. And, unlike the central characters in the more literary novels intended for adults, the girls in these books usually have normal, loving, middle-class parents, with whom they tend not to have angst-ridden, existential conflicts. The father is usually employed in a respectable job and the mother stays at home cooking and baking and so tends to be slightly overweight and homely.

One of the earliest examples of this genre was the short story 'Sixteen' by Maureen Daly – later the editor of the *Ladies' Home Journal's Sub-Deb* column – which won first prize in a short story competition in 1938 when Daly was herself sixteen and still at school; the previous year she had entered a story called 'Fifteen' and won third prize. The narration foreshadows the knowing, conspiratorial tone of many of the subsequent novels about sixteen-year-old girls, many of which were influenced by it. The unnamed narrator is confident, modern and independent; like some of her successors (and of course Cinderella) she has two older sisters as role models.

Now don't get me wrong. I mean, I want you to understand from the beginning that I'm not really dumb. I know what a girl should do and what she shouldn't. I get around. I read. I listen to the radio. And I have two older sisters. So, you see, I know what the score is . . . I'm not exactly small-town either. I read Winchell's column. You get to know what New York boy is that way about some pineapple Princess on the West Coast and what Paradise pretty is currently the prettiest. It gives you that cosmopolitan feeling. And I know that anyone who orders a strawberry sundae in a drugstore instead of a lemon Coke would probably be dumb enough to wear colored ankle-socks with high-heeled pumps or use Evening in Paris with a tweed suit. But I'm sort of drifting. This isn't what I wanted to tell you. I just wanted to give you that the general idea of how I'm not so dumb. It's important that you understand that.

The narrator is ice-skating when a boy comes up and says: 'Mind if I skate with you?' She agrees. 'That's all there was to it. Just that and then we were skating. It wasn't that I'd never skated with a boy before. Don't be silly. I told you before, I get around. But this was different. He was a big shot at school and he went to all the big dances and he was the best dancer in town.' Afterwards, walking home in the snow they talk, softly, 'as if every little word were secret... A very respectable Emily Post sort of conversation and then finally – how nice I looked with snow in my hair and had I ever seen the moon so close?' As he leaves her at her door the boy says he will call her.

And that was last Thursday. Tonight is Tuesday. Tonight is Tuesday and my homework is done and I darned some stockings that didn't really need it, and worked a crossword puzzle, and I listened to the radio and now I'm just sitting. I'm sitting because I can't think of anything, anything but snowflakes and ice skates and a yellow moon and Thursday night. The telephone is sitting on the corner table with its old black face turned to the wall so I can't see its leer. I don't even jump when it rings any more. My heart still prays but my mind just laughs... And so I'm just sitting here and I'm not feeling anything. I'm not even sad because all of a sudden I know. All of a sudden I know. I can sit here now for ever and laugh and laugh and laugh while the tears run salty in the corners of my mouth. For all of a sudden I know. I know what the stars knew all the time – he'll never never call – never.

As a sixteen-year-old herself, Daly fully understands and beautifully communicates this life-altering tragedy in a way that no adult novelist could.

ANGIE MORROW: *SEVENTEENTH SUMMER* BY MAUREEN DALY, 1942.

One of the earliest full-length teen girl books of the 1940s, and arguably the first Young Adult novel, is Maureen Daly's first novel, *Seventeenth Summer*. Since the category did not exist at that time it was issued as an adult novel though Irish-born American writer Daly (1921-2006) was still – just – a teenager; she was still at college when she finished writing it. It continues the theme of the short story 'Sixteen' and foreshadows many of the features of the later books aimed at teenage girl by Rosamond du Jardin and others, with its almost-seventeen narrator whose world consists entirely of her family – conventional middle-class father, mother and three sisters – her school and her first boyfriend; the novel covers just the summer of their relationship. It opens rather like Daly's earlier 'Sixteen': 'I don't know just why am telling you all this. Maybe you think I'm being silly. But I'm not, really, because this is *important*. You see, it was different!' Of course, it is only important within Angie's small world and only different compared her previously very limited experience. She says to her date, Jack: 'I just want to read a lot and learn everything I can,' but she is just trying to impress him. In return he says he wants to go to an opera wearing a cape and white gloves, 'I don't know much about music,' he says. 'I don't even like it a lot but I could learn.' But Jack's family are socially one step down from Angie's and she notices the difference even if he doesn't. Her mother notices too. 'It isn't that my mother doesn't like boys, as I explained, but because we are girls and because we are the kind of family who always use top sheets on the beds and always eat our supper in the dining room and things like that – well, she just didn't want us to go out with *anybody*.' Her mother probably reads *Ladies Home Journal*.

This social difference is put under the microscope the first time Jack comes for dinner. Angie's older sister Lorraine shows off her knowledge of literature, deliberately – at least in Angie's mind – to expose Jack; she asks him if he has read various books.

Jack looked at her in her embarrassment and his lips were awkward with his words. 'I don't read much,' he confessed and my heart slipped down a little 'I don't read at all as much as I'd like to,' he went on, 'but, gee, with school and everything . . .' He looked at her in apology and then at me, adding feebly, 'I play a lot of basketball and things . . .'

Angie defends him, but only in her mind, she does not speak up in his defence. Her sisters do not realise, she thinks, that 'he could dance to any kind of music at all, fast or slow, and that any girl in town would be glad to wear his basketball sweater even for one night.' But the disastrous meal is soon made even worse by Jack's eating habits and even Angie starts to look down on him.

> In our house where we had never been allowed to eat untidily, even when we sat in highchairs! It all seemed so suddenly and sickeningly clear – I could just see his father in shirtsleeves, piling food onto his knife and never using napkins except where there was company. And probably they brought the coffee pot right in and set it on the table. My whole mind was filled with a growing disdain and loathing. His family probably didn't even own a butter knife! No girl has to stand for that. Never. If a boy gets red in the face, sputters salad dressing on the tablecloth, and hasn't even read a single book to talk about when you ask him over for dinner, you don't have to be nice to him – even if he has kissed you and said things to you that no one has ever said before!

Daly became a journalist after leaving college – she graduated in English and Latin – working as a reporter and book reviewer on the *Chicago Tribune* and *Saturday Evening Post* as well as at one point editing the *Sub-Deb* column at the *Ladies' Home Journal*. But, despite the success of *Seventeenth Summer*, which sold over 1 million copies, and was reissued in 2002, Daly wrote no more novels until the mid-1980s.

BEANY MALONE BY LENORA MATTINGLY WEBER, 1948

Lenora Mattingly Weber (1895–1971) grew up on the plains of Colorado and by the time she was sixteen was riding in rodeos; she later had six children of her own. Over a period of over forty years Weber published stories in most of the women's magazines, including *Ladies Home Jour-*

nal and *Good Housekeeping*. The first Malone book, which concerns the whole family, was followed by *Beany Malone*, 1948 which has the sixteen-year-old Beany as its central character. There were twelve books in the Malone series, which ran until 1969, plus *The Beany Malone Cookbook*, 1972. Weber also wrote the Katie Rose Belford series: five books from 1964-1968 about the twenty-year-old Katie Rose, the Stacey Belford Series, three books from 1970-1972 and ten non-series novels.

'Sixteen-year-old Catherine Cecilia Malone – known as Beany to family and friends,' like other tomboy heroines, has a gender-neutral nickname with no hint of femininity or sexual attractiveness. She has a 'sprinkling of freckles' across her nose and a 'square-chinned face,' with 'stubby brown braids, which she wore pinned up now that she was a high school sophomore.' Her father is a writer, a journalist rather than a creative writer and, like Tobey Haydon, she has an older sister, Elizabeth, who is married with a child and who lives with her family while her husband is absent – in this case he is a soldier who has not yet returned from abroad.

Elizabeth was lovable and loving – and so lovely! Oh, why couldn't I, Beany often thought, have hair that makes a shining aureole about my face (as they say in books? Why couldn't boys send me violets and say they were pale compared to my eyes? 'Beany is so capable,' everyone said . . . But doggonit, when you were a high school sophomore and your heart's eyes always followed one certain boy down the hall, it wasn't enough to be tagged as capable.

The 'one certain boy' is Norbett, for whose benefit she is 'secretly ordering freckle cream.' She sits next to him in typing classes, where he asks her advice on spelling. 'Oh, thank goodness, she could spell! Maybe he hadn't noticed the freckles, or her hair, which Beany, in her pessimistic moments, called "roan."' In the middle of making a cake, Beany goes to the drugstore.

Then her heart did a hollow hop, skip, and jump. Norbett Rhodes was standing at the magazine rack, thumbing through a magazine.
Instinctively Beany's two hands reached out and caught her short flappy braids under her combs. Oh, why did she have to meet Norbett

Rhodes, wearing this messy plaid seersucker under Johnny's faded, shapeless jacket!

Norbett said, 'Hi, Beany!' and she said, 'Hi, Norbett!' and stood so he wouldn't see the dab of icing on her skirt.

But the fountain mirror, with its pasted-on patches telling of sundaes and sandwiches, showed a girl with cheeks as pink as the peppermint-stick ice cream that she had mixed earlier. Her eyes weren't the violet blue of Elizabeth's, but a grey-blue shadowed by short but very thick eyelashes. Her 'roan' hair hadn't the golden highlights of Elizabeth's, but it had a soap-and-water, well-brushed shine. Beany's prettiness was of the honest, hardy variety.

The druggist, behind the fountain, called out, 'Beany, the freckle cream I ordered for you came. Want to take it?'

'No – no – ' she faltered. 'I just want some pink candle holders.' If only Norbett was too preoccupied with his magazine to notice.

Yes, Beany. If only.

SALLY BURNABY: *SENIOR YEAR* BY ANNE EMERY, 1949

Anne Emery (1907-1984), who was a teacher for ten years and had five children of her own, wrote five books in the Sally and Jean Burnaby series, four in the Dinny Gordon series, three each in the Jane Ellison and Pat Marlowe series and two Sue Morgan books as well as a large number of non-series novels.

Like Rosamond du Jardin's twins Penny and Pam Howard, whom we will meet in a minute, sisters Sally and Jean Burnaby are chalk and cheese: one is quiet and bookish, unconcerned about clothes and boys, while the other is fashion conscious, outgoing and interested in dating. Except that in this case the narrative focus, unusually, is the 'shallow' sister, Sally. Their family is typical of this kind of novel: middle-class, confident consumers. The father is 'slender and wiry... Sometimes you'd never think he was a dignified college professor.' Their mother, 'looking like one of the girls, with her trim figure and dark hair,' is like a big sister to them. 'Mother was something to rejoice in – young looking as an older sister, tolerant and easy to talk to. She seemed to know how things happened without being told. And she had as much energy as one of the high school crowd.'

Sally is constantly annoyed by Jean's sloppiness in her dress and untidiness in their shared bedroom, and when they return from a family holiday it all gets too much for her.

Sally had made firm resolutions every night of their trip not to nag at Jean anymore. But this time she couldn't help herself. 'Your jeans are filthy. You look simply awful! Aren't you going to clean up and unpack?'

'Who cares?' yawned Jean, her feet, in thick socks and dirty saddle shoes, sprawling over most of the floor.

'Oh, honestly!' Sally snapped. 'I don't see how you can stand it! All you have to do is clean up a little!'

'Go fly a kite!' Jean instructed her in lazy cheerfulness. 'I'm tired, and I want to lie down and read a good book!'...

Sally's considered opinion was that her sister was hopeless. It wasn't just that she never pick things up and never closed her dresser drawers entirely and never put shoe trees in her shoes; those things at least Sally could bear, in the bosom of the family. But she refused to do anything about her hair. Said she hadn't time – she'd rather read. She wouldn't put on lipstick. And she didn't care if she wore the same dress two days in a row when everyone knew *that* simply was not done.

As well as being a keen reader, Jean is musical. 'Sally wished now that she could play as well as Jean. But there never seemed to be time to practice.' This of course is because Sally spends her time with friends – especially her best friend Kate – and boys; she is exactly the kind of outgoing, popular girl Betty Cornell was to write about a few years later. Conversely, Jean typically looks 'bleak and discontented,' as she goes round with 'her arms full of books.' But in fact, when she was 'in a good humor, there was something sparkly and fresh about Jean, an elusive charm that surprised Sally every time she noticed it. Jean's mouth was lovely when she smiled, but for schoolmates that was seldom. They knew her only as she was now, sulky and plain.' Unlike Sally, she does not like to join in school activities. 'I loathe clubs,' she says. Sally on the other hand had 'joined any activity with Kate and enjoyed them all.'

The tragedy of Sally's summer is that Kate, with whom she is very close, is going away to school. 'I think that's nice for Kate," says their mother. 'But what about me?' replies Sally.

That's how it always was, Sally thought bitterly. No one cared how she felt at all. All through high school she and Kate had done things together. And now Kate wouldn't be there for senior year.

What about the crowd? The double dates for dances and movies? And the football games! It would be no fun at all to go to them alone. Even at lunch hours! There were lots of other girls. But there wasn't anyone else like Kate.

Bleakly Sally faced herself in the mirror. She was going to be on her own this year. And what on earth was she going to do?...

High school *wasn't* the same without Kate. There was the same gay crowd in the halls, the same excited gossip, but none of it seemed important without Kate to share it. Sally missed her coming out of the classrooms, going to hockey, and especially on the way home. Warmed-over news in letters was highly unsatisfactory. Without Kate, Sally felt as if she had an amputation.

Of course, the word 'gay' in the previous paragraph does not mean what it means now; there is no explicit suggestion that Sally and Kate have any kind of physical relationship, and presumably the female teenage readers of the time would not have thought about their relationship that way – unless they themselves had sexual feelings about girls. Sally likes to be popular with boys but it seems to be the popularity she likes rather than the boys themselves; she certainly is not passionate about anyone. Her friends seem to think that Scott, with whom Sally has been friends since fourth grade, is her boyfriend; 'I don't know if I actually go with him,' she says, 'at least not steady.' Sally had 'not the slightest reason to think Scotty was mad about her, but it was pleasant to hear it.' 'Pleasant' is very faint praise indeed from a girl of this age. But it does not seem that Scotty is particularly passionate about her either: Sally's new friend Millie says, 'Eddie told me that Red told him that Don said he heard Scotty say he thought you were quite a girl.' Jean tells Sally not to let Millie 'give you all that stuff about Scotty!' Sally takes this like 'cold water on her face,' but she 'recovered and pretended indifference,' defending her new friend, while staying cool about Scott and trying to make her sister feel not so bad about being unpopular.

It would be nice if true. I never liked her much – but I thought today she wasn't as bad as I expected. At least she isn't snippy to girls who aren't popular – like us!

ROSAMOND DU JARDIN'S PRACTICALLY SEVENTEENS

Rosamond du Jardin (1902-1963) had published five adult novels and a large number of short stories in women's magazines – she published over a hundred stories in all – before she started to write books for the teenage market. Once she started she became very prolific and very successful, publishing seventeen Young Adult novels including four Tobey Haydon books, beginning with *Practically Seventeen*, from 1949 to 1951; two books about Midge Haydon (Tobey's younger sister) from 1958 to 1961; four books in the Marcy Rhodes series from 1950 to 1957 and four in the Pam and Penny Howard series from 1950 to 1959. (All of these, as well as many of the authors in the previous chapter, have recently been republished as physical and electronic books by specialist publisher Image Cascade.)

TOBEY HAYDON: *PRACTICALLY SEVENTEEN*, 1949.

'My name is Tobey Haydon and I am practically seventeen years old, since my sixteenth birthday was five whole months ago.' According to Tobey she is, 'older than my sixteen years in lots of ways, I think.' This of course is how most sixteen-year-olds feel, including the fictional ones. Tobey (note the gender-ambiguous name) begins by introducing herself and her family, including her sisters and her 'fairly modern' parents (bear in mind that du Jardin was forty-seven years old with three children, including two girls, when this was published):

Ours is quite a large family, as families go nowadays. First there are my mother and father, who are pretty old, in their 40s. Still they are fairly modern in their ideas. My father is tall and thinnish and has a pleasant face with lots of laugh wrinkles. He claims that any man, completely surrounded by females in his own home, would go crazy without a sense of humour and that he has had to develop his in self defense. Sometimes his wit is a little corny, as is often the case with older people. But none of us mind. He is really sweet, as fathers go. My mother is very well satisfied with him, too. Her only complaint is that his job as a salesman of plumbing supplies takes him away from home on occasional out-of-town trips, during which time she seems to miss him very much indeed.

My mother thinks she is overweight and she is always talking about dieting and losing ten pounds, although compared with the mothers of some of my friends she has a very nice figure.

Like Mick Kelly and Maureen Daly's Angie Morrow, Tobey has two older sisters though unlike Mick's and Angie's sisters they are horrid to her; she acts as a kind of Cinderella to them, though the sisters are by no means ugly. She also has a younger sister. Janet, the eldest, is twenty-three with 'dark red hair and very blue eyes and the kind of figure that rates admiring whistles on street corners,' though she is married and has a baby known as Toots, 'a bundle of fiendish energy aged three,' who is living with the family while Janet's husband is working away. Next is her sister Alicia, who is 'twenty and beautiful, if you care for blondes.' (The stage show of *Gentlemen Prefer Blondes* opened in 1949, the same year as *Practically Seventeen*; Anita Loos' novel had come out in 1925, and the first film of it in 1928. The more famous film version, with Marilyn Monroe and Jane Russell did not come out until 1953.) Alicia, who has just got engaged, is mean and spiteful to Tobey and 'hasn't a smidgen of a sense of humour, although how this can be true of one of my father's daughters is difficult to see.' Finally, Tobey has 'quite a young sister named Marjorie, but inevitably called Midge. She has a lot more freckles than I, sandy hair that she wears braided in pigtails, and skinny legs. She may improve, though, as she gets older. Right now she is only eight and my father frequently refers to her as The After-thought, this being an example of one of his more corny jokes.'

The recently-engaged Alicia and her fiancé are 'always kissing. Now I personally, have nothing against this form of amusement, particularly for engaged couples. Still I should think they might want to do something else for a change now and then.' Tobey does not specify, indeed does not appear to know, what other things engaged couples might do for a change. Tobey has a boyfriend called Brose who takes her to the movies but does not apparently do very much else with her; on one date with him she puts on lipstick which she has 'borrowed' from one of the sisters but she finds it 'very difficult to maintain any glamour whatever in a family with so many women around, especially sisters.' They all, including Midge and her mother, mock Tobey's attempts to look grown-up.

Tobey, like most of the heroines in this genre, is bookish and serious rather than glamorous and flirtatious. Her mother, sounding like Betty Cornell, tries to get Tobey her to make more of herself: 'do stop slumping. You have curvature of the spine.' But still, Tobey has learned some womanly wiles from her older sisters. 'Brose is really wonderful. I wouldn't admit this publicly, because it doesn't pay to let your true opinion of a man get around. Either it goes to his head, or some of your girlfriends decide to try to take him away from you if he's that terrific. But I am pretty crazy about Brose.' Tobey certainly does not want to rush into marriage; she has the example of Janet, at twenty-four, who 'sees life sort of passing her by and her husband's faraway and she is growing old and older and what does the future hold for her?' What indeed.

MARCY RHODES: *WAIT FOR MARCY*, 1950

Marcy is a tomboy. But for Christmas her grandmother has bought her – at Marcy's request – a white net 'formal,' a dress to be worn to parties or other formal occasions; another Cinderella reference perhaps (Disney's film of *Cinderella* appeared in 1950, too late for du Jardin to have seen it before she wrote these last two novels; Marcia Brown's popular, illustrated retelling of Perrault's version of the story was not published until 1955). Marcy does not really do parties and has never worn the dress. As the novel opens she is sitting 'sprawled comfortably crosswise in a slip-covered chair, deeply engrossed in her favourite magazine. The white shirt she wore had long since been discarded by her father, her blue jeans were deeply cuffed. Floppy moccasins hung from her toes. At fifteen Marcy was dark and slim, with brown hair curled under in a soft bell. Hers were a sort of looks that might easily develop into real loveliness as she grew older.' Still, despite her tomboyish dress sense, Marcy envies her best friend's looks; she 'would gladly have traded high cheek bones, wide dark eyes and golden tan skin for the blonde, blue-eyed prettiness possessed by her closest friend, Liz Kendall.'

Unlike Tobey and Cinderella, Marcy has no sisters, though she does have an older brother, Ken. Older brothers of course are an annoyance, always seeking to embarrass their sister, though Betty Cornell advised that 'an older brother is about the best social insurance any teen-ager can have.' Like Tobey's, Marcy's mother is 'an agreeable-looking woman, just verging on plumpness, whose fair hair was only lightly frosted with grey.' Also like Tobey, she considers that her parents, 'on the whole, were fairly reasonable,' though not when her mother starts urging her to go to the school dance, if only so she can wear the formal dress.

> Marcy felt a sick sort of sensation in her tummy. The very first suitable occasion. A dance in the big gym at High, with paper festoons and the lights softened and all the couples, all the girls and their dates, whirling and swaying to just the sort of music that was coming from the radio now. Her lovely white formal would fit into the picture perfectly. But before she could wear it, before she could be a part of the entrancing scene in her mind, someone – who, she wondered a little desperately? – would have to invite her to go with him.
>
> Grow up, why don't you? That was what Ken had said just now. Marcy was trying, but in some respects it wasn't easy.

It never is, Marcy.

PENNY HOWARD: *DOUBLE DATE,* 1951

Penny and Pam Howard are twin sisters but have very different personalities; authors of teen novels often use the device of a sister or best friend with an opposite personality to the protagonist; usually she is shy and bookish while the sister/friend is glamorous and popular. The four Penny and Pam novels, though written in the third person, are seen from the perspective of Penny, the introverted one. Pam is outgoing and popular, a Sub-Deb who has seems like read and digested Betty Cornell's advice, though it did not come out until two years later. Although they are physically identical, Penny is less gregarious, more shy and reticent. When we see the twins at home, 'Penny had been intent on her homework, curled on the couch, surrounded by books. Pam had been lying in front of the record-player, dreamily listening to Perry Como.' Du Jardin gives us access to Penny's thoughts while Pam is chatting to two boys they have just met:

> How could twin sisters, who looked so much alike that most people couldn't tell them apart, be so unlike inside? She had pondered the question many times before and found no answer. How could Pam chat on so animatedly, so effortlessly, keeping these boys she scarcely knew interested and amused, instilling in them a desire to get better acquainted? Penny could think of nothing at all to add to Pam's running comments. Beside her sister she felt leaden and dull and miserably aware of the poor impression she was making. Trudging along with the others, Penny spoke only when spoken to directly. Casual, friendly talk eddied about her like a warm current, while she contributed little more than monosyllables. Not that the others seemed to notice. Pam's voice filled any void that might otherwise have been left by Penny's silence.

Du Jardin has presumably chosen to focus on the socially-awkward twin deliberately – she probably assumed, and probably correctly, that teenage girls who read novels like hers rather than *Ladies Home Journal* columns would themselves be socially awkward and identify more with Penny than Pam, the girl curled up on the couch surrounded by books rather than the girl dreamily listening to crooners. Read in another way of course, Penny is Pam's alter ego, the girl she wants to be, the girl she – and her readers – aspire to be.

DADDY'S GIRLS

Although it is strictly outside the scope of *Girls in Bloom*, which is about fiction written by women, I want to briefly consider some novels from the period that are about teenage girls but were written by the fathers of teenage daughters; heroines who are literally daddy's girls, or at least based on them. Of course, the ultimate wayward (step)daddy's girl of the 1950s is Dolores Haze, from Vladimir Nabokov's *Lolita*, published in 1955. Not many writers contribute new words to the English language but Nabokov contributed two new nouns related to adolescent girls: *lolita* and *nymphet*. neither of these words existed before 1955. Now they are everywhere, including places Nabokov cannot possibly have had in mind, like Japan, where the Japanese male fascination with schoolgirls is called roricon (lolicon, short for Lolita Complex). For young Japanese women there is an enormous Lolita fashion sub-culture, with sub-sub cultures like Lolita Goth Punk. *Lolita* is undoubtedly a coming of age novel in its unique way, but Dolores' story is not told from her point of view; all we know about her is what the narrator tells us, and we know how unreliable he is. *Lolita* is like *Little Red Riding Hood* as told by the wolf. Even the name we know Dolores by, Lolita, is not her own but is given to her by her narrator Humbert; she is indeed seen through a haze.

Another underage, virgin temptress from around the same time who may be called a daddy's girl but was created by a woman, is the terrifying fifteen-year-old Sabbath Lily Hawks (a girl with a mythic/biblical name) in *Wise Blood*, 1952, by Flannery O'Connor (a female author with a gender-neutral name) who ferociously protects her preacher father while trying to seduce Hazel Motes (a man with a woman's name). We will look in detail at Sabbath Lily later. In her name and personality, Sabbath Lily is the opposite of Scout Finch, a girl with a boy's name in *To Kill a Mockingbird*, 1960, written by another author with a gender-ambiguous name: Harper Lee. Tomboy Scout is another daddy's girl who ferociously protects her father, though she is too young to be considered in *Girls in Bloom*.

In several of the novels we are considering in *Girls in Bloom*, the girl's father is a writer even though the novel was written by a woman; the novels I want to look at in this chapter actually *were* written by the heroine's father. In these books we have male authors writing coming of age novels using their own daughters as material – potentially a very disturbing idea, or at least so it seems today. The first of these authors was F Hugh Herbert and the second was Frederick Kohner. Herbert was born in Austria and moved to Hollywood, as did Kohner, the author and father of *Gidget*. Herbert wrote screenplays for at least sixty three movies, starting with *The Waning Sex* in 1926, finishing with *This Happy Feeling* in 1958, the year of his death. This was based, like several of his screenplays, on his own original script. Many of Herbert's screenplays involved relationships between willing, not to say eager younger women or girls who believe they have come of age and older male authority figures: he co-wrote *That Certain Age*, 1938 from his own original story, where a seventeen-year-old Deanna Durbin, playing a fifteen-year-old girl, pursues a thirty-seven-year old Melvyn Douglas (she is his boss's daughter), the provocatively-titled *My Heart Belongs to Daddy*, 1942, where a burlesque dancer seduces a professor (taglines: 'When she takes over the professor . . . she's in a class by herself,' and 'Professor, here's where I add a few degrees to your name . . . and your blood pressure.') and *Margie*, 1946, about a high school girl's crush on her French teacher.

Herbert's screenplay for the 1953 movie *The Moon is Blue*, directed by Otto Preminger, ran into trouble with the Motion Picture Production Code because of its 'light and gay treatment of the subject of illicit sex and seduction.' The first revision was also rejected because of 'an unacceptably light attitude towards seduction, illicit sex, chastity, and virginity.' In the end, Preminger pressed ahead without approval, releasing the film without a certificate. It was banned in some Midwestern areas, the studio appealed and eventually the US Supreme Court allowed it to be shown; it thus became part of a landmark decision that helped to weaken censorship in America.

PAMELA COTRELL: *A LOVER WOULD BE NICE* BY F HUGH HERBERT, 1935

As well as his plays and screenplays, the prolific Herbert also wrote novels about old/young romance: in 1935, before he struck gold with the Corliss Archer franchise he published *A Lover Would Be Nice*. It opens with not so much an April/September romance as early March/late November flirtation: a young woman – we don't know at this point how young – is toying shamelessly with a much older man, a cartoonish English admiral. Note that one of Herbert's real-life daughters was called Pamela.

Pamela, destined to be kissed innumerable times, remembered her first one only because it was given to her by a retired English Admiral, aged sixty, and old enough to have known better. Rear Admiral Sir Lionel Leghorn K. C. B., did, in fact know better. But Pam was looking rather beautiful.

An attractive little devil, was the way Sir Lionel put it to himself. He met her at a New Year's Eve dance in her mother's big country house on Long Island. It was a thoroughly informal affair with many of the guests in masquerade costumes. Pam represented an Oriental slave girl. She had very little on.

She tells him, 'warmly' that he is 'the first real live Admiral I've ever spoken to.' She tells him that she does not like younger men. 'Don't you hate boys of nineteen?' she asks him. 'They have no poise, no repose, no sense, and no money.' Pam takes the Admiral to the billiard room, where she asks him if he would like to play a game. 'Do you know any good games?' he asks her, 'coyly'. 'I meant a game of billiards,' says Pam, virtuously.' The Admiral wonders how old she might be and guesses anywhere from eighteen to twenty-two. Her mother disabuses him: 'She was fourteen two weeks ago.'

Pamela's actual adolescence is dismissed in half a paragraph on page twelve so that Herbert can get on with the novel of adultery his readers have been promised on the first page where, in the cast of characters, it is revealed that: 'Pamela Cotrell, who had beauty, brains and a healthy, reckless lust for life, was merely being her own normal, rational self when she decided it would take more than one man to keep her satisfied.' Herbert therefore fast forwards through her 'dull' adolescence and coming of age.

Between the ages of fourteen and nineteen, Pam gained two pounds, grew by an inch, and learned, if not wisdom, at least discrimination, which is often a better thing to learn. It is a five-year stretch in a woman's life interesting only to those who find adolescence charming. Pam found it very dull and silly.

CORLISS ARCHER: *MEET CORLISS ARCHER* BY F HUGH HERBERT, 1944

Fortunately for *Girls in Bloom*, many authors have not found adolescence to be dull and silly; including, a few years later, Herbert himself when he combined his own daughters into Corliss Archer, a completely different kind of bad girl to Pamela Cotrell. Herbert made it clear in the epigraph to *Meet Corliss Archer* where the inspiration for her character came from:

Through these pages walk the most wonderful girls in the world – my daughters,

DIANA AND PAMELA

– whose endearing struggles with adolescent problems have given me most of the material for this, their book.

The jacket blurb for the 1944 edition of the novel *Meet Corliss Archer* – it was originally published in 1942 and the play *Kiss and Tell* which was based on it was published in 1943 – emphasised this connection; it runs:

Not so very long ago, F. Hugh Herbert was driving down Hollywood Boulevard with his sixteen-year-old daughter when he stopped to give a lift to a personable young infantry-man. His daughter's spontaneous 'charm act' not only devastated the soldier, it sent Herbert himself to his typewriter to record the incident for *Good Housekeeping Magazine* and posterity. He called his heroine Corliss Archer. He little knew it at the time, but he was creating a new industry.

Corliss Archer stories became a regular and increasingly popular feature of *Good Housekeeping*. Then they became a radio show. Then Herbert fashioned them into a play called *Kiss and Tell*, which has four companies playing to capacity as this is written. Now, finally, Mr.

Herbert has collected the best of them into a book which will carry the name of the irresistible Corliss and her long-suffering admirer, Dexter, even further afield. If you haven't met Corliss yet yourself, for heaven's sake don't waste another second reading jacket blurbs.

Corliss Archer became a widespread franchise, including, as well as the novel and the play, both radio and TV series and a comic strip in which the illustrator uses highlighting to emphasise Corliss' prominent and pointed breasts in every frame; it looks as if he had in mind the young Marilyn Monroe and the (in)famous stills of Jane Russell from 1943's *The Outlaw* for which billionaire Howard Hughes, an engineer by background, designed a cantilevered, seamless bra.

Nothing very much happens to the bland and harmless fifteen-year-old Corliss in any of these formats – even the novel is just a series of short scenes, as if the author had intended it to be made into a series which, given his background, he probably did. Still, Corliss is as sharp, knowing and wisecracking as no doubt her real-life father was. Like several heroines in female coming of age novels, she adores her father, and like Natalie Waite in Shirley Jackson's *Hangsaman* and Cassandra Mortmain in Dodie Smith's *I Capture the Castle* she writes poetry for her father's approval; however, unlike Kate Chopin's Charlie Laborde, her poetry is awful.

Although her character is almost entirely asexual, and she never so much as kisses her boyfriend-next-door, the long-suffering, dumbly adoring Dexter, her foil, she does know how to seductively manipulate both of the men in her life (she also has a brother, but he is away at war, like Frankie Addams' brother). Corliss' family also have a dog, Moronica, dumber than Dexter but not nearly so adorable.

Dexter was a gangling, amiable boy just short of seventeen whose years of adolescence were being sorely complicated by the fact that he adored Corliss with all his large and extremely vulnerable heart – a circumstance of which Corliss was pleasantly aware and of which she took full advantage. She adored him too, but, being of the feminine gender, was far more shrewd and reticent about her emotions. It was Corliss' pleasure, particularly during the last few years, to harass, bewilder and humiliate the adoring Dexter whenever she deemed such a course advisable – which was pretty often.

Corliss and Dexter disagree about the film version of *Gone with the Wind*, 1939, the story of Scarlett O'Hara's coming of age: Dexter likes Clark Gable's strong silent type of masculinity whereas Corliss prefers Ashley Wilkes. Corliss cries at the movie whereas Dexter is completely unmoved; she tells him he has no soul.

'I only kiss men with souls,' she murmured seductively.

Under the amused scrutiny of his parents and Corliss, Dexter, despite the temptation, stayed firm in character as a man without sentiment.

'I guess that lets me out,' he said coldly.

'It certainly does,' Corliss declared. 'And it only goes to show that not only haven't you got a soul, but you haven't even got a heart!'

Dexter plunged his hands in his pockets and jingled his loose change in a worldly and callous fashion.

'Too bad you don't admire the Gable type,' he said cynically. 'Personally, I find that's the only way to treat women.'

'Atta boy, Dexter,' Mr. Archer encouraged him. 'Treat 'em rough.'

Corliss was wearing her Mona Lisa smile.

'Dexter,' she murmured temptingly, 'I'm going to tidy the porch after mummy and daddy go to bed. Would you like to stay and help me?'

It was the opportunity for which Dexter had connived, but now masculine pride impelled him to spurn it.

'Not interested, thanks,' he said in a bored voice.

He waved to her disdainfully and, without a backward glance, followed his parents into the night.

Corliss, helping to fold the bridge chair, giggled happily.

'Poor drip,' she said fondly. 'He is *so* cute, and such *fun* to rib.'

'You're a sadistic little beast,' Mr. Archer said, 'and I shall advise Dexter to sock you right in the nose.'

Spoken, no doubt, from the author's heart – assuming that, unlike Dexter, he had one.

DOLORES KEITH: *I'D RATHER BE KISSED*, BY F HUGH HERBERT, 1954

Some years after F Hugh Herbert turned his daughters into Corliss Arch-er, he wrote another novel about a teenage girl, Dolores Keith. Like many of the adolescents in *Girls in Bloom*, Dolores keeps a diary and expresses herself through it. Also like many of her literary sisterhood, the diary is a desirable physical object of itself; she has made a New Year's resolution to use it when she 'happened to find this perfectly gorgeous diary in my underwear drawer under a pile of old slips. It is a perfectly beautiful dia-ry, bound in leather, and it smells simply divine.' The diary is 'going to be the first thing that I ever wrote in my life that I didn't have to write;' the beginning of her career as a professional writer – something she has in common with several of the characters in *Girls in Bloom*: Shirley Jack-son's Harriet Merriam for instance. 'You see, I made up my mind years ago when I was just a little kid of eleven that when I grow up I want to be a writer. I want to be a famous novelist and make millions of dollars. '

FRIDAY, JANUARY 1, 1954

My name is Dolores Keith.
I put that on a separate line because I wanted to see how it looks. I think it looks okay. Anyway, I think if you are going to *keep* a diary which is what I've just *decided* to do, the first thing is to let people know who you *are*.

I don't know very much about diaries. I never even *tried* to keep one before in my whole life, and the only one I ever *read* was the Dia-ry of Samuel Pepys which we read in school last year. It bored me stiff. Miss Sloman said it was a classic of English literature and she ought to know because she teaches me English and I am crazy about her, but it *still* bored me stiff.

So I guess I will just have to sort of grope around in this diary without any pattern to go by, and just put down whatever I *feel* like putting down, so that people will know what I'm like *inside* and not just who I *am*.

It is now exactly six PM Pacific Standard Time on New Year's Day. At this very moment I am exactly fifteen years, one month, nineteen days, five hours, eight minutes, and twenty-five seconds old. But I look a *lot* older. When people ask how old I am I generally always tell them I going on sixteen, which of course is perfectly true and *has* been true from the *moment* I was fifteen.

Dolores is in many ways typical of the girls in *Girls in Bloom*, including the fact that she wants to be a writer and that she has a crush on her female teacher – given Herbert's track record one does not have to be too cynical to see this as a fantasy on behalf of her author – though in fact she likes men, and especially older men; this is definitely a fantasy on behalf of her author/father. 'I must admit I am very much interested in men. I don't mean just the carpet man, even though he really is very cute. I guess I am just very much interested in men period. And I don't care how old they are either.' According to her diary, on New Year's Day she had been kissed 'seventeen times in nineteen hours. I just checked through the list I kept and I think the score is quite interesting. Only five were boys of about my age. Twelve were their fathers and uncles and relatives. And, kiss for kiss, I must say the fathers and uncles are much better than the sons or nephews.'

Dolores, as the title implies, likes to be kissed, and has no difficulty persuading men to kiss her. 'I suppose you could say that I was very pretty. Oh, why not be honest. I think you could say more than that. I guess I am really quite pretty. I guess I could even say very pretty and not be too far off the mark.' A girl her age with her looks who likes to be kissed by all the men is bound to come adrift at some point, even in a relatively harmless fantasy like this one. And she does. Like Corliss Archer, she has a family friend a little older than her who likes her a lot, but unlike Corliss she prefers his father. 'Terry is a very nice boy, despite all his faults, and I am very fond of him. I enjoy our dates a lot but to be perfectly frank about it I would *much* rather kiss his father.' On a trip to New York with her parents, they run into Terry's father, Mr Duffy, and things pan out so that she is left alone with him one evening on the understanding that he will take her to dinner and a show while her parents are elsewhere. They appear not to be worried when Mr Duffy 'jokes' that Dolores' father is cramping his style and pulls her onto his knee in his hotel room in their presence. 'I haven't sat on Mr Duffy's lap since I was about ten. I have *wanted* to ever *since* then because of the way I felt, but I never did.' Her parents leave and Dolores soon wishes they hadn't.

I didn't know *what* to do. I felt so *silly* sitting on his lap, and when he kissed my neck again I sort of laughed and said his moustache was tickling me and tried to get up. But he had his arms around my waist and I *couldn't* get up without sort of struggling and I thought that would make me feel even *sillier*. I mean once you have struggled it is no use even pretending any longer that everything is okay and that you don't mind.

So he held me on his lap and asked me what show would I like to see and he kissed the tip of my ear. I wanted to tell him to not *do* that and to let me get up off of his lap but somehow I couldn't. I was frightened. I didn't know *what* to do or what to *say*, even. I don't think I ever felt so awful in my life. Mr Duffy was holding me very tight with his arm around my waist. He wasn't *hurting* me, of course, but he was holding me so tight I could hardly breathe. I honestly didn't know what to *do*.

Then Mr Duffy asked what was the matter, why was I so silent, didn't I *want* to paint the town red with him? He took my chin and turned my face around and kissed me. He kissed me on my lips. I didn't *imagine* it. He really did. I wish it *was* my imagination. Then he left in a sort of funny way and sort of pushed me off his lap and said I was getting to be a big girl now and maybe he shouldn't let me sit on his lap. Then he walked over to the window and looked out. Over his shoulder the asked me again what show did I want to see because he would telephone for seats. Even his voice didn't sound like Mr Duffy's.

I was absolutely shaking all over. I was afraid I was going to pass out cold, I felt so awful. Finally I said I felt a terrific headache coming on. I said I thought maybe I'd better go to bed right away and would he mind if I didn't go out with him?

It is not entirely obvious whether this novel is intended for teenage girls or adults; perhaps it is meant as a cautionary tale for girls the age of his own daughters. Certainly, Dolores later explains to her readers that she was partly at fault, and that girls her age should not flirt with older men. The narrative device for this is a conversation with an older woman who is not her mother. Left alone in her hotel room, Dolores phones an old family friend who lives in New York, and goes to see her. She tells the wise and sympathetic Mrs McCracken what has happened. She asks Dolores: 'Are you quite sure that he always knew you were kidding' when she was flirting with him. Dolores has a coming of age moment. 'Mrs McCracken is right. I have known inside me, for the last year, anyway, that Mr Duffy wasn't just pretending and that he did get a kick out of it when I squeezed his hand while I was sat next to him on the couch. And I shouldn't have done it.' Mrs McCracken says to her 'I'm sure this man meant no harm to you. But you are a very pretty girl, almost a woman. He wanted to make love and he thought it would be a thrill for you. He is to blame for trying to make love. You are to blame for leading him to think it would be fun.'

Really?

FRANZIE HOFER: *GIDGET, THE LITTLE GIRL WITH BIG IDEAS* BY FREDERICK KOHNER, 1957

Like F Hugh Herbert's daughters, Kathy Kohner was a normal teenage girl with an Austrian screenwriter father who inspired a novel and its successful film and TV franchise: in this case *Gidget*. The name is short for the combination of girl and midget: she is less than five feet tall. Her actual name is Franzie in the original novel (Zuckerman's wife's name was Fritzie; the surname Hofer only occurs in the sequel, *Cher Papa*, 1960). In the *Gidget* films and TV series made at the height of the Cold War her name is anglicised to Francie Lawrence – another literary Frances. Like F Hugh Herbert, Kohner was born in Austria and he had been a screenwriter in Berlin; in America he was a refugee from Nazi Germany with a Jewish-sounding name. The McCarthy witch hunts had only just finished and studios were still afraid of being considered un-American. In any case Francie Lawrence sounds a lot more like an all-American, Californian surfer girl. In the films (the first one was released in 1959) she is blonde, unlike Kathy Kohner in real life, though like Franzie in the book. The film role was played by Sandra Dee, though in the later TV series (1965/66), still called Frances Lawrence, she reverted to a brunette and was played by a young Sally Field.

The timing of the original novel caught the incoming wave (pun intended) of the new surfing culture, which emerged in music through the

Beach Boys, the Ventures, Jan and Dean and others in the late 1950s and early 60s; *The Jan and Dean Sound* and The Ventures' first album, *Walk Don't Run*, came out in 1960. 1961 was the year of the Beach Boys' first album and Elvis Presley's film *Blue Hawaii* as well as both the book and the film of *Gidget goes Hawaiian*. Two more *Gidget* novels followed, both in 1963: *Affairs of Gidget* and *Gidget goes to Rome*.

In her introduction to a later reissue of *Gidget*, Kathy Kohner tells the story of how the original novel came about.

> One day I told my dad that I wanted to write a story about my sum-mer days at Malibu: about my friends who lived in a shack on the beach, about the major crush I had on one of the surfers, about how I was teased, about how hard it was to catch a wave – to paddle the long board out – and how persistent I was in wanting to learn to surf and be accepted by the 'crew,' as I often referred to the boys that summer.
>
> My father, Frederick Kohner, was a Hollywood screenwriter at the time. He became absorbed and amused with my tales of the beach. He told me he would write the story for me. He wrote the book *Gidget* in six weeks. It was his first novel. It became a bestseller and the basis for subsequent popular movies and television shows.

The real-life Kathy seems to have been happy to hand over her story to her father, and seems to have coped relatively well with the subsequent fame, though it seems not to have had much of a financial benefit for her, since she later worked as a waitress for many years. Perhaps, though, that was because she simply wanted to stay close to where the surf was, which she did well into middle age.

Neither Kathy nor her father seem to have worried about the implica-tions of a father writing about his daughter's sexual awakening. But by the third novel, *Affairs of Gidget*, this becomes hard to ignore. The blurb on the front of the paperback edition runs: 'Let me clue you in, fans. Un-der-sized girls have over-sized drives, says my analyst uncle – well, there were these three terrific men last year at Cascadia College . . .' Kohner was not a native English speaker; he probably learned and used his daughter's surfer-girl language the way he used regular English: as an outsider. The book is written in the first person in the style in which one imagines, or at least he imagined, Kathy would herself have written it. The literary style is therefore in contrast to the writing of most first person novels purporting to be by a teenage girl but actually written by a mature woman. Kohner is clearly enjoying the irony of writing it – for example, in the novel Franzie (i.e. Kohner) describes her father and his friends 'talking a lot of boring stuff, intellectual and such, my old man being a professor of German Literature at USC.' Kohner's joy in writing the novel is obvious.

> I'm writing this down because I once heard that when you're getting older you're liable to forget things and I'd sure be the most miserable woman in the world if I ever forgot what happened this summer. It's probably a lousy story and can't hold up a candle to those French novels from Sexville, but it has one advantage: it's a true story on my word of honor. On the other hand, a true story might not be a good story. That's what my English-comp teacher says – Mr. Glicksberg, that barfy-looking character who's practically invented halitosis. But then, he's dishing out a lot of bilge water if you ask me and what does a creep of an English teacher know about writing anyhow?

Gidget's story is not exactly lousy, though it is not of much interest to the average adult literary reader, being an everyday tale of surfing and teenage love affairs. The 'French novel from Sexville' that Kohner alludes to is presumably Françoise Sagan's *Bonjour Tristesse*, a female coming of age novel narrated by the seventeen-year-old Cécile, which was written by Sagan while a teenager herself; it was first published in English in 1955 and was highly influential (the English language movie came out in 1958). Despite having a first name similar to Sagan's, the perky, enthusiastic Franzie is the completely opposite kind of teenager to world-weary, languid Cécile, and Franzie's naive, innocent beach summer is completely opposite to Cécile's amoral, sexually-charged beach summer, with her borderline-incestuous relationship to her father that Franzie certainly does not have.

However, Franzie's first description of herself can only be read in the knowledge that this is in fact her father's description of a just-sixteen-year-old girl; she is both his real daughter and not – his real daughter was not blonde, though the other details may be accurate, including what her 'bosom' looks like when she is undressed.

When someone asks me about my height, I always say five foot, naturally, like when someone wants to know my age, I say going on seventeen.

I was sixteen last month.

I'm really quite cute.

I've real blonde hair and wear it in a horse tail. My two big canines protrude a little, which worries my parents a great deal. They urge me to have my teeth pushed back with the help of some crummy piece of hardware, but I've been resisting any attempt to tamper with my personality. The only thing that worries me is my bosom. It's there all right and it sure looks good when I'm undressed, but I have a hard time making it count in a sweater or such. Most of those kids in Franklin High are a lot taller and have a lot more to show, but most of them wear those damn falsies that stick out all over the place and I'd rather be caught dead than be a phoney about things like your bosom. Imagine what a boy thinks of you once he finds out. And he finds out sure as hell the first time he takes you to a show.

It's different in a bathing suit of course. Nothing helps there – no falsies or such phoney stuff.

I got a couple of real sexy-looking bathing suits that're pretty low-cut and have skintight fit.

Unlike many teenage narrators, Franzie makes no pretence of being literary. 'I'm really horrible about reading. It's embarrassing, especially for my old man who is a doctor of literature, but it just seems impossible for me to concentrate. To be honest, I'd rather write a book than read it.' Franzie's brother-in-law, a 'professional headshrinker' tells her that she is 'suffering from an inferiority complex on account of my old man having zillions of books around the house and reading like a maniac.' Nevertheless, books seem to be the main source of her knowledge – such as it is – about sex. One night she has a dream about Jeff in which she appears to have an orgasm: 'I got hot. And then chilled. And then hot again. It had been that kind of sensation. It must have been what they write about in all the books my ma wants me to read all the time and I never could buckle down to – except for the real sexy passages.' Again, remember that this is a real girl's father writing about a real girl.

Franzie fits in well with the surfer boys she hangs out with, mostly being part of the gang except when talk turns to sex, 'especially at the publication date of Playboy or such pornographic stuff. Someone would sit up and point at some sex display, "Look at those boobs!"' Franzie pretends not to listen but gets 'hot and hotter. Bosom talk brings out the worst in me. I'm so self-conscious on account of my meager output and in desperation had turned to some ointment which is supposed to work when you rub it in for three weeks.' There is a discussion of the difference between a good girl and a nice girl, which Franzie does not get. 'A *good* girl goes on a date, goes home goes to bed,' explains one boy. 'A *nice* girl,' continues another, 'goes on a date, goes to bed, goes home.' Another boy asks her what kind of girl she is but she is saved by Jeff, the boy she likes but who has never taken her out tandem on a surfboard. 'I was glad he asked me, though, on account of not having to answer those dirty questions. It didn't occur to me then that they were dirty – only afterward.'

When it looks like things are beginning to get serious with Jeff, her parents dispatch the psychoanalyst brother-in-law, Larry, to have a 'casual' chat with her to find out the state of the relationship. Franzie is a course not fooled but Larry apparently is; she portrays a physical relationship with Jeff which is entirely fictional – the 'feverish night' consisted just of her dream. Larry asks her what is so different about Jeff.

'For one thing, he's older. Nineteen. He goes to college. And he was in Alaska . . . and in Europe . . . and in Japan too.'

I was really flying high.

'That doesn't necessarily make him a great guy.'

'It does – in my book. He knows how to handle girls. He has finesse. No sweaty hands, no making out in drive-in movies.'

'Making out??'

'My God, Larry, where've you been living. I guess you still call it necking.'

'Oh, I see. And you kids – er – don't neck?'

'*I* don't,' I said with dignity.

'Well, then you and this boy, Jeff, you're just pals?'

'Pals??' I smiled. The torrid love scenes of my feverish night flashed through my mind. And something else too.

'Oh – er – has it gone a little further?' Larry asked.

'A *little*??'

His mouth sagged.

'Keep on trying,' I said. I got a great charge out of it.

'I guess he's just like any other college boy then,' Larry said, still hopeful. 'Trying to find out how far a girl like you would go.'

There was a pause. Then I said sort of matter-of-fact: 'If a girl goes all the way, a boy doesn't have to find out.'

Poor Larry. He almost toppled of his chair. The edges of his mouth began to pucker. He looked sick.

Franzie eventually lets Larry off the hook; his 'relief over my well-preserved virginity was so fierce that he had called my old man the very afternoon of our luncheon and sold him a double size of Freud and Adler, well mixed'. Franzie listens in on their phone call. Larry tells her father that her behaviour is 'quite harmless, believe me, and just the normal pattern. She wants to be free from control, and she wants to show her independence. All this dirty language and smoking cigarettes and putting on mascara are just the obvious signs of juvenile rebellion. The best way to get her over it is to give her all the freedom she wants with certain limitations.' The father is not convinced: 'I hear those boys out there do a lot of funny things – drinking, smoking, and God knows what else.' Larry asks him if he means sex. 'Damn right, sex!' answers her father. 'And Franzie is snoopy as a cat in that department. Maybe just because she's not quite developed for her age.' Again, it is difficult to read this book, published the year after *Lolita*, without worrying about the author's feelings for his daughter.

Meanwhile, the 'snoopy' Franzie really is a virgin. She finally kisses Jeff but she is worried about going any farther. 'I wanted to tell him that I was only fifteen and that all the love affair I had had was with him, Jeff, and that one only in my dream. I wanted to tell him to love me just a little bit and have patience and we would love each other forever.' But Jeff doesn't think enough of her to be patient. She is still the girl midget to him.

'I love you,' I said.

'Please,' Jeff said, and backed away.

'Don't you want me to?'

'No,' he said. Then he added quickly, 'you can kiss me though. I like the way you kiss.'

'And you don't want me to love you?'

'Do I have to spell it out?'

'But why not? Don't you like me?'

'Yes and no.'

'Why "no"?'

'You're too young for it, Gidget.'

There it was again. It takes so long to get old. I wished I could have grown up overnight.

'I'm getting older every day,' I said. 'It's the way you feel inside that counts.'

'The crew would think I've gone in for cradle-snatching.'

And that of course is the problem: any nineteen-year-old boy needs the approval of his 'crew.' Jeff admits that he has been seeing someone else: a tall, eighteen-year-old girl. Briefly, Franzie thinks she might die before she gets home then she realises she is happy to share him; if Jeff is getting what he wants from the older girl, Franzie can behave as she wants. 'Didn't I always see me as the heroine in a tragically beautiful melodrama? Now I wouldn't have to act grown-up and sophisticated, and I could go on loving him and wouldn't have to do the things that I didn't understand and that frightened me.' The other girl 'had the cake, but I had the frosting.'

Towards the end of the novel, Kohner the doctor of literature says, through the mouth of Gidget, the fifteen-year-old girl: 'And now I embark on that portion of my story which I promised myself to put down in my most elegant English. It has real drama and contains that very important element labelled by my teacher Glicksberg as the "clincher" or climax.' In fact it is not so dramatic: Franzie ends up having to spend the night on the beach next to Cass, who is known as the big Kahuna. She seems prepared to offer herself to him when he asks if he can lie down with her.

It was shocking and overwhelming, feeling a man's body like that. At this moment I knew that I had never lived at all. Maybe I had not even be born yet. All my fears and frustrations seemed to melt away in a sudden blaze.

Yes, this was the moment I had been waiting for.

Now it would happen. He would make me a woman.

And then I could have any man I wanted to. I could have Jeff.

Nothing happened.

They lie together 'like a man and a woman, but also like brother and sister.' Cass knows that she is in love with Jeff and respects it; the crew always come before the girl. 'You're everything a man would ever want. You're sweet, you're young, and you're in love with life. Remember this. So when it happens between you and a man it must be beautiful.' Cass kisses her but 'like a father. Different from Jeff. Tender.' The 'clincher' comes in two waves (pun and innuendo both intended): first, Jeff hits Cass out of jealousy; 'this wasn't a crummy movie I was watching. Two grown-up men had almost killed each other on account of little me – the gnomie, the shortie – the Gidget!' The final, and most important, twist of the whole story is when Franzie finally successfully surfs her own wave, solo; this, not love or sex, is what makes her a complete woman. 'There was the shore, right there. I could almost reach out and touch it.' The orgasmic symbolism of this image might have been lost on some of its teenage readers and perhaps even on its author's daughter, but almost certainly was not lost on its author.

In the final chapter of the book, almost as an epilogue, Franzie, newly come of age, tells us: 'Now I'm middle-aged, going on seventeen. I've learned so much in between. I've learned that virtue has its points. That you can grow up even if you don't grow.'

NECK OR NOT? SEX AND THE TEENAGE GIRL

We saw earlier that teenage girls read and wrote to advice columns like the *Sub-Deb* for guidance on how far to go with boys (though not with girls), on the difference between necking (sometimes okay) and petting (never okay), how to avoid 'parking' after a date and so on. Most of the girls in the books we are considering don't go the whole way and there is very little physical sex in any of the books in *Girls in Bloom*, though we will encounter liberal amounts of it in the novels of Maude Hutchins; of course the censorship of the time would have prevented anything too explicit being published anyway. But some of the girls offer themselves, usually unsuccessfully, to boys and in some cases to older men, even if they don't always know exactly what it is they are offering. We have just seen how F Hugh Herbert's Dolores Keith flirts with her boyfriend's father and goes too far, though in the end nothing actually happens and how Gidget offered herself unsuccessfully to Jeff, but these examples were in novels written by men and fathers; in this chapter we see how four adolescent girls are prepared to go 'the whole hog' with older men: one succeeds on a regular basis, two are unsuccessful and one has such a bad experience she wipes it from her mind and her author wipes it from the book.

ANNA MORGAN: *VOYAGE IN THE DARK* BY JEAN RHYS, 1934

Jean Rhys (1890-1979) is of course best known for her late novel *Wide Sargasso Sea*, her take on the *Jane Eyre* story seen from the point of view of the 'madwoman in the attic', Rochester's wife, who, like Rhys, came from the Caribbean. This was finally published in book form in 1966 after years of tinkering and after a very long gap following her early novels, the first of which, *Quartet*, was published in 1928. *Voyage in the Dark* was published before our official start date of 1940, but it does not read at all like a pre-war novel, it feels far more like the British kitchen-sink novels and dramas of the late 1950s/early 1960s where amoral young women with either no parental influence or a very bad one float aimlessly through a world of seedy boarding houses and casual sex: *A*

Taste of Honey by Shelagh Delaney, 1958, *The L-Shaped Room* by Lynne Reid Banks, 1960, which became the 1962 film and *Up the Junction* by Nell Dunn, 1962, which also became a film as well as a TV play.

Voyage in the Dark is to a large extent autobiographical, following an eighteen-year-old girl who has come to a cold, damp England from the warm, sunny Caribbean, as Rhys herself did. Anna is no English rose; she has a totally opposite life experience to the upper-middle-class English girls of Rosamond Lehmann and her peers: she is travelling around England working as a 'showgirl,' both in the sense of acting on the stage and in the pejorative sense the word had at the time of a 'woman of easy virtue.' Though by no means a prostitute, Anna certainly seems to be prepared to have relationships with men for money, as do all the women she knows, most of whom are older than her. One friend calls her 'the Virgin,' though it is not absolutely clear whether at the start of the novel she is.

One of the men who gives her money believes she is a virgin but when she goes to his room she denies it; oddly, because virginity is presumably a very valuable commodity. 'I'm not a virgin if that's what's worrying you,' she says. 'You oughtn't to tell lies about that,' the man replies. She denies that she is telling lies and says it does not matter anyway. The man replies: 'Oh yes, it matters. It's the only thing that matters.' She tells him she wants to leave, but then she doesn't. 'When I got into bed there was warmth from him and I got close to him. *Of course you've always known, always remembered, and then you forget so utterly, except that you've always known it. Always – how long is always?*'

Anna is travelling and rooming with Maudie who is ten years older than her and highly cynical; hardly the ideal role model. She sees that Anna is reading *Nana*, Zola's 1880 novel about an eighteen-year-old showgirl who becomes a highly successful prostitute, casually ruining all the men around her; Anna is of course an anagram of Nana. In its way, *Nana* is a coming of age novel, if an extremely dark one: 'All of a sudden, in the good-natured child, the woman stood revealed, a disturbing woman with all the impulsive madness of her sex, opening the gates of the unknown world of desire.'

'That's a dirty book, isn't it?'

'Bits of it are all right,' I said.

Maudie said, 'I know; it's about a tart. I think it's disgusting. I bet you a man writing a book about a tart tells a lot of lies one way and another. Besides, all books are like that – just somebody stuffing you up.'

In fact, apart from *Nana* and Alexandre Dumas' *Lady of the Camellias*, most courtesan novels were written by women who actually were courtesans: Colette's *Claudine*, 1920 was a late addition the genre established by French nineteen century authors like Liane de Pougy, Céleste de Chabrillan and Valtesse de la Bigne.

Anna and Maudie always seem to be poor and always have trouble getting landladies to accommodate 'professionals,' as one landlady calls them. Maudie encourages Anna; she is not entirely reluctant, has no qualms about accepting money from men, and is not even especially repulsed by the physical side of it. 'You shut the door and you pull the curtains over the windows and then it's as long as a thousand years and yet so soon ended.' But Anna wonders when and how her life will change; how, even if, she will come of age as a woman, where she will end up; she has none of Nana's or Dumas' Marguerite Gautier's single-minded drive to become rich through exploiting men and just seems to have fallen into this way of life. 'Of course, you get used to things, you get used to anything. It was as if I had always lived like that. Only sometimes, when I got back home and was undressing to go to bed, I would think, "my God, this is a funny way to live. My God, how did this happen?"'

'But it isn't always going to be like this, is it?' I thought. 'It would be too awful if it were always going to be like this. It isn't possible. Something must happen to make it different' and I thought, 'yes, that's all right. I'm poor and my clothes are cheap and perhaps it will always be like this. And that's all right too.' It was the first time in my life I'd thought that.

The ones without any money, the ones with beastly lives. Perhaps I'm going to be one of the ones with beastly lives. They swarm like woodlice when you push a stick into a woodlice-nest at home. And their faces are the colour of woodlice.

In a way, Anna cannot wait to get old; when an older woman says to her that this is no way for a young girl to live, she thinks: 'people say "young" as though being young were a crime, and they are always scared of getting old. I thought, "I wish I were old and the whole damned thing were

finished; that I shouldn't get this depressed feeling for nothing at all.'"
But in Anna's way of life, youth is the most valuable commodity, as a
male acquaintance tells her in a letter informing her that Walter, one of
the men who has been giving her money, and of whom she has become
quite fond, cannot see her again; it is a rather standard Dear Jane letter,
telling her she would be better off without him.

> *I'm quite sure you are a nice girl and that you will be understanding
> about this. Walter is still very fond of you but he doesn't love you like
> that anymore, and after all you must always have known that the
> thing could not go on forever and you must remember too that he is
> nearly 20 years older than you are. I'm sure that you are a nice girl
> and that you will think it over calmly and see that there is nothing to
> be tragic or unhappy or anything like that about. You are young and
> youth as everybody says is the great thing, the greatest gift of all.
> The greatest gift, everybody says. And so it is. You got everything in
> front of you, lots of happiness. Think of that. Love is not everything –
> especially that sort of love – and the more people, especially girls,
> put it right out of their hands and do without it the better... Walter
> has asked me to enclose this cheque for £20 for your immediate ex-
> penses because he thinks you may be running short of cash. He will
> always be your friend and he wants to arrange that you should be
> provided for and not have to worry about money (for a time at any
> rate).*

In this demimonde everything has a price, though not necessarily a high
price; life is cheap, and women are cheaper: £20 to buy off Anna must
have seemed a reasonable amount, though at least one man 'gave me fifteen quid' for a single experience. Maudie tells Anna that a man said to
her, 'have you ever thought that a girl's clothes cost more than the girl
inside them?... You can get a very nice girl for five pounds, a very nice girl
indeed; you can even get a very nice girl for nothing if you know how to
go about it. But you can't get a very nice costume for her for five pounds.'
Anna is not in fact deeply upset about Walter and she has no hesitation in
asking him for more money later when she needs an abortion, illegal and
very dangerous in those days, and costing £50. But even this does not
seem to make Anna want to change her way of life; everything in grey,

miserable England seems like a bad dream to her anyway, even though the dream is interspersed with pleasant interludes.

> Sometimes not being able to get over the feeling that it was a dream. The light and the sky and the shadows and the houses and the people – all parts of the dream, all fitting in and all against me. But there were other times when a fine day, or music, or looking in the glass and thinking I was pretty, made me start again imagining that there was nothing I couldn't do, nothing I couldn't become. Imagining God knows what. Imagining Carl would say, 'When I leave London, I'm going to take you with me.' And imagining it although his eyes had that look – this is just for while I'm here, and I hope you get me.
>
> 'I picked up a girl in London and she . . . Last night I slept with a girl who . . . ' That was me.
>
> Not 'girl' perhaps. Some other word, perhaps. Never mind.

PORTIA QUAYNE: *THE DEATH OF THE HEART* BY ELIZABETH BOWEN, 1938

This novel is also slightly before our official start date and, very much unlike the previous book, is in many ways a traditional English 1930s novel, a comedy of manners – the manners of pre-war, upper-middle-class London which Elizabeth Bowen (1899-1973), like Rosamond Lehmann, whom we looked at earlier, knew well; she was born in Ireland but moved to England as a child. But it is also a coming of age novel and Portia undoubtedly belongs in this chapter about adolescent girls and their sexual experiences. She does, in her way, come of age in the course of the story though she does not have the novel to herself; she is just one of the cast of unappealing characters examined in forensic detail by the witty, sardonic and ruthless Bowen in this chamber piece.

Among her many novels, Bowen had already included girls as central characters in at least two others: *The House in Paris*, 1926, is about a day in the life of eleven-year-old Henrietta Mountjoy – not a long enough period to see Henrietta coming of age – and one of the major characters in *The Last September*, 1929, is eighteen-year-old Lois Farquar, whose coming of age is just one of the stories in this vast, sweeping novel about an upper-class family during the Anglo-Irish troubles of the time.

Sixteen-year-old Portia Quayne is a recent orphan, and is being brought up, like Jane Eyre and other girls in coming of age novels, by unsympathetic relatives who make it clear that they do not want her. She has been sent to live with her much older half-brother Thomas and his snobbish wife Anna in their stylish and fashionable central London home after Portia's mother has died. Thomas's father had much earlier left his mother for a woman of a much lower social class, who then gave birth to Portia; the father then died and Portia continued to live with her mother, moving around and living in cheap hotels. Thomas and Anna have no children of their own and Anna clearly does not want Portia cluttering up her pristine house. Portia's only ally is the older female servant Matchett, who was in service with her and Thomas's father and was left to Thomas in his father's will, like a chattel, along with 'the furniture that had always been her charge.' Portia seems to realise that she is *in* the house but not *of* it; even though she is hardly a mousy Cinderella/Jane Eyre character she tries to make herself as unnoticed as possible with her 'orphaned un-ostentation'.

> Getting up from the stool carefully, Portia returned her cup and plate to the tray. Then, holding herself so erect that she quivered, taking long soft steps on the balls of her feet, and at the same time with an orphaned unostentation, she started making towards the door. She moved crabwise, as though the others were royalty, never quite turning her back on them – and there, waiting for her to be quite gone, watched... Her body was all concave and jerkily fluid lines; it moved with sensitive looseness, loosely threaded together: each movement had a touch of exaggeration, as though some secret power kept springing out. At the same time she looked cautious, aware of the world in which she had to live. She was sixteen, losing her childish majesty.

As the novel opens Portia is being discussed by Anna and her friend, the novelist St Quentin. Anna has recently found Portia's diary in which she has written about her host and hostess – it is not that Portia has written unkindly that has upset Anna, just the fact that she has written about her at all. Anna claims that she was not looking for the diary or searching

FRANCIS BOOTH

Portia's room, just entering to hang up a dress that had come back from the cleaners.

> Her room looked, as I've learnt to expect, shocking: she has all sorts of arrangements Matchett will never touch. You know what some servants are – how they ride one down, and at the same time make all sorts of allowance for temperament in children or animals.'
> 'You would call her a child?'
> 'In many ways, she is more like an animal. I made that room so pretty before she came. I had no idea how blindly she was going to live. Now I hardly ever going there; it's simply discouraging.'

Portia is, by any normal standard, a polite, intelligent and respectful girl but by the standards of Anna's finicky fastidiousness Portia is a rogue element in her otherwise immaculate house; especially in the way she keeps her room. 'I really did feel it was time I took a line. But she and I are on such curious terms – when I ever do take a line, she never knows what it is. She is so unnaturally callous about objects – she treats any hat, for instance, like an old envelope.' Anna has given Portia a 'little *escritoire* thing' that had been Thomas's mother's with locking drawers, hoping it 'would make her see that I quite meant her to have a life of her own.' The symbolism of this object seems to be lost on Portia. 'Nothing that's hers ever seems, if you know what I mean, to belong to her.' Anna should not really be surprised at this, as Portia has grown up moving around from one hotel to another.

One of the things that has most upset Anna about Portia's diary is the quality of the book it is written in: unlike several of the diary-keepers in *Girls in Bloom*, Portia does not write in a beautiful leather journal: 'One of those wretched black books one buys for about a shilling with *moiré* outsides.' Anna is clearly horrified to have such a seedy object in her house, but in any case she has never liked Portia – or her late mother, who may have been pregnant with Portia when Thomas's father ran off with her – even before Portia moved in. 'She's made nothing but trouble since before she was born.' St Quentin replies: 'You mean, it's a pity she ever was?' Anna agrees that that is how she feels. Thomas also seems to have resented Portia, and especially her mother, from before her birth. 'From the grotesqueries of that marriage he had felt a revulsion. Portia, with her suggestion – during those visits – of sacred lurking, had stared at him like a kitten that expects to be drowned.'

St Quentin, as a writer, is interested in the style rather than the content or physical form of Portia's diary; his dialogue with Anna allows Bowen to have some authorial fun.

'Was it affected?'

'Deeply hysterical.'

'You've got to allow for style, though. Nothing arrives on paper as it started, and so much arrives that never started at all. To write is always to rave a little – even if one did once know what one meant, which at her age seems unlikely. There are ways and ways of trumping a thing up: one gets more discriminating, not necessarily more honest. *I* should know, after all.'

'I am sure you do, St Quentin. But this was not a bit like your beautiful books. In fact it was not like *writing* at all.' She paused and added: 'She was so odd about me...'

'A diary, after all, is written to please oneself – therefore it's bound to be enormously written up. The obligation to write it is all in one's own eye, and look how one is when it's almost always written – upstairs, late, overwrought alone.'

This is of course a good point about diaries purporting to have been written by young girls: they are indeed written alone and at night in the privacy of their own room where their thoughts can run free. Bowen has more fun with the idea of diaries as a form of fiction later on in the novel; Portia is talking here to St Quentin.

'Now what can have made me think you kept a diary? Now that I come to look at you, I don't think you'd be so rash.'

'If I kept one, it would be a dead secret. Why should that be rash?'

'It is madness to write things down.'

'But you write those books you write almost all day don't you?'

'But what's in them never happened – it might have, but never did. And though what is felt in them is just possible – in fact, it's much more possible, in an unnerving way, than most people will admit – it's fairly improbable. So, you see, it's my game from the start. But I should never write what had happened down... I dare say,' said St

Quentin kindly, 'that what you write is quite silly, but all the same, you are taking a liberty. You set traps for us. You ruin our free will.'

'I write what has happened. I don't invent.'

'You put constructions on things. You are a most dangerous girl.'

Writing, of course, is about the most dangerous thing woman can do.

Like Rosamond Lehmann's heroines, Portia does not go to a normal school but attends a small, special private institution for 'delicate girls, girls who did not do well at school, girls putting in time before they went abroad, girls who were not to go abroad at all.' But this seems to be quite an intellectual finishing school, not one designed to turn out dim, obedient, marriageable girls. According to Portia's diary, a typical day is: 'today we began Sienese Art, and did Book Keeping, and read a German play.' She has only one friend there: Lilian, whom Anna does not think 'very desirable, but this could not be helped.' Lillian 'walks about with the rather fated expression you see in photographs of girls who have subsequently been murdered,' after she had 'had to be taken away from her boarding school because of falling in love with the cello mistress, which had made her quite unable to eat.' (Although ten years later than Lehmann's *Dusty Answer*, this is one of the first coming of age novels to explicitly mention lesbianism, though not in relation to the principal character and only in relation to a schoolgirl crush on a teacher.)

Portia does not do well at the school, she cannot concentrate, cannot 'keep her thoughts at face-and-table level; they would go soaring up through the glass dome.' Because of her upbringing so far, Portia is 'unused to learning, she had not learnt that one must learn.' She is also socially out of place with all these future debutantes; while they had been learning art, languages and social graces, Portia and her mother Irene 'had been skidding about in an out-of-season nowhere of railway stations and rocks, filing off wet third-class decks of lake steamers, choking over the bones of *loups de mer*, giggling into eiderdowns that smelled of the person-before-last. Untaught, they had walked arm-in-arm along city pavements, and at nights had pulled their beds closer together or slept in the same bed overcoming, as far as might be, the separation of birth. Seldom had they faced up to society.'

But now, Portia must face up, alone and motherless, to not only society, but older male attention; Anna is entirely incapable of acting *in loco parentis*. Anna's shiftless friend Eddie, like an impecunious and disrespectable member of Bertie Wooster's Drones Club, and the slightly seedy, older hanger-on Major Brutt both seem to have feelings for her, though neither of them seems particularly eager to turn them into physical form. At first it seems that Portia has set her cap squarely at Eddie. 'Portia's life, up to now, had been all subtle gentle compliance, but she had been compliant without pity. Now she saw with pity, but without reproaching herself, all the sacrificed people – Major Brutt, Lilian, Matchett, even Anna – that she had stepped over to meet Eddie.' Eddie refuses to let her write about him in her diary, but she tells him that, now she has him, she may not need the diary anymore. Nevertheless, she still writes down thoughts and deeds, some of which Bowen gives us, in a style not entirely unlike that of her friend Virginia Woolf.

> Today I have had a sort of conversation with Thomas. When he came in he asked if Anna was there, so I said no and said should I come down and he was not sure but said yes. He was leaning on his desk reading the evening paper, and when I came in he said it was warmer wasn't it? He said in fact he felt stuffy. As he had not seen me last night, because of the dinner party, he asked had I had a nice weekend? He said he hoped I had not been at all lonely, so I said oh no. He asked if I thought it was nice. I said oh yes, and he said, he was round here yesterday, wasn't he? I said oh yes and said we had sat down here in the study, and that I did hope Thomas did not mind people sitting down here in his study. He said oh no, oh no in a sort of far-off voice. He said he supposed I and Eddie were rather friends, and I said yes we were. Then he went back to reading the evening paper as if there was something new in it.

But things with Eddie do not work out: he is not the settling down type. 'I used to think that we understood each other. I still think you're sweet, though you do give me the horrors. I feel you're trying to put me into some sort of trap. I'd never dream of going to bed with you, the idea would be absurd.' Towards the end of the novel, on the rebound from Eddie as it were, Portia tries to give her virgin self to the Major, who has been sending her presents of jigsaw puzzles. She visits him at his down-at-heel hotel and proposes marriage to him. 'I could cook; my mother cooked when we lived in Notting Hill Gate. Why could you not marry me?

I could cheer you up. I would not get in your way, and we should not be half so lonely... Do think it over, please,' says Portia calmly.

> With a quite new, matter-of-fact air of possessing his room, she made small arrangements for comfort – peeled off his eiderdown, kicked her shoes off, lay down with her head in his pillow and pulled the ei- derdown snugly up to her chin. By this series of acts she seemed at once to shelter, to plant here, and to obliterate herself – most of all the last... 'I suppose,' she said, after some minutes, 'you don't know what to do.'

But the Major turns out to be a confirmed bachelor – though not neces- sarily in the sense that 'confirmed bachelor' was used in those days to connote homosexuality. She looks at the rows of his military-shiny shoes and offers to clean them for him. 'For some reason, women are never so good at it.' He picks up the brushes and begins to clean the shoes himself.

> Portia, watching him, had all in that moment a view of his untouched masculine privacy, of that grave abstractedness with which each part of his toilet would go on being performed. Unconscious, he could not have made plainer his determination to always live alone. Clapping the brushes together, he put them down with a clatter that made them both start. 'I'm sure you will cook,' he said, 'I'm all in favour of it. But not for some years yet, and not, I'm afraid, for me.'

And that is that; Portia returns 'home.' But of course it is only home in the sense of Philip Larkin's famous definition: 'home is where, when you have to go there, they have to let you in.'

SABBATH LILY HAWKS: *WISE BLOOD* BY FLANNERY O'CONNOR, 1952

Sabbath Lily Hawks is about as different from Portia Quayne as it is pos- sible for a girl to be and the steamy, fervid, Deep South world of O'Connor's novel is about as far from Bowen's and Lehmann's polite, middle-class England as it is possible to get. Best known for her Southern

Gothic short stories, Flannery O'Connor (a woman, like fellow-southerner Carson McCullers, with a gender-neutral name) also wrote the highly Gothic novel *Wise Blood* about a former soldier, Hazel Motes – a man with a woman's name, the opposite of many of the characters in *Girls in Bloom* – who comes into a small southern town and meets an array of strange, intense characters who make Carson McCullers' creations seem quite benign. Among them is the 'blind' preacher Asa Hawks – he is not in fact blind, it is just a scam – and his precocious, fifteen-year-old daughter Sabbath Lily who 'guides' him around as he preaches and distribute leaflets. Hazel at first follows them and is determined to seduce Sabbath, but things soon go the other way. Sabbath tells Hazel that her parents were not married and therefore she is a bastard; she has been wondering whether this means it is okay for her to have sex and has been consulting advice columns, though she does not at all seem either the *Sub-Deb* or the *Seventeen* magazine type. In this scene, they are in Hazel's car driving down a dirt road; Sabbath had been hiding on the back seat waiting for him.

'A bastard?' he murmured. He couldn't see how a preacher who had blinded himself for Jesus could have a bastard. He turned his head and looked at her with interest for the first time.

She nodded and the corners of her mouth turned up. 'A real bastard,' she said, catching his elbow, 'and do you know what? A bastard shall not enter the kingdom of heaven!' she said.

Haze was driving his car toward the ditch while he stared at her. 'How could you be . . .' he started and saw the red embankment in front of him and pulled the car back on the road.

'Do you read the papers?' she asked.

'No,' he said.

'Well, there's this woman in it named Mary Brittle that tells you what to do when you don't know. I wrote her a letter and ast what I was to do.'

'How could you be a bastard when he blinded him . . .' he started again.

'I says, "Dear Mary, I am a bastard and a bastard shall not enter the kingdom of heaven as we all know, but I have this personality that makes boys follow me. Do you think I should neck or not? I shall not enter the kingdom of heaven anyway so I don't see what difference it makes.'"

'Listen here,' Haze said, 'if he blinded himself how . . .'

'Then she answered my letter in the paper. She said, "Dear Sabbath, light necking is acceptable, but I think your real problem is one of adjustment to the modern world. Perhaps you ought to re-examine your religious values to see if they meet your needs in Life. A religious experience can be a beautiful addition to living if you put it in the proper perspective and do not let it dwarf you. Read some books on Ethical Culture."'

'You couldn't be a bastard,' Haze said, getting very pale. 'You must be mixed up. Your daddy blinded himself.'

'Then I wrote her another letter,' she said, scratching his ankle with the toe of her sneaker, and smiling, 'I says, "Dear Mary, What I really want to know is should I go the whole hog or not? That's my real problem. I'm adjusted okay to the modern world."'

'Your daddy blinded himself,' Haze repeated.

'He wasn't always as good as he is now,' she said. 'She never answered my second letter.'

Soon, Hazel moves into the same rooming house as Asa and Sabbath and soon after, the preacher leaves his daughter and disappears. Sabbath turns up in Hazel's room. "'Are you going to hit me not?' she asked. "If you are, go ahead and do it right now because I'm not going. I got no place to go."' Hazel doesn't want to hit her and is not sure whether he wants her to go or not.

'Listen,' she said, with a quick change of tone, 'from the minute I set eyes on you I said to myself, that's what I got to have, just give me some of him! I said look at those pee-can eyes and go crazy, girl! That innocent look don't hide anything, he's just pure filthy right down to the guts, like me. The only difference is I like being that way and he don't. Yes sir!' she said. 'I like being that way, and I can teach you how to like it. Don't you want to learn how to like it?'

He does. 'Come on! Make haste,' she says to him. 'Take off your hat, king of the beasts.' The relationship doesn't last; Hazel, who does not believe in anything except that 'Jesus was a liar,' tries to form the Church Without Christ, leaves town and leaves Sabbath Lily. Never realising that Sabbath's father was a fake, and not blind, he blinds himself.

NATALIE WAITE: *HANGSAMAN* BY SHIRLEY JACKSON, 1951

Because she had children of her own, and, as we saw, wrote innocuous magazine pieces about her charming but chaotic family life, Shirley Jackson presumably found it quite difficult to write about sex. Does Natalie Waite in *Hangsaman* go the whole hog? If so, with whom: is it with an older man, one of her father's friends, or even perhaps her father himself? We don't know, though despite the Oxford critic who, as we saw earlier branded *Hangsaman* a lesbian novel there is no hint that it was with a woman. As in Heinrich von Kleist's *The Marquise of O* there is gaping hole in the story, a lacuna around Natalie's first – possible – experience of sex; perhaps the experience was so awful that she has erased from her mind and Jackson has erased it from the novel. It feels almost as if some clumsy censor has excised a whole section that would have described her experience. But neither at the time it happens nor later in the novel are we given any idea of what actually happened; we know Natalie has been irrevocably changed but not by what exactly.

The critics were not kind, though they mostly saw it as a coming of age novel. *The Saturday Review*, May 5, 1951, compared *Hangsaman* to Jackson's notorious short story 'The Lottery,' where villagers choose one person a year to be stoned to death, which had been published not long before and caused an enormous – almost entirely negative – response.

Now in the novel *Hangsaman* and on its much larger scale Miss Jackson again proceeds from realism to symbolic drama. Here the method fails. The tones do not flow into one another... Like many another story, this one is about the maturing of an adolescent. Natalie Waite, though, is a very special seventeen; not so much in her un-adult trick of occasionally blurting out exactly what she is thinking as in the quality of her thinking and in her literary background. Natalie is an exceptionally talented, intellectual child, already supervised by her father, who is apparently a sort of critic and certainly an egotistical fool... Natalie was raped or seduced offstage at her father's cocktail party. Presumably the emotional effects were profound, but we don't know any more about them than we know, for instance, about the effects of a flock of martinis Natalie absorbed one afternoon and for the first time. Miss Jackson's method of not-quite-telling begins to show its disadvantages. We know from her diary that Natalie is schizoid, but when she traverses a period of paralytic madness we can never be sure whether her girl-friend Tony, kleptomaniac and Tarot card reader, is real or imagined. We are too fragmentarily informed to be fairly prepared for what happens. We can move from the vacuum of a June morning to cold horror but we cannot stride, believing, from social comedy to hallucination.

Another review of the time, in *The Age*, from Melbourne Australia, February 1952, was titled 'A Novel of Emotional Bewilderment'.

Shirley Jackson, with the acuteness of a surgeon, lays bare the tissue and nerves of adolescent emotions in her novel, *Hangsaman*. She portrays the period between childhood and maturity in the life of an American girl when self assumes immense proportions and demands constant dramatization, gaining importance and size in these imaginary flights.

Natalie Waite, seventeen years old, comes from a home where there is disunity. Both the father, who is a not very successful writer, and the mother, who feels she has set herself off from her own people by her marriage, seek to find solace in the girl. At some sacrifice they send her to college.

Loneliness descends on her like a pall while she struggles to find some place amongst her housemates. Her unhappiness culminates in a nightmare in which her experiences at home and in the college are massed in horrible shape. She finds only one friend in the college, a girl who is an echo of herself but stronger, who shows her the dark places into which her wallowing in her own ego might lead her.

This story is one to bring terror to the heart of a parent sending an unadaptable child out among her fellows. One would think that it must surely be autobiographical, so deeply has the author plunged in her description of the cruelty girls can deal one to another and of the brutality with which the can win a place in the mob.

It is a harrowing and particularly vicious picture and not an easily assimilated one. Incidents are part of the general emotional bewilderment of scenes that build to a climax, leaving the reader to wonder to the last moment whether Natalie will escape.

Despite the critics however the writing in *Hangsaman* is controlled and masterly; it is one of the finest of all coming of age novels. There is a wonderful passage where Jackson describes the crucial moment of adolescence where the girl becomes the woman, with her own will and a personality separate from that of her parents and family. For Jackson, naturally, this transition is effected by creativity, in this case, as in Jackson's, the creativity of writing.

> There was a point in Natalie, only dimly realised by herself, and probably entirely a function of her age, where obedience ended and control began; after this point was reached and passed, Natalie became a solitary functioning individual, capable of ascertaining her own believable possibilities. Sometimes, with a vast aching heartbreak, the great, badly contained intentions of creation, the poignant searching longings of adolescence overwhelmed her, and shocked by her own capacity for creation, she held herself tight and unyielding, crying out silently something that might only be phrased as, 'Let me take, let me create.'
>
> If such a feeling had any meaning to her, it was as the poetic impulse which led her into such embarrassing compositions as were hidden in her desk; the gap between the poetry she wrote and the poetry she contained was, for Natalie, something unsolvable.

Along the same lines, one of Natalie's father's friends says to her: 'Little Natalie, never rest until you have uncovered your essential self. Remember that. Somewhere, deep inside you, hidden by all sorts of fears and worries and petty little thoughts, is a clean pure being made of radiant colours.' This is 'so much like the things that Natalie sometimes suspected about herself,' that she asks, 'how do you ever know?'

Like a true creative spirit, Natalie lives mainly in her head, in a fantasy world which includes, as the novel opens, a kind of noir detective story where she is a suspect. Whatever she is doing, the story keeps playing out in her mind; in the narrative she is the central figure, the protagonist, the heroine and the detective is her antagonist. Natalie's character in her own story is rather like the many girl detective stories of the time, though at seventeen she is rather too old for this kind of fiction, at which her pretentious, writer father would no doubt sneer.

> Natalie, fascinated, was listening to the secret voice which followed her. It was the police detective and he spoke sharply, incisively, through the gentle movement of her mother's voice. 'How,' he asked pointedly, 'Miss Waite, *how* do you account for the gap in time between your visit to the rose garden and your discovery of the body?'...
>
> 'You realise,' detective said silently, 'that this discrepancy in time may have very serious consequences for you?'
>
> 'I realise,' Natalie said. Confess, she thought, if I confess I might go free...'
>
> 'Do you think that you alone can stand against the force of the police, the might and weight of duly constituted authority, against *me*?'
>
> A lovely little shiver went down Natalie's back. 'I may be in danger every moment of my life,' she told the detective, 'but I am strong within myself.'
>
> 'Is *that* an answer?' the detective said. 'What if I told you that you were seen?'
>
> Natalie lifted her head, looking proudly off into the sky.

This particular fantasy stops when she goes to college, to be replaced by another, her imaginary friend Tony (female, despite her name); more of her shortly. Natalie is about to leave for college as the novel opens; she is 'desperately afraid,' even though the college is only thirty miles away and is the one that her father has chosen for her. Here Jackson describes the unbridgeable gulf between a teenager and her parents.

> Natalie Waite, who was seventeen years old but who felt that she had been truly conscious only since she was about fifteen, lived in an odd corner of a world of sound and sight past the daily voices of her father and mother and their incomprehensible actions. For the past two years – since, in fact, she had turned around suddenly one bright morning and seen from the corner of her eye a person called Natalie, existing, charted, inescapably located on a spot of ground, favored with sense and feet and a bright-red sweater, and most obscurely alive

– she had lived completely by herself, allowing not even her father access to the farther places of her mind.

Nevertheless, like other teenage girls in *Girls in Bloom*, she is close to her father who critiques her writing as if he were her mentor rather than her father. In this she is very close to Cassandra Mortmain in *I Capture the Castle* by Dodie Smith, which we will look at shortly, a novel which also prefigures Jackson's *We Have Always Lived in the Castle*. Her father is kindly but patronising towards Natalie, who he says, being an adolescent, is 'too untaught for literature and too young for drink.' One of Natalie's school writing projects has been to write a description of her father; she has shown it to him. In his pomposity and vanity he is amused by her honesty.

'I am not finding fault with your interpretation. You are of course completely free to write whatever you please about me or anything else. I am interested in seeing you write what you please, and in encouraging you to write more. But you *must*, if you are ever to be a *good* writer, understand your own motives'...

'That does not mean,' he continued thoughtfully, '– although, remember, this is actually a new experience for me as well as for you – that does not mean that I am not able to help you, or advise you, or sympathise with you; it only means that we must recognise now that you are a growing girl and I an old man, and that a basic sex antagonism, combined with a filial resentment, separates us, so that we cannot always be honest with one another as we have been up to now.'

If it's happening does he tell me? Natalie thought briefly, and heard from faraway the police detective demanding, 'Are you prepared to confess that you killed him?'

Natalie's father is also no doubt to some extent a portrait of Jackson's own husband, Stanley Edgar Hyman, a critic and book reviewer who taught at Bennington women's college, whose relationship with Jackson is presumably in some ways portrayed in Natalie's relationship with her father. 'Do you realise I'm two weeks behind in my work?' he asks his wife. 'I've got to review four books by Monday; four books no one in this house has read but myself... Not to mention the book.' At the mention of his book, 'his family glanced at him briefly, in chorus, and then away;' no doubt Hyman and Jackson's children reacted similarly. Hyman's heavy-weight *The Armed Vision: A Study in the Methods of Modern Literary Criticism* was published in 1947 his next book, *The Critical Performance: An Anthology of American and British Literary Criticism in Our Century* was published in 1956, nine years later and his third, *Poetry and Criticism: Five Revolutions in Literary Taste* in 1961. In this period Jackson published five novels (with another in 1962), two collections of her lightweight – as both she and Hyman no doubt saw them – though lucrative magazine pieces, a collection of short stories and numerous individual stories in magazines. But this was at a time when a woman's place was in the kitchen and her role was, as Virginia Woolf said, to magnify her man's reflection in the mirror of her self; no doubt both Hyman and their friends saw his work as the most important, the most serious, as do Natalie's family. Unlike Woolf, Jackson did not have a room of her own and had to be Woolf's 'angel in the house', though she was hardly the soft, gentle, beautiful, radiant type of angel. In the introduction to *Just an Ordinary Day*, a posthumous collection of Jackson's stories, two of her children wrote about how she balanced domesticity and creativity.

> Our mother tried to write every day, and treated writing in every way as her professional livelihood. She would typically work all morning, after all the children went off to school, and usually again well into the evening and night. There was always the sound of typing. And our house was more often than not filled with luminaries in literature and the arts. There were legendary parties and poker games with visiting painters, sculptors, musicians, composers, poets, teachers, and writers of every leaning. But always there was the sound of her typewriter, pounding away into the night.

This is very much a description of the literary garden parties that Natalie's father hosts on Sundays, which are rather reminiscent of the Ramsays' dinner party in Woolf's *To the Lighthouse*, whose modernist pretensions Jackson nicely deflates. 'The books they were likely to want to consult during discussion (*Ulysses*, CS Lewis, *The Function of the Orgasm*, the newest English homosexual novel, *Hot Discography*, an abridged *Golden Bough*, and an unabridged dictionary) were set in the small bookcase.' It is after one of these parties that Natalie – probably – has her first sexual experience; it is foreshadowed when her father says to her: 'Daughter mine... has anyone yet corrupted you?' Someone is about to; 'she was almost sure of this, the preliminary faint stirrings of something about to happen. The idea once born, she knew it was true; something incredible was going to happen, now, right now, this afternoon, today; this was going to be a day she would remember and look back upon, thinking, That wonderful day ... the day when *that* happened.'

An older man, who is not named and whom she does not seem to know, asks her to sit down; 'he was old, she could see now, much older than she had thought before. There were fine disagreeable little lines around his eyes and mouth, and his hands were thin and bony, and even shook a little.' He tells Natalie that her father has described her as 'quite the little writer... Obviously meaning to make her sound less like her mother and more like a frightened girl not yet in college.' Natalie is hurt by this and responds, 'I suppose you probably want to write too?' Natalie tries to get up to leave but he holds onto her. 'A little chill went down Natalie's back at his holding her arm, at the strange unfamiliar touch of someone else.' In Natalie's head the detective says to her: '*This* you will not escape.' The 'strange man' leads Natalie away. She has been telling him about 'how wonderful I am.'

'Now then,' he said. 'Tell me what she thinks is so wonderful about herself.'

How far wrong, Natalie thought, can one person be about another? Perhaps in that little time I have grown in his mind and he is now talking to some Natalie he thought he had hold of by the arm. She felt the grass under her feet, the soft brush of bushes against her hair, and his fingers on her arm. It was no longer afternoon; the time had slipped away from under Natalie and while she had been behaving in her mind, under the lights, as though it were 5 o'clock, she found now in the darkness that it was much, much later, long past dinnertime, long past any daylight.

They end up in the woods where Natalie used to play when she was a child; 'the trees were really dark and silent, and Natalie thought quickly The danger is in here, in *here*, just as they stepped inside and were lost in the darkness.' They sit down the grass. 'Oh my dear God sweet Christ, Natalie thought, so sickened she nearly said it aloud, is he going to touch me?'

If he does, Jackson does not tell us. The next paragraph has Natalie waking up the next morning, 'to bright sun and clear air,' before burying her head in the pillow and saying:

'No, please no'.

'I will not think about it, it doesn't matter,' she told herself, and her mind repeated idiotically, It doesn't matter, it doesn't matter, it doesn't matter, it doesn't matter, until, desperately, she said aloud, 'I don't remember, nothing happened, nothing that I remember happened.'

Slowly she knew she was sick; her head ached, she was dizzy, she loathed her hands as they came toward her face to cover her eyes. 'Nothing happened,' she chanted, 'nothing happened, nothing happened, nothing happened, nothing happened.'

'Nothing happened,' she said looking at the window, at the dear loss today. 'I don't remember.'

'I will not think about it,' she said to her clothes, lying on the chair, and she remembered as she saw them how she had torn them off wildly when she went to bed, thinking, I'll fix them in the morning, and a button had fallen from her dress and she had watched it roll under the bed, and thought, I'll get it in the morning, and I'll face it all in the morning, and, in the morning it will be gone.

If she got out of bed it would be true; if she stayed in bed she might just possibly be really sick, perhaps delirious. Perhaps dead. 'I will not think about it,' she said, and her mind went on endlessly, Will not think about it, will not think about it, will not think about it.

Someday, she thought, it will be gone. Someday I will be sixty years old, sixty-seven, eighty, and, remembering, will perhaps recall that something of this sort happened once (where? when? who?) and will perhaps smile nostalgically thinking, What a sad silly girl I was, to be sure.

Before whatever happened, happened, the detective in Natalie's head had said to her: 'No one can live through such things and not *remember* them,' but Natalie is determined not to remember and Jackson is determined not to tell us. She does tell us that 'the most horrible moment of that morning or any morning in her life, was when she first looked at herself in the mirror, at her bruised face and her pitiful, erring body,' but none of her family notice anything wrong with her face and perhaps the bruising is entirely internal. Later, at college, she writes in her private journal, where she splits off a separate personality and talks to herself in the third person (in Jackson's next novel, *The Bird's Nest*, 1954, the central character will be a schizophrenic young woman, but there is nothing unusual about adolescents in fiction talking themselves through their journals):

> Perhaps, you thought, Natalie is frightened and perhaps she even thinks sometimes about a certain long ago bad thing that she promised me never to think about again. Well, that's why I am writing this now. I could tell, my darling, that you are worried about me. I could feel you being apprehensive, and I knew what you were thinking about was you and me. And I even knew that you thought I was worried about that terrible thing, but of course – I promise you this, I really do – I don't think about it at all, ever, because both of us know that it never happened, did it? And it was some horrible dream that caught up with us both. We don't have to worry about things like that, you remember we decided we didn't have to worry.

Natalie does leave for college, where, unlike her mother and her author, Natalie has a room of her own, 'the only room she had ever known where she would be, privately, working out her own salvation.' The college is described as being very much like the liberal, girls-only Bennington College where Jackson's husband taught and she meets a professor, Arthur Langdon, who seems to be another portrait of Edgar Hyman (even their names are concordant). Langdon has a wife who, like Natalie's mother but completely unlike Jackson herself is entirely subsumed under her husband's ego and has, as Hyman undoubtedly did, a circle of young, devoted female admirers. Langdon soon steps into the role that had been filled by Natalie's father, and gives Jackson another chance to muse on the absurdity of being a writer.

> 'I find your criticisms very helpful,' Natalie said demurely. 'My father discusses my work with me very much as you do.' She thought of her father with sudden sadness; he was so far away and so much without her, and here she was speaking to a stranger.
> 'Do you plan to be a writer?'

A what? Natalie thought; a writer, a plumber, a doctor, a merchant, a chief; the best-laid plans of; a writer the way I might plan to be a corpse? 'A writer?' she repeated, as though she had never heard the word before.

He was staring at her with his mouth half-open; she must have delayed her idiotic answer beyond any reasonable time for thought. 'Do you plan to be a writer?' he asked again.

He *did* mean it, then. 'Look,' Natalie said, 'why does everyone say they're going to be writers? When they're not? I mean, why do you and my father and everybody say 'to be a writer' as though it were something different? Not like anything else? Is there something special about writers?'

Her delay had not helped him any. 'It's because writing itself,' he began, hesitated, and then, 'I suppose it's because writing – well it's something important, I suppose.'

'Well, then, what am I going to write?'

'Well . . .' he said. He looked at her and then irritably at the papers on his desk. 'Stories,' he said. 'Poems. Articles. Novels. Plays.' He shook his head and then said, 'Anything – well, creative.'

'But why is it so important, this creating?'

Why indeed, Jackson must herself have wondered while juggling family life and writing.

Natalie make some friends at the college and fits in well enough, though she is never part of any crowd, too bookish and self-sufficient for the rest of the girls. One friend says that the other girls accuse her of sitting in her room all day and never going out; 'They say you're crazy. You sit in your room all day and all night and never go out and they say you're *crazy... you're spooky.*' Natalie's answer to this comes in her own private journal, which Jackson allows us limited access to.

Dearest dearest darling most important dearest darling Natalie – this is me talking, your own priceless own Natalie, and I just wanted to tell you one single small thing: you *are* the best and they *will* know it someday, and someday no one will ever dare laugh again when you are near, and no one will dare even *speak* to you without bowing first. And they *will* be afraid of you. And all you have to do is wait, my darling, wait and it will come, I promise you.

Later it seems that Natalie has split herself into two in a different way: by inventing a female friend Tony. It is not entirely clear at first that Tony is imaginary but after much romantic talk – not romantic in the lesbian sense, despite what Jackson's Oxford critic said – about travelling the world together they end up alone in a dark wood, where Tony disappears. This time, nothing bad happens to Natalie in the woods and a friendly couple in a car pick her up and take her back to town, drop her off at the bridge where she appears for a moment to contemplate suicide. But then, one with herself again, she heads back to the college; she has come of age. 'As she had never been before, she was now alone, and grown-up, and powerful, and not at all afraid.'

In most of the novels we are looking at the adolescent heroine's world is largely made up of three overlapping spheres: parents and siblings; her school and school friends; boys. But in some cases the girl is part of a community which shapes her life and the novel – the 'we' of her 'me' as Frankie Addams would say. In some of these cases the novels are chamber pieces where the teenage girl is merely one of the cast of characters, even if she believes herself to be someone special.

HARRIET MERRIAM: *THE ROAD THROUGH THE WALL* BY SHIRLEY JACKSON, 1948

Fourteen-year-old Harriet lives in a middle-class suburb in California – not completely unlike the one where Jackson herself was born – where everyone knows everyone else's business. Like *Peyton Place*, which we will look at next, this is a chamber piece where many characters have an equal part and Harriet is simply one of the actors in the drama. Nevertheless, she is drawn in great detail and the novel does show her awkwardly coming of age, at least in one sense. *Saturday Review*, February 28, 1948 said, 'the story is a good one, set down with neither hope nor despair. It is the story of Sidestreet, USA, where the children reflect the life of their parents with its bickering futility and its moral bankruptcy.' As in several of Jackson's stories and novels, we do indeed see the world – and in this case Pepper Street is its own world – largely through children and their mothers; Jackson didn't – possibly couldn't – ever write a sympathetic male character.

Like several of the central figures in *Girls in Bloom*, Harriet wants to be a writer, but unlike many of them she is dumpy, unattractive and awkward; Jackson herself was consistently overweight – at the age of forty she weighed over 200 pounds – and by no means conventionally beautiful or glamorous even in her publicity photos; she creates Harriet with obvious love and a great deal of empathy. 'Harriet was a big girl, large-boned and stout, and Mrs Merriam braided Harriet's hair every morning and dressed her in bright colors. For the last year or so, from twelve to almost fourteen, Harriet had begun to speak awkwardly when she was uneasy, missing her words sometimes, and stammering.' Her mother confides to a friend that she worries about Harriet, 'about her being so heavy, I mean. It's very hard on a girl.' Harriet does not join in with the other children playing 'baseball or tag or hide-and-seek, actually because she was fat and the other children made fun of her, ostensibly because her mother had forbidden her to play.' She tells her friends that she has 'a sort of weak heart... My mother thinks and the doctor thinks I shouldn't do much running around like the other kids.' Jackson herself died of a heart attack in her forties.

Harriet's trouble with her mother starts when, following other girls in her class, she writes a letter to a boy which only the most prudish of mothers, even in the 1940s, would consider risqué. Unfortunately for Harriet, her mother is one of those mothers. Harriet has chosen to write to George 'because he was dull and unpopular and she felt vaguely that she had no right to aim any higher than the one boy no one else would have.' Harriet had not sent the letter, nor even finished it. It begins, 'Dearest George,' and continues, 'Let's run away and get married. I love you and I want to – ' The letter ends here because 'Harriet had not been able to think of what she wanted to do with George.' Her friend Helen's letter had ended 'kiss you a thousand times' but Harriet 'could not bring herself to write such a thing, at least partly because the thought of kissing George Martin's doll face horrified her.'

Harriet sees that her mother has been looking through her desk drawers, a private world which contains her notebooks labelled, respectively, Poems, Moods, Me and Daydreams. The mothers of the various girls are appalled to various degrees at this wanton, lustful collective display on the part of their daughters. Harriet's mother is distraught.

'I try to make my daughter into a good decent girl in spite of –' Mrs Merriam sobbed, '– in spite of everything, and I work all day and I worry about money and try to make a good decent home for my husband and now my only daughter turns out to be –'

'Josephine,' Mr Merriam said strongly. 'Harriet, go upstairs again.'

Harriet went upstairs away from her mother's sorry voice. Her desk was unlocked; instead of eating dinner, she and her mother had stood religiously by the furnace and put Harriet's diaries and letters and notebooks into the fire one by one, while solid Harry Merriam sat eating lamb chops and boiled potatoes upstairs alone.

Harriet's mother soon comes down and 'Harriet felt at last like crying. She loved her mother again, as one should love a mother, tenderly and affectionately. She put her arm around her mother and kissed her. "I'm sorry," she said.' Her mother says to Harriet: 'We'll spend more time together from now on. Reading, and sewing. Would you like to learn to cook, really *cook*?' She even offers to help Harriet write her poetry. 'I used to write poetry, Harriet, not very *well*, of course, but that's probably where you get it.' Her father insists that she shows her mother everything she writes; Harriet, earnestly, says she will. Unusually for the characters in *Girls in Bloom*, Harriet's father is not at all close to his daughter and has no idea what is going on in her life. Unlike Natalie Waite's father he has no interest in literature or his daughter's interest in it.

'Can you sew?' Mr Merriam asked with interest.

'Not very well,' Harriet said. 'Mostly I'm a writer.'

'I see,' Mr Merriam said. 'What do you do with yourself all the time, Harriet?'

'I write,' Harriet said, 'and I play with the kids, and mother is teaching me to cook.'

'When are you going to make me a cake?' Mr Merriam asked cheerfully.

'I can't make *cakes* yet,' Harriet said.

Harriet's friend Virginia very nearly leads her into serious trouble when she takes Harriet with her to the apartment of a Chinese man she has met on the street. Harriet has been nervous of doing anything her mother would not approve of and wants to go the long way home so they will not run into him but Virginia tells her, 'if you're going to be scared all the time and always be wanting to go around the other way and afraid of your mother and everything I'll just go on down to the store by myself and not talk to you anymore.' Harriet doesn't know what to do, she doesn't want to go into the apartment but 'she couldn't let Virginia go alone, and never be friends again afterward, but once inside they were no longer right where they could call for help.' She tries to stop Virginia. 'We *can't* go in, Ginnie. My *mother*.' The girls do go inside but nothing bad happens, except that they discover the Chinese man is simply a servant in the apartment and the owners are away. Afterwards she is nervous that Virginia will let slip something to her mother and is hoping that the family moving into the vacant house on the street may provide a new friend for her to replace the risky Virginia. Harriet quite naturally – for a girl in *Girls in Bloom* – sees the world in terms of *Little Women*, though unusually she does not want to be Jo.

Perhaps one of the new girls who would live in the house – they would be like in *Little Women*, and Harriet's friend would be Jo (or just possibly Beth, and they could die together, patiently) – would love and esteem Harriet, and some day their friendship would be a literary legend, and their letters –

Marilyn Perlman walked past, slowly, and then stopped and turned back. 'Hello,' she said.

'Hello,' Harriet said. Marilyn came over and stood beside Harriet, looking back at the house-for-rent.

'I guess someone's going to move in,' she said.

'Sure,' Harriet said. She was bewildered; she had never spoken particularly to Marilyn; why should Marilyn stop and speak to her?... Marilyn sat down, suddenly, next Harriet on the curb.

'Listen, she said in an honest voice, 'I wanted to talk to you for a long time.'

'What about?' Harriet said.

Marilyn put her chin on her hands and stared straight ahead. 'Just about everything,' she said. 'You like to read, don't you?' When Harriet moved her head solemnly Marilyn said, 'so do I,' and then stopped to think. 'Do you get library books? she asked.

'No,' Harriet said. 'I've never been to the library yet.'

'Me neither,' Marilyn said. 'We could get library cards you know.'

'Have you read *Little Women*?' Harriet asked.

Marilyn shook her head and asked, 'have you read *Vanity Fair*?'

'I haven't read that yet,' Harriet said. 'I liked *Little Women*, though.'

Harriet's mother would presumably be apoplectic if Harriet were to read *Vanity Fair*. Marilyn tells Harriet about the girls she does not like, including Virginia. 'She's not much,' says Harriet and in 'a final recognition of her bond with Marilyn,' she says, 'I know something about *her.*' Marilyn is from the only Jewish family in the neighbourhood. Harriet's parents are not at first especially anti-Semitic, and the subject only arises in relation to readings of Shakespeare that are being organised; someone mentions that it might be insensitive to read *The Merchant of Venice* with Marilyn present. Eventually, Harriet's parents tell her she must not see Marilyn again but before that Harriet and Marilyn have become close, especially in their literary tastes.

One time, Marilyn is talking about reincarnation; she tells Harriet that she might have been Becky Sharp before she was Harriet Merriam, even though Harriet is far closer to Emmy Sedley than to Becky Sharp, who is more like Virginia. '"Or Jo March," Harriet replied, fascinated;' clearly her friendship with Marilyn has given her the confidence to move up the ladder of the March sisters. Marilyn suggests that they should both write down where they think they will be in ten years' time, bury the notes and never look at each other's for the next ten years. 'Rest here, all my hopes and dreams,' says Marilyn as they bury the paper. 'The curse be on whoever touches these papers,' adds Harriet. 'Now you're my closest and dearest friend, Harriet.' After Harriet's parents have forbidden her to see Marilyn again, Harriet meekly agrees but handles the breakup very badly. Marilyn calls her a fat slob and Harriet now sees Marilyn as being ugly. They never do see each other's ten-year plans, but we do: a neighbourhood boy finds them and Jackson shows them to us. As we have already seen, Jackson knows a thing or two about what teenage girls want. Cunningly, she does not tells which note is which but we can probably work it out.

> *In ten years I will be a beautiful charming lovely lady writer without any husband or children but lots of lovers and everyone will read the books I write and want to marry me but I will never marry any of them. I will have lots of money and jewels too.*

> *I will be a famous actress or maybe a painter and everyone will be afraid of me and do what I say.*

ALLISON MACKENZIE: *PEYTON PLACE* BY GRACE METALIOUS, 1956

Peyton Place, like Shirley Jackson's *The Road Through the Wall*, is set in a community where everyone knows everyone's business; in this case a small New England town quite similar to the one where Jackson herself lived. The novels are similar in that they are both chamber pieces with an ensemble cast of characters Their communities are similar too, though the inhabitants of Peyton Place seem to have a lot more sex – more than the censors and many critics were prepared to put up with: the novel was banned in Knoxville, Tennessee in 1957 and in Rhode Island in 1959. But the censors were far too late. *Peyton Place* was already a bestseller by September 1956, and would remain so well into 1957. It sold over 100,000 copies in its first month, compared to the average first novel which sold 3,000 copies, if it was lucky, in its lifetime. *Peyton Place* eventually sold over 12 million copies but even then is most widely re-membered for its film and TV adaptations.

Grace Metalious (1924-1964), born Marie Grace DeRepentigny, unlike most of the authors in *Girls in Bloom*, was born into poverty, in New England. She married George Metalious (unusually for the writers in this survey, she published under her husband's name) before she was twenty years old and the couple immediately had a child. Despite their poverty, George attended university and became principal of a school while Grace continued to write, something she had done since she was at school and in which George encouraged her. George later said that the novel's epon-ymous town and its name were 'a composite of all small towns where ug-liness rears its head, and where the people try to hide all the skeletons in their closets.' Grace was thirty when she finished the manuscript; she found a literary agent but had trouble finding a publisher because of the amount of sex it contained.

Reviews in serious newspapers condemned the book but that did not stop people buying it. Much later Metalious said, 'If I'm a lousy writer, then an awful lot of people have lousy taste.' She was right. Less than a month after the novel was published, producer and screenwriter Jerry Wald paid her $250,000 for the film rights. He also paid her as a story consultant though she was not in the end responsible for any of the screenplay and in fact she hated Hollywood, hated the way her novel was sanitised and was appalled by the suggestion that Pat Boone – who, as we know, wrote a bland advice column for teenagers in *Ladies Home Jour-*

nal – be cast in a leading role. Still, the $400,000 she made from the film was probably some consolation. The film came out in 1957, featuring nineteen-year-old newcomer Diane Varsi who was far too beautiful and mature for the role but was nominated for an Academy Award anyway. Varsi did not continue in the movie business but went on to study poetry, coincidentally at Bennington College, where Shirley Jackson's husband had taught. The TV series of Peyton Place began in 1964, running for five seasons until 1969. Like the film, it was a very toned down version of the novel, starring Mia Farrow, aged nineteen when the series began, as twelve-year-old Allison Mackenzie. Unlike Varsi and Farrow, but like Harriet Merriam, Allison is plain and quite chubby and has very few friends.

> Allison hadn't one friend in the entire school, except for Selena Cross. They made a peculiar pair, those two, Selena with her dark, gypsyish beauty, her thirteen-year-old eyes as old as time, and Allison Mackenzie, still plump with residual babyhood, her eyes wide open, guileless and questioning, above that painfully sensitive mouth.

Selena is indeed entirely different from Allison: as we have seen, in many female coming-of-age novels the blameless, bookish, shy, unattractive central character has a foil who is pretty, popular and outgoing, and very often with looser morals. In this case the contrast is extreme. Selena is by no means a virgin, though we only find out later how and to whom she loses her virginity; the truth when it comes is like nothing else in *Girls in Bloom*. There is also a huge social difference between the two girls: Allison's mother Constance is discreet and aloof and runs a very high-class dress shop – 'the women of the town bought almost exclusively from her' – while Selena lives in a rundown shack with her hopeless mother and vile, violent, drunken and lecherous stepfather who rapes her and takes her virginity. (In the original manuscript, he was her father; the one change that Metalious agreed with her publisher before publication was that he should become her stepfather – it hardly lessens the shock when the rape happens.) 'Selena was beautiful while Allison believes herself an unattractive girl, plump in the wrong places, flat in the wrong spots, too long in the legs and too round in the face.' Selena on the other hand is 'well-developed for her age, with the curves of hips and breasts already discernible under the too short and often threadbare clothes that she wore.' She has 'long dark hair that curled of its own accord in a softly beautiful fashion. Her eyes, too, were dark and slightly slanted, and she had a naturally red, full lipped mouth over well shaped startlingly white teeth.' Selena is nowhere near as well read as Allison but she is much wiser; 'wiser with the wisdom learned of poverty and wretchedness. At thirteen, she saw hopelessness as an old enemy, as persistent and inevitable as death.' Selena cannot understand 'what in the world ailed Allison that she could be unhappy in surroundings like these, with a wonderful blond mother, and a pink and white bedroom of her own.'

Unlike Allison, Selena covets the dresses in Constance's shop. Constance 'could understand a girl looking that way at the sight of a beautiful dress. The only time that Allison ever wore this expression was when she was reading.' When Constance asks Selena to work part-time in her shop, Selena thinks she is in heaven. Wearing one of the dresses, Constance thinks Selena has 'the look of a beautifully sensual, expensively kept woman.' Selena adores Constance; she thinks: 'Someday, I'll get out, and when I do, I'll always wear beautiful clothes and talk in a soft voice, just like Mrs McKenzie.'

Allison may not be popular with the girls – or indeed the boys, not that she cares about boys – but her teacher Miss Thornton likes her. She has a mission: 'If I can teach something to one child, if I can awaken in only one child a sense of beauty, joy in truth, and admission of ignorance and a thirst for knowledge then I am fulfilled. One child, thought Miss Thornton, adjusting her old brown felt, and her mind fastened with love on Allison Mackenzie.' Allison knows about Miss Thornton's feelings for her – an unusual example of a teacher having a crush on a girl – but she believes it is 'only because Miss Thornton was so ugly and plain herself'.

Allison's mother has never told her the truth about her father, whom Allison believes to be dead, but who is in fact alive and well. Constance had an affair with him but they never married; he is a Scottish businessman and his name was also, confusingly, Allison. But he had a wife at the time of the affair and had no intention of marrying Constance, though he has always provided for her and their daughter financially. Constance left town, pregnant, before Allison's birth and invented a fictitious, short lived marriage, coming back after Allison was born with a story that her imaginary husband was dead. To make the story work, she has had to subtract a year from Allison's real age – Allison is a year older than she and everybody else believes.

Allison loves her absent father – or at least the false image she has built up of him – as well as her mother, though they have 'little in common with each other; the mother was far too cold and practical a mind to understand the sensitive, dreaming child, and Allison too young and full of hopes and fancies to sympathise with her mother.' Like many of the characters in *Girls in Bloom*, Allison is bookish but does not get her love of reading from her mother: Constance 'could not understand a twelve-year-old girl keeping her nose in a book. Other girls her age would have been continually in the shop, examining and exclaiming over the boxes of pretty dresses and underwear which arrived there almost daily.'

Unlike Selena, all Allison knows about life she has got from her reading. She has discovered a box of old books in the attic, and is fascinated by them; 'she went from de Maupassant to James Hilton without a quiver. She read *Goodbye, Mr Chips* and wept in the darkness of her room for an hour while the last line of the story lingered in her mind. "I said goodbye to Chips the night before he died." Allison began to wonder about God and death.'

But what Allison loves most of all, better than books even, is being alone in the countryside just outside the town where she can 'be free from the hatefulness that was school... For a little while she could find pleasure here and forget that her pleasures would be considered babyish and silly by older, more mature twelve-year-old girls.'

Now that she was quiet and unafraid, she could pretend that she was a child again, and not a twelve-year-old who would be entering high school within less than another year, and who should be interested now in clothes and boys and pale rose lipstick... But away from this place she was awkward, loveless, pitifully aware that she lacked the attraction and poise which she believed that every other girl her age possessed...

There would not be many more days of contentment for Allison, for now she was twelve and soon would have to begin spending her life with people like the girls at school. She would be surrounded by them, and have to try hard to be one of them. She was sure that they would never accept her. They would laugh at her, ridicule her, and she would find herself living in a world where she was the only odd and different member of the population.

Allison does not want to turn from a girl into a woman, does not want come of age, mentally or physically; the outward attributes of woman-hood repel her. She hates the idea of 'hair growing anywhere on her body. Selena already had hair under her arms which she shaved off once a month.' Selena tells Allison that she gets it all over with at once, 'my peri-od and my shave.' Allison agrees this is a good idea but 'as far as she was concerned, "periods" were something that happened to other girls. She decided that she would never tolerate such things in herself.' Allison sends off for a sex education book which she reads carefully to find out about periods; she clearly cannot contemplate asking her mother.

> Phooey, she thought disdainfully when she had finished studying the pamphlet. I'll be the only woman in the whole world who won't, and it'll be written up in all the medical books.
> She thought of 'It' as a large black bat, with wings outspread, and when she woke up on the morning of her thirteenth birthday to dis-cover that 'It' was nothing of the kind, she was disappointed, disgust-ed and more than a little frightened.
> But the reason she wept that she was not, after all, going to be as unique as she had wanted to be.

Despite its mauling by 'serious' critics and its mangling by film and TV producers, the original novel's reputation for lowbrow sleaze is complete-ly unjustified: in its sensitive and perceptive treatment of both Allison and Selena it is as good a coming of age novel as any in *Girls in Bloom*. It is certainly much better than her later novels, including its hastily written sequel, *Return to Peyton Place*, 1959, which follows Allison as she grows up to become a writer, writing scurrilous, thinly disguised portraits of the people in Peyton Place and, like her mother, has an affair with a married man. Success did not bring happiness to Metalious and she died of liver failure following years of heavy drinking at the age of thirty-nine in 1964, eighteen months before Shirley Jackson died of a heart attack at the age of forty-eight.

IN THE CASTLE

'Last night I dreamt I went to Manderley again'. In some novels, like Daphne du Maurier's *Rebecca*, a large house forms more than just the backdrop to the story – it becomes a key part of the story, not just the physical but also the emotional setting for the action, forming the boundaries of the characters' world and the possibilities of the plot, as it did in many Gothic novels and as it had in Shirley Jackson's *The Sundial* and *The Haunting of Hill House*. There is undoubtedly a tradition of female Gothic novels centred on a gloomy, secluded house or castle which contains, as one critic described it, 'virgins in distress and demons in disguise.'

The tradition started with Clara Reeve's *The Old English Baron*, 1777 and Anne Radcliffe's *Mysteries of Udolpho*, 1794, which followed the first male-authored Gothic novel, Horace Walpole's the *Castle of Otranto*, 1764. This tradition includes novels as diverse as *Northanger Abbey*, *Wuthering Heights*, *Jane Eyre*, *The Tenant of Wildfell Hall*, *Frankenstein*, *Lady Audley's Secret*, *Cold Comfort Farm*, *Rebecca*, Angela Carter's *The Bloody Chamber*, Anne Rice's vampire stories and Stephenie Meyer's *Twilight* series. Many of these books include teen heroines and their coming of age stories, though they are mostly dark and unsettling ones.

Although the dark, damp Gothic houses and castles in the stories are in many ways womb-like, they are nevertheless often the seat of male power and female imprisonment, the extreme example perhaps being Bluebeard's castle, in which all his former wives are entombed. This trope was set early in the genre: travelling to Udolpho to marry Count Murano, Radcliffe's Emily is rightly afraid of what she is going to find.

> From the deep solitudes, into which she was immerging, and from the gloomy castle, of which she had heard some mysterious hints, her sick heart recoiled in despair, and she experienced, that, though her mind was already occupied by peculiar distress, it was still alive to the influence of new and local circumstance; why else did she shudder at the idea of this desolate castle?

I want to look in this chapter at three coming of age novels where the house is itself a character in the novel but where the female characters, unlike the heroines in most Gothic literature, dominate both their novels and the house/castle they live in. The first and last of these have similar titles and quite similar adolescent female characters.

CASSANDRA MORTMAIN: *I CAPTURE THE CASTLE* BY DODIE SMITH, 1949

British writer Dodie Smith (1896-1990) is best known for the children's book *101 Dalmatians*. But this heavyweight book (in physical size rather than literary style), written after the war while Smith was living in California and writing scripts for the movies, was her first novel, published when she was fifty-one, older than Shirley Jackson was when she died. It is very much in the female *bildungsroman* tradition; though it concerns a teenage girl it is oriented at an adult, literary audience. It foreshadows many of the characteristics of Shirley Jackson's novels and central characters: the spooky house acting as almost a character in the novel (*The Sundial*; *The Haunting of Hill House; We Have Always Lived in the Castle* – even Jackson's title here is very similar to Smith's); the narrator being the younger of two sisters who live close to a village but do not interact with the villagers (*We Have Always Lived in the Castle*); the heroine writing poetry and being unfeasibly well-read (*Hangsaman*); the dead mother (*We Have Always Lived in the Castle*; Smith's own mother died when she was fourteen, but not her father) and the narrator's father being a self-absorbed writer (*Hangsaman*).

In Greek myth, Cassandra was cursed to utter predictions which were true but which no one would believe, and in real life Cassandra Austen was Jane's elder sister, so Cassandra Mortmain's name has multiple resonances. Her castle, unlike Mary Katherine's in *We Have Always Lived in the Castle* is a real one: literary rather than metaphorically Gothic. Mediaeval, literally crumbling, unheatable and virtually uninhabitable, the family inhabit the parts of it which still have some vestiges of a roof in virtually total poverty. 'I must admit that our home is an unreasonable place to live in. Yet I love it. The house itself was built in the time of Charles II, but it was damaged by Cromwell.' The family live in entirely different kind of poverty to Francie Nolan's or Francie Withers' in the next chapter: theirs is a genteel, intellectual and eccentric – in a very English sense – poverty. The castle, which they rent on a forty year lease, was at one time superbly furnished but all the furniture has been sold to raise money.

Unlike Shirley Jackson's *Hill House*, the castle is not literally haunted: 'there are said to be ghosts – which there are not. (There are some queer things up on the mound, but they never come into the house.)' Cassandra's sister Rose says the castle is 'like the tower in *The Lancashire Witches* where mother Demdike lived.' (Shirley Jackson was interested in witchcraft and wrote a book on the Salem Witches, very much the American equivalent to the English Lancashire Witches.)

Like Natalie Waite's father, Cassandra's father is a writer and had some years earlier published the avant-garde book *Jacob Wrestling* (a reference to Kierkegaard) to great critical acclaim though to no great sales; there is virtually no revenue from the book anymore and he has now stopped writing altogether following a short stay in prison as a result of a dispute with a neighbour. He now spends most of his time locked away in a study, apparently doing puzzles. As well as the narrator, shy, bookish Cassandra – 'I am seventeen, look younger, feel older. I am no beauty but have a neatish face.' – and her father, the household includes Cassandra's more outgoing older sister Rose – 'nearly 21 and very bitter with life,' their younger brother Thomas and their father's young but rather ghostlike wife Topaz.

> Three years ago (or is it four? I know father's one spasm of sociability was in 1931) a stepmother was presented to us. We *were* surprised. She is a famous artists' model who claims to have been christened Topaz – even if this is true there is no law to make a woman stick to a name like that. She is very beautiful, with masses of hair so fair that it is almost white, and quite extraordinary pallor.

If anyone is haunting the castle it is Topaz, a very fey character who likes to stride around the estate naked under her raincoat and play *Greensleeves* on the lute upstairs – not that she is exactly the madwoman in the attic; she is too fashionable and stylish for that. Cassandra says she is 'tall and pale, like a slightly dead goddess.' It is not at all clear why she stays in the dilapidated castle but she genuinely seems to love Cassandra's father and gets on well with his daughters.

Unlike Cassandra, the younger brother Thomas attends school. 'I rather miss school itself – it was a surprisingly good one for such a quiet little country town. I had a scholarship, just as Thomas has at his school; we are tolerably bright.' There is another male character in the household who is not part of the family: Stephen, whose mother was the maid to the family and who now lives with them; he is infatuated with Cassandra but not vice versa. 'He is eighteen now, very fair and noble-looking but his expression is just a fraction daft. He has always been rather devoted to me; Father calls him my swain. He is rather how I imagine Silvius in *As You Like It* – but I am nothing like Phoebe.' Stephen writes poetry to Cassandra, or rather he copies out classic poems and pretends he has written them himself. Literary Cassandra of course recognises them but says nothing to avoid hurting Stephen's feelings. The household is completed by two dogs, Abelard and Heloïse.

Sheila Jackson's *We Have Always Lived in the Castle*, which we will come back to later, is famous for its first paragraph, but *I Capture the Castle* can match it for grabbing our attention.

> I write this sitting in the kitchen sink. That is, my feet are in it; the rest of me is on the draining-board, which I have padded with our dogs' blanket and the tea-cosy. I can't say that I am really comfortable, and there is a depressing smell of carbolic soap, but this is the only part of the kitchen where there is any daylight left. And I have found that sitting in a place where you have never sat before can be inspiring – I wrote my very best poem while sitting on the hen-house. Though even that isn't a very good poem. I have decided my poetry is so bad that I mustn't write any more of it.

Like the equally poor Francie Nolan, Cassandra keeps a journal and aims to write a novel. 'I am writing this journal partly to practice my newly acquired speed-writing and partly to teach myself how to write a novel.' Like Natalie's father in Shirley Jackson's *Hangsaman*, though more reluctantly, Cassandra's father critiques her writing, without much sympathy or enthusiasm. 'The only time Father obliged me by reading one of them, he said I combined stateliness with a desperate effort to be funny. He told me to relax and let the words flow out of me.'

The only way out of their poverty appears to be Rose making a good marriage, but this seems to be impossible; we are not in Jane Austen territory though at one point Rose enviously mentions *Pride and Prejudice* to Cassandra.

'How I wish I lived in a Jane Austen novel!'
I said I'd rather be in a Charlotte Brontë.
'Which would be nicest – Jane with a touch of Charlotte, or Charlotte with a touch of Jane?'
This is the kind of discussion I like very much but I wanted to get on with my journal, so I just said: 'Fifty percent each way would be perfect,' and started to write determinedly. Now it is nearly midnight. I feel rather like a Brontë myself, writing by the light of a guttering candle with my fingers so numb I can hardly hold the pencil.

Later though Cassandra veers back inevitably to Austen, after whose sister she is of course named: 'I don't intend to let myself become the kind of author who can only work in seclusion – after all, Jane Austen wrote in the sitting room and merely covered up her work when a visitor called (though I bet she thought a thing or two) – but I am not quite Jane Austen yet and there are limits to what I can stand.' The village vicar, also apparently highly literary, tells Cassandra that she is 'the insidious type – Jane Eyre with a touch of Becky Sharp. A thoroughly dangerous girl.' Like many of the heroines in Girls in Bloom, Cassandra is more Emmy Sedley than Becky sharp, but calling an adolescent would-be novelist a dangerous girl is exactly what the novelist St Quentin did to Portia Quayne in Elizabeth Bowen's *The Death of the Heart*, which we looked at earlier; as I remarked at the time, writing is considered by many men to be the most dangerous thing woman can do. Later in the novel, Cassandra is tempted to take confession with the vicar, 'as Lucy Snowe did in *Villette*,' she says – reverting from Austen to Charlotte Brontë – though the vicar is not 'High Church enough for confessions.'

As the extreme poverty wears them all down, Rose at one point tells Cassandra and Topaz she is considering a radical way to earn money, using her looks but without being married. 'It may interest you both to know that for some time now, I've been considering selling myself. If necessary, I shall go on the streets.' Cassandra points out that she cannot go street walking in the 'depths of Suffolk.' Rose asks Topaz to lend her the fare to London, but Topaz tells her to continue looking for a wealthy man to marry.

> Rose... has always hoped that the man would be handsome, romantic and lovable into the bargain. I suppose it was her sheer despair of ever meeting any marriageable men at all, even hideous, poverty-stricken ones, that made her suddenly burst into tears. As she only cries about once a year I really ought to have gone over and comforted her, but I wanted to set it all down here. I begin to see that writers are liable to become callous.

This is one of many knowing asides that Betty Smith indulges in via her narrator; she obviously loves and identifies with Cassandra, as will most readers. Smith makes sure that Cassandra is undefeated by her circumstances; chapter 1 ends:

> I finish this entry sitting on the stairs. I think it worthy of note that I never felt happier in my life – despite sorrowful Father, pity for Rose, embarrassment about Stephen's poetry and no justification for hope as regards our family's general outlook. Perhaps it is because I have satisfied my creative urge; or it may be due to the thought of eggs for tea.

But then a potential saviour arrives: the owner of the large house next door from whom the Mortmains lease the castle has died and the house has passed to the Fox-Cottons, a family who include two young single men from America, both of marriageable age and attractive, though one of them has a beard which all three women consider unacceptable. Worse, this is Simon, the actual heir to the estate and the most marriageable of them all. Nevertheless, despite the beard, Rose decides she must marry Simon. Cassandra will have no part in talk of marriage; she says that she would 'approach matrimony as cheerfully as I would the tomb and I cannot feel that I should give satisfaction.' It is the physical side of marriage, of which she has no personal experience, that revolts Cassandra.

> Am I really admitting that my sister is determined to marry a man she has only seen once and doesn't much like the look of? It is half real

and half pretence – and I have an idea that it is a game most girls play when they meet any eligible young men. They just . . . wonder. And if any family ever had need of wondering, it is ours. But only as regards Rose. I have asked myself if I am doing any personal wondering and in my deepest heart I am not. I would rather die than marry either of those quite nice men.

Nonsense! I'd rather marry both of them than die. But it has come to me, sitting here in the barn feeling very full of cold rice, that there is something revolting about the way girls' minds so often jump to marriage long before they jump to love. And most of those minds are shut to what marriage really means. Now I come to think of it, I am judging from books mostly, for I don't know any girls except Rose and Topaz. But some characters in books are very real – Jane Austen's are; and I know those five Bennets at the opening of *Pride and Prejudice*, simply waiting to raven the young men at Netherfield Park, are not giving one thought to the real facts of marriage. I wonder if Rose is? I must certainly try to make her before she gets involved in anything. Fortunately, I am not ignorant in such matters – no stepchild of Topaz's could be. I know all about the facts of life. And I don't think much of them.

Nevertheless, despite their aversion to physical contact with men and her constant fighting off of the attentions of Stephen, Cassandra does become attracted to Simon, unlike Rose, who, although she has agreed to marry Simon, does not love him; something of a Jane Austen situation. The turning point comes when the sisters and Topaz are looking at old paintings in the Fox-Cottons' grand house with the brothers' father and mother, Aubrey and Leda.

Topaz and Aubrey Fox-Cotton looking at pictures too; they were with the eighteenth-century Cottons. 'I've got it,' he said suddenly to Topaz, 'you are really a Blake. Isn't she, Leda?'

Mrs F-C seemed to take a mild interest in this. She gave Topaz a long, appraising stare and said: 'Yes, if she had more flesh on her bones.'

'Rose is a Romney,' said Simon. 'She's quite a bit like Lady Hamilton.' It was the first time I had heard him use her Christian name.

'And Cassandra's a Reynolds of course – the little girl with the mouse-trap.'

'I'm not!' I said indignantly. 'I hate that picture. The mouse is terrified, the cat's hungry and the girl's a cruel little beast. I refuse to be her.'

'Ah, but you'd let the mouse out of the trap and find a nice dead sardine for the cat,' says Simon. I began to like him a little better.

Cassandra briefly considers whether she should marry Simon's brother, Neil and, like Rose, have a thousand pounds spent on her trousseau with furs and jewellery to match, 'everything we can possibly want and, presumably, lots of the handsomest children. It's going to be "happy ever after", just like the fairy tales.' But, she decides, it wouldn't be so happy, and not just because of the physical side. 'I am not so sure I should like the facts of life, but I have got over the bitter disappointment I felt when I first heard about them, and one obviously has to try them sooner or later.' What Cassandra resists is 'the settled feeling, with nothing but happiness to look forward to.' She realises what has been happening: Rose has come of age without her.

> I suddenly know what has been the matter with me all week. Heavens, I'm not envying Rose, I'm missing her! Not missing her because she is away now – though I *have* been a little bit lonely – but missing the Rose who has gone away forever. There used to be two of us always on the look-out for life, talking to Miss Blossom at night, wondering, hoping; two Brontë – Jane Austen girls, poor but spirited, two Girls of Godsend Castle. Now there is only one, and nothing will ever be quite such fun again.

In Rose's absence, Simon has turned his attention to Cassandra. 'You are far prettier than any girl so intelligent has a right to be,' he says to her, sounding 'fairly surprised.' Cassandra tells him she's prettier when Rose is not around. They dance to gramophone records – a luxury Cassandra has never experienced before, and he kisses her. 'I have tried and tried to remember what I felt. Surely I must have felt surprised, but no sense of it comes back to me. All I can recall is happiness, happiness in my mind and in my heart and flowing through my whole body.' Simon calls her an 'astonishing child,' hardly the ideal compliment, then tells her she kisses 'very nicely.' 'I never kissed any man in my life before,' she says. 'Instantly I wished I hadn't said it – for I saw that once he knew I wasn't used to kissing, yet had returned his kiss, he might guess how much it had meant to me.' Simon takes her home in his car. 'Well, I've managed to get Cinderella home by midnight.' The Cinderella aspect of the story has of course long been apparent, as it is in many female coming of age novels, though neither the stepmother nor the sister are horrible to Cassandra and there are two princes here – enough to go round if things are to work out in Jane Austen fashion.

The tipping point comes perhaps when Rose overhears Simon and his mother talking about Proust; she has ever heard of Proust. Later, Cassandra asks Simon if she should read Proust too. 'Apparently that was more amusing than it was intelligent, because it made him laugh. "Why wouldn't say it was a *duty*," he said, "but you could have a shot at it. I'll send you *Swann's Way*.' This is very much like the slightly patronising conversation Olivia Curtis has with Rollo in Rosamond Lehmann's *Invitation to the Waltz*, which we looked at earlier. Simon has now started to see Cassandra as an adult, partly because of the new dress she is wearing – another Cinderella reference perhaps. 'I don't know that I approve of you growing up. Oh, I shall get used to it,' he says, 'but you are perfect as you were.' Cassandra realises that it was 'the funny little girl that he had liked – the comic child playing at Midsummer nights; she was the one he kissed.' He preferred her before she began to come of age.

Cassandra does not marry Simon; she realises that 'when he nearly asked me to marry him it was only an impulse – just as it was when he kissed me on Midsummer Eve; a mixture of liking me very much and longing for Rose.' As narrator, she ends her novel at the end of the journal she is writing in – the third she has used to write this book.

The daylight is going. I can hardly see what I am writing and my fingers are cold. There is only one more page left in my beautiful blue leather manuscript book; but that is as much as I shall need. I don't intend to go on with this journal; I have grown out of wanting to write about myself...

It isn't a bit of use pretending I'm not crying, because I am . . . Paused to mop up. Better now.

Perhaps it would really be rather dull to be married and settled for life. Liar! It would be heaven.

Only half a page left now. Shall I fill it with 'I love you, I love you' – like Father's page of cats on the mat? No. Even a broken heart doesn't warrant a waste of good paper.

There is a light down in the castle kitchen. Tonight I shall have my bath in front of the fire, with Simon's gramophone playing. Topaz has it now, much too loud – to bring Father back to earth in time for tea – but it sounds beautiful from this distance. She is playing the Berceuse from Stravinsky's 'The Firebird'. It seems to say: 'what shall I do? Where shall I go?

You were going to tea, my girl – and a much better tea than you would have come by this time last year.

A mist is rolling over the fields. Why is summer mist romantic and autumn mist just sad?

There was mist on Midsummer Eve, mist when we drove into the dawn.

He said he would come back.

Only the margin left to write now. I love you, I love you, I love you.

MORGAN HARVEY: *GUARD YOUR DAUGHTERS* BY DIANA TUTTON, 1952

This novel, by the English writer Diana Tutton (1915-1991) forms a sort of bridge between *I Capture the Castle* and *We Have Always Lived in the Castle*. It was recently republished by Persephone Books, an English publisher which specialises in reprinting 'interwar novels by women'. Tutton published three novels, all written in Malaya where her British army officer husband was stationed.

The physical presence of the house itself does not loom so large over this narrative as it does over the other two in this chapter, but the novel does concern an eccentric, exotically-named and very self-contained family who live apart from their neighbours and from most of society and have very little life outside of the house. The centre of the house is called the Room. A rare visitor asks why it is called that.

'The Room?'

'Yes. It's – well it's always call that. Mother and father couldn't agree on a name for it.'

'Mother objected to drawing room –' said Cressida.

'Because we don't withdraw there,' said Thisbe.

'And father wouldn't let us have sitting room –' said I.

'Because he says it's always so full of women there is never a chair left for him.'

'Of course that's quite untrue, but it's what he says.'

'And smoking-room's silly.'

'And it's not a library or study –'

'it's only incidentally a music room –'

'No one ever even *suggested* lounge –'

We might have had saloon, all Regency –'

'Common-room would have been good. Why didn't someone think of common-room?'

'Anyway, it's just the Room, with a capital R, and that saves a lot of trouble.'

The nineteen-year-old narrator Morgan (she is named after Morgan La Fée, as she spells it, though she is not fey and there is nothing remotely witchy or evil about her) is the middle one of five sisters (Tutton herself was the youngest of four sisters): Pandora, who has recently married and gone to live in London; 'little swashbuckling Thisbe,' whom Morgan calls a *belle laide*; 'tall redhead Cressida,' who has 'red hair and green eyes and lovely long slim legs,' and Teresa. 'Mother chose them all except Teresa, and by then she got tired, so father had a go. That's why Teresa has such a common name.'

On the whole we have adapted our parents' handsome features rather successfully. Thisbe is the only ugly one (you could never insult her by calling her plain) and she certainly does make up for it with her bright dark eyes and rather thin, ironic mouth. Cressida is quite perfect in every part, and I am not bad, though my face is too round and my legs the *least* little bit bandy. We all have good teeth and skins, and I hope we remember to be grateful.

Like Cassandra Mortmain, Morgan has a father who is a famous writer, though in this case he writes detective stories that are both critically and commercially successful and makes a lot of money. The children, who, also like Cassandra, are all unfeasibly literate and, in two cases also highly musical, do not go to school. (Like some of her English contemporaries and their young female characters, Tutton herself was educated at home.) Thisbe says to one of their rare visitors – a young man, the rarest of the rare: '*None* of us ever went *any* sort of school. We regard them as sinks of ignorance and unnatural vice.' Although she is being ironic, this kind of intellectual snobbishness means they have very few friends, which means that the girls have very little chance of meeting husbands. It is never made entirely clear how Pandora met her husband or why their mother, who jealously guards the unity of the family, let her marry him and move away.

Pandora has not entirely integrated into her new married life in London; referring to her husband's family she calls them: 'Rather lace-curtainy, a lot of them. I think they think I'm very badly brought up because I don't say pardon and I do say sweat.' Snobby Thisbe says Pandora is: 'Lost in trackless Suburbia.' When Pandora returns for a visit, she is naturally concerned that 'you never, any of you, meet any young men, and something's really got to be done about it.' Not that any of the girls show any signs of wanting to marry, leave home or start careers; they all resist coming of age. All of them are dilettantes at various artistic pursuits, but pursue these interests entirely at home, including their mother. 'I realise that her gift is small and perfect and could never have been enlarged into a great one. A year ago I was certain that she could have been a great artist if she had had the opportunity. I was also certain that I was meant to be a great pianist, just as Thisbe had a fine future before her as a poet.' In the absence of any need to make money, the girls all stay at home, Cressida gardening and cooking and fifteen-year-old Teresa devouring heavyweight literature voraciously in lieu of any formal education.

It was odd, I thought, how people seemed to expect me to go out and work for a living. I didn't need to work and I thought mother was quite right – I was lucky to be out of the turmoil, to be able to play my piano without material anxieties. At the same time, I had to suppress the inkling that a little competition might have made me work harder.

When the girls are invited to a cocktail party by neighbouring aristocrats, Morgan asks their mother if they can go. 'Do you know none of us have ever been to one?' 'I'm very glad of it,' replies the mother, who stops them from going; despite their age, all the girls except Pandora behave with complete obedience and without any resentment toward their parents. Their visiting uncle intercedes on their behalf, to no avail. 'Mother clutched desperately at the banisters, and I went and took her other arm. She said: "I don't want to – I'm never happy unless – oh, Gregory it's so *safe* here!"' Eventually, eighteen-year-old Cressida rebels and leaves home suddenly. She writes a letter to her parents telling them not to try to find her and airs all her grievances as well as telling them the home truths she has not been able to say to them face-to-face. She also discusses her sisters, including Morgan.

> As for Morgan, I don't know what to think. I know she is older than me but she does seem to treat Life rather as a joke at times, and I don't believe she's really very *integrated*. Unless she will really get down to her music and be willing to give up other things for its sake, I believe she would do better to buy a typewriter and teach herself touch-typing. I believe one can learn shorthand from a book, too. Then, as I don't expect she'd be allowed to do a real job away from home, she could take in people's MSS. And type them at home. If she mastered that she'd have earned a little money of her *own* and done something to be proud of, then perhaps she could go on to something more exciting. Do please think about this *carefully* and write and let me know your views.

After Cressida leaves, Thisbe and Morgan do attend a party at the local Lord and Lady's house; the first time they have been out in society, though this is not a formal coming out and they are not properly introduced. The sisters do not have the impact they were hoping for and are virtually ignored. 'Morgan, the awful thing is – I don't believe we're as unique as we think we are. No one's looking at is at all. Do you think we are really quite ordinary?' Without their eccentricity, the girls have very little. Nevertheless, Morgan has her first kiss that evening, though it is entirely platonic and shared by her sister. Meanwhile, the mother has taken Cressida's absence very badly and the family are worried about her. 'Father was very angry with Cressida for tearing the delicate fabric across, that had lasted for so long.' The father is even worried that the mother is losing her mind and the family doctor calls in psychiatric specialists. But Cressida becomes ill while separated from the family and returns home.

> She had wanted, she told me later, to die.
> I protested when she said that: 'Oh, Cressida, you don't really mean it. You *couldn't* want to die however awful things looked.' I was – and am – quite unable to imagine such a wish.
> 'But I did, Morgan. It seemed the only thing to do. No one wanted me, I was a failure, and I'd sent mother to – Well, I'd wrecked all our lives, I thought.'
> 'But the future. There's always the future.'
> 'That was the worst of all. I wasn't fit to marry – probably none of us were, I thought then.'

After the specialists have told him that there is nothing wrong with the mother, the father finally sets the girls free from their cage. 'You must all get away from this morbid atmosphere and have some fun. I've saved some money, enough to settle a sum on each of you.' He sends them off to a seaside hotel for Easter following which Cressida has chosen to attend a 'college of domestic science,' and Thisbe has received a marriage proposal, which she is considering; meanwhile she is going to live in a hostel in London with Morgan.

> My own plans were still uncertain. I had faced facts, and had bitterly decided that I could never succeed as a concert pianist, and that I should not therefore make music my career. It seemed hard at this moment to depart from another cherished illusion. During Easter I will decide what I want to learn and to be, and then Thisbe and I would go out daily to lectures at one of the polytechnics.

> I would meet new people, hundreds of young men and women, and among them would be my friends. I would become famous at – something or other, and I would be much beloved. In about ten years' time I would marry.
> I lay smiling in the dark. There were wonderful things ahead, and I would not look back or regret what was gone. 'But,' I thought with a

pang, 'we shall never really be a family again. That part is done, and it was everything while it lasted.

'That part of our story is ended now.'

MARY KATHERINE BLACKWOOD: *WE HAVE ALWAYS LIVED IN THE CASTLE* BY SHIRLEY JACKSON, 1962

Shirley Jackson is a kind of Virginia Werewoolf among the séance-fiction writers. By day, amiably disguised as an embattled mother, she devotes her artful talents to the real-life confusions of the four small children (*Life Among the Savages, Raising Demons*) in her Vermont household. But when shadows fall and the little ones are safely tucked in, Author Jackson pulls down the deadly nightshade and is off. With exquisite subtlety she then explores a dark world (*The Lottery, Hangsaman, The Haunting of Hill House*) in which the usual brooding old houses, fetishes, poisons, poltergeists and psychotic females take on new dimensions of chill and dementia under her black-magical writing skill and infra-red feminine sensibility.
Time Magazine, 1962

We have already seen how, in Shirley Jackson's *The Sundial* and *The Haunting of Hill House*, she used an old house as a brooding, malign presence in the novel, almost a character in its own right. She did the same, though in a completely different way, in *We Have Always Lived in the Castle*, her last completed novel. It was well received at the time – the reception of Jackson's books got warmer with each new one she published – and has been well-regarded ever since, generally being considered her best work. But it is strange that little attention has been paid to the similarity in title and content to Dodie Smith's *I Capture the Castle*; both are narrated by strange, isolated adolescent women living in fortress-like solitude, though Smith's Cassandra Mortmain is perhaps more like Jackson's Natalie Waite than Merricat Blackwood. Shirley Jackson's previous adolescent heroines, including Natalie, have all been a little bit unhinged, but of this novel she said that the heroine was '*really* crazy.' Jackson's older daughter Jannie told her mother's biographer Judy Oppenheimer that the character of Merricat was based on her younger sister

Sally and the character of the older sister Constance was based on herself. As we saw earlier, Jackson understood teenage girls and saw how really crazy they could be. In this case, the crazy girl is the narrator so that we see the story, indeed the whole world through her rather myopic, out of focus eyes. The opening paragraph is often quoted, and rightly so, as one of the best opening paragraphs in modern fiction; it is worth quoting again.

> My name is Mary Katherine Blackwood. I am eighteen years old, and I live with my sister Constance. I have often thought that with any luck at all I could have been born a werewolf, because the two middle fingers on both my hands are the same length, but I have had to be content with what I had. I dislike washing myself, and dogs, and noise. I like my sister Constance, and Richard Plantagenet, and *Amanita phalloides*, the death-cup mushroom. The rest of my family is dead.

Actually this is not completely true: her uncle Julian is not dead and still lives with them, though he is in a wheelchair and has advanced dementia – he never speaks to Merricat and seems to think she is dead, along with the rest of the family who used to live in the house. It becomes apparent that the rest of the family have been poisoned and that Constance – ten years older than Merricat – was tried for their murder but not convicted. The remaining three family members live in a large rambling house on the edge of the village – presumed to be based on the New England town of Bennington where the Jacksons lived and her husband taught. The inhabitants have always resented the old and wealthy family, who have lived in the house for generations, for their pretensions and even more so after Merricat's late father had fenced off the shortcut through the estate that the villagers used to use. 'The people of the village have always hated us.' Merricat is the only one who leaves the grounds of the house and only then twice a week to do the shopping and go to the library; Constance, who is an excellent gardener and cook gives her a shopping list. Merricat gets through the shopping and comes home as quickly as possible, though she always briefly stops for coffee just to show that she does not care what people think, even though she does; whenever any of the surly and suspicious villagers come in they always taunt her. Merricat hates them in return.

Constance said, 'Never let them see that you care,' and 'If you pay any attention they only get worse,' and probably it was true, but I wished they were dead. I would have liked to come into the grocery some morning and see them all, even the Elberts and the children, lying there crying with the pain and dying. I would then help myself to groceries, I thought, stepping over their bodies, taking whatever I fancied from the shelves, and go home, perhaps a kick for Mrs Donell while she lay there. I was never sorry when I had thoughts like this; I only wished it would come true. 'It's wrong to hate them,' Constance said, 'it only weakens *you*,' but I hated them anyway, and wondered why it had been worthwhile creating them in the first place.

Merricat seems to have a degree of what would now be called OCD; whenever she leaves the house she plays a superstitious kind of children's game of gaining and losing points depending on which route she can take.

The library was my start and the black rock was my goal. I had to move down one side of Main Street, cross, and then move up the other side until I reached the black rock, when I would win. I began well, with a good safe turn along the empty side of Main Street, and perhaps this would turn out to be one of the very good days; it was like that sometimes, but not often on spring mornings. If it was a very good day I would later make an offering of jewelry out of gratitude.

Merricat is superstitious to the point of believing in sympathetic magic; she buries objects and uses coins and mirrors to bring luck. She lives in her own private world, on the moon, as she puts it, though she does not mean this literally. 'I am living on the moon, I told myself, I have a little house all by myself on the moon.' Like all young girls she has a private world to which she can retreat in her head – taking with her her cat Jonas, who acts as kind of a witch's familiar; Jackson had written a nonfiction book the children about the Salem witch trials, where adults believed that young girls believed that they could harm people with sympathetic magic. But of course Merricat is not a young girl, she is eighteen, even if she is mentally not even the twelve years old she was at the time of the death of her family. 'I liked my house on the moon, and I put a fireplace in it and a garden outside (what would flourish, growing on the moon? I must ask Constance).' Constance, who is more like a loving mother than an older sister, always indulges Merricat in her fantasies. One morning she tells Merricat that uncle Julian is not well.

'If I had a winged horse I could fly him to the moon; he would be more comfortable there.'
'Later I'll take him out into the sunshine, and perhaps make him a little eggnog.'
'Everything's safe on the moon.'
She looked at me distantly. 'Dandelion greens,' she said. 'And radishes.'
'I love you, Constance.'
'And I love you. Now what will you have for breakfast?'
'Pancakes. Little tiny hot ones. And two fried eggs. Today my winged horse is coming and I am carrying you off to the moon and on the moon we will eat rose petals.'
'Some rose petals are poisonous.'
'Not on the moon.'

Merricat and Constance are extremely fond of each other, complementing each other perhaps to the extent of being two halves of the same character; we have seen this several times in *Girls in Bloom*: two sisters with opposing personalities who are both to sides of the same coin. 'When I was small I thought Constance was a fairy princess... Even at the worst times she was pink and white and golden, and nothing has ever happened to dim the brightness of her. She is the most precious person in my world, always.' In return, Constance loves and looks after Merricat with great affection and solicitude, sometimes calling her 'silly Merricat', but never chiding her or getting cross with her. It emerges that, before the poisoning, Merricat had been considered wayward and disobedient and had often been sent to bed with no supper, as she was on the night of the poisoning.

The remaining family members are quite content with their strange life, which they have lived for the six years since the poisoning. Uncle Julian never leaves the house, Constance never leaves the grounds and only leaves the house to tend to her garden; practically no one ever comes to visit them. 'Don't you ever want to leave here, Merricat?' asks Constance. 'Where would we go?' she replies. 'What place would be better for us than this? Who wants us, outside? The world is full of terrible people.' The two sisters are even fond of uncle Julian, who is happy enough pottering around taking notes and claiming to be writing a book about the poisoning, though he gets confused and very often has to ask if the poisoning actually happened. The two sisters never talk about it and Merricat never reveals anything to us, but we are slowly coming to think that perhaps it was she who did the poisoning and not Constance.

The finely balanced domestic harmony is shattered when the sisters' cousin Charles comes to visit and seems intent on staying. Merricat had already foreseen something: 'All the omens spoke of change.' Change of course being the last thing that Merricat wants; she never wants to come of age. 'There's a change coming,' she says to Constance. 'It's spring, silly,' she replies.

It is quickly apparent to us, if not to Merricat and Constance, that Charles is after their money: it seems that the father had had a large amount of money in his safe when the family all died. There are also many silver coins, which Merricat has buried for superstitious reasons. 'On Sunday mornings I examined my safeguards, the box of silver dollars I had buried by the creek, and the doll buried in the long field, and the book nailed to the tree in the pinewoods; so long as they were where I put them nothing could get in to harm us.' Charles, who seems to be broke, becomes almost hysterical at this disregard of money but of course the two sisters are not concerned about money as such, they only need enough to live on; uncle Julian has no idea where the money comes from to provide the food that Constance prepares for him three times a day.

Merricat tries various kinds of sympathetic magic to get Charles to leave, but he is intent on staying and Constance seems to become almost fond of him. 'It was important to choose the exact device to drive Charles away. An imperfect magic, or one incorrectly used, might only bring more disaster upon our house.' Merricat tries everything, including not only symbolic magic like smashing mirrors but also practical attacks on him like pouring a pitcher of water over his bed. She even says to Constance: 'I was thinking that you might make a gingerbread man, and I could name him Charles and eat him.' This is a very similar idea of sympathetic magic to the 'poppets' that the so-called Salem Witches used, as Jackson had said in her book on them and Arthur Miller showed in his play *The Crucible* of 1955. There is even more explicit reference to this kind of magic when Merricat finds a stone the size of a head, draws a face on it, buries it in the ground and says, 'Goodbye, Charles.' But Charles' presence seems to be making Constance reconsider their life.

'I never realised until lately how wrong I was to let you and Uncle Julian hide here with me. We should have faced the world and tried to live normal lives; Uncle Julian should have been in a hospital all these years, with good care and nurses to watch him. We should have been living like other people. You should...' She stopped, and waved her hands helplessly. 'You should have boyfriends,' she said finally, and then began to laugh because she sounded funny even to herself.

'I have Jonas,' I said, and we both laughed and Uncle Julian woke up suddenly and laughed a thin old cackle.

'You are the silliest person I ever saw,' I told Constance, and went off to look for Jonas.

Merricat is appalled at the way Charles brings newspapers into the house; they have no phone, never open mail and have received no news since Constance was released from prison. Another of Charles' annoying habits for Merricat is his pipe-smoking, which leaves smell and mess in the pristine house – ever since the poisoning the two sisters have 'neatened' the house weekly, leaving everything undisturbed and as it was when the whole family was living there. She finds a saucer with his burning pipe on it; 'I brushed the saucer and the pipe of the table into the wastebasket and they fell softly onto the newspapers he had brought into the house.' If it does occur to her that this will cause a fire, she does not tell us. But of course it does cause a fire. The local fire brigade attend, though all the neighbours stand around watching and tell them to let it burn. The villagers then go in to the house and start smashing objects and breaking windows in a frenzy of hatred that again recalls the days of witch hunting; the burning of 'witches' – the *auto da fé* or act of faith – was supposed to free their souls.

Uncle Julian dies in the fire and Charles leaves but the two sisters remain in what is left of the house, which is pretty much only the kitchen. 'Our house was a castle, turreted, and open to the sky.' (This makes their house even more like Cassandra Mortmain's castle.) They decide that they will continue their lives as before; the kitchen was the centre of their existence anyway. They have no clothes, as everything has been destroyed, but Constance says she will wear uncle Julian's shirts, which have survived and Merricat will wear a tablecloth made into a dress. There is preserved food in the cellar, and the garden, though covered in ash, will still produce fresh food for them. They board up the door so that no one can see in, now that the village children have started to play on the path that their father had blocked off. And then, after only a few days, villagers start to leave food outside the door with apology notes for their behaviour; they will not starve and they have each other.

> One of our mother's Dresden figurines is broken, I thought, and I said aloud to Constance, 'I am going to put death in all their food and watch them die.'
>
> Constance stirred, and the leaves rustled. 'The way you did before?' she asked.
>
> It had never been spoken of between us, not once in six years.
>
> 'Yes,' I said after a minute, 'the way I did before.'

This is the nearest Merricat comes to a coming of age moment: admitting guilt and taking responsibility for her actions, though she does not have any regret. 'Although I did not perceive it then, time and the orderly pattern of our old days had ended.' The new Merricat accepts the changes; she stops believing in the power of magic and turns more practical things. 'My new magical safeguards were the lock on the front door, and the boards over the windows, and the barricades along the sides of the house.'

> We were going to be very happy, I thought. There were a great many things to do, and a whole new pattern of days to arrange, but I thought we were going to be very happy.

COMING OF AGE IN POVERTY

Most of the central figures in *Girls in Bloom* are comfortably middle-class, or at least belong to families who have enough money for the girls not to have to worry about where the next meal is coming from, not to mention the next book, dress or instalment of school fees. However, there are some examples of novels where girls come of age in poverty; in two of the cases I will consider in this chapter it is so extreme that they and their siblings have to scour rubbish dumps to supplement the family's meagre, even non-existent income.

In both these cases the girls are called Francie. We have already seen girls in coming of age novels named several variants of Frances: Francie, Frankie, Fancy, Franzie and Fanny; Maude Hutchins' daughter Frances was known as Franja and JD Salinger's *Franny* first appeared in the New Yorker in 1955. There are earlier examples too: in Jane Austen's *Mansfield Park*, 1814, arguably one of the first coming of age novels, Fanny Price, 'with all her faults of ignorance and timidity,' is brought up, like Jane Eyre, by her relatives. Like some of her namesakes she is not very feminine, though she is no tomboy. 'She was small for her age, with no glow of complexion, nor any other striking beauty; exceedingly timid and shy, and shrinking from notice.' And of course another orphan, Frances Hill, better known as Fanny, had already narrated her own rather different kind of coming of age, as published by John Cleland in 1749.

> My education, till past fourteen, was no better than very vulgar; reading, or rather spelling, an illegible scrawl, and a little ordinary plain work composed the whole system of it; and then all my foundation in virtue was no other than a total ignorance of vice, and the shy timidity general to our sex, in the tender stage of life when objects alarm or frighten more by their novelty than anything else. But then, this is a fear too often cured at the expense of innocence, when Miss, by degrees, begins no longer to look on a man as a creature of prey that will eat her.

In 1778, Frances Burney, also known as Fanny, published *Evelina or the History of a Young Lady's Entrance into the World*, a very rare combination of *bildungsroman* and epistolary novel: a seventeen-year-old girl's coming of age told in letters. Burney described the intent of this early coming of age novel in her Preface.

> To draw characters from nature, though not from life, and to mark the manners of the times, is the attempted plan of the following letters. For this purpose, a young female, educated in the most secluded retirement, makes, at the age of seventeen, her first appearance upon the great and busy stage of life; with a virtuous mind, a cultivated understanding, and a feeling heart, her ignorance of the forms, and inexperience in the manners of the world, occasion all the little incidents which these volumes record, and which form the natural progression of the life of a young woman of obscure birth, but conspicuous beauty, for the first six months after her *Entrance into the world*.

Frances, spelled Francis, is of course also a man's name. Betty Smith's second novel, *Tomorrow Will Be Better*, which is almost a sequel to *A Tree Grows in Brooklyn*, being also set in the grinding poverty of Brooklyn, follows the fortunes of a twenty-year-old woman who falls in love with a man called Frankie. At that time Francis was the name of a very famous real-life, indeed larger than life man. At the exact moment *A Tree Grows in Brooklyn* was being published, Francis Albert Sinatra, possibly *the* man of that particular time, was creating a sensation among the new bobby-soxer movement, causing near-riots every time he appeared in public, beginning with his December 30, 1942 appearance at the Paramount Theater in New York City. When Sinatra arrived in Los Angeles in 1943, huge numbers of fans went into 'a squealing ecstasy,' according to *Time* magazine. And when he returned to the Paramount Theater in October 1944, the month after *Seventeen* magazine first appeared, it was estimated that 30,00 to 50,000 fans – all actual or potential *Seventeen* readers – were waiting for him outside; the press called it the Columbus Day Riot.

FRANCIE NOLAN: *A TREE GROWS IN BROOKLYN* BY BETTY SMITH, 1943

The first published novel by the American Betty Smith (1896-1971) is a wonderful example of the female *bildungsroman*, following the central character Francie in an epic sweep from age eleven to seventeen. In addition to its similarities, *A Tree Grows in Brooklyn* also has many differences to most of the novels in *Girls in Bloom*, one of which is its length: at around 500 pages it is much longer than most of the other novels are considering. It is also unusual for this genre in that it is historical, beginning in summer 1912. Another major difference is that Francie's family are very poor; they live in a Brooklyn slum where the children pick rags to make a few cents. Like Cassandra Mortmain and like some other girls in this genre – Natalie Waite in Shirley Jackson's *Hangsaman* is another example – Francie is very, perhaps unfeasibly, literate, even more so given her poor background. She loves the local public library.

Francie thought that all the books in the world were in that library and she had a plan about reading all the books in the world. She was reading a book a day in alphabetical order and not skipping the dry ones. She remembered that the first author had been Abbott. She had been reading a book a day for a long time now and she was still in the B's. Already she had read about bees and buffaloes, Bermuda vacations and Byzantine architecture. For all of her enthusiasm, she had to admit that some of the B's had been hard going. But Francie was a reader. She read everything she could find: trash, classics, time tables and the grocer's price list. Some of the reading had been wonderful; the Louisa Alcott books for example. She planned to read all the books over again when she had finished with the Z's.

We are not told what Francie thought of Jane Austen or whether she has yet reached the Brontës. Francie lives out the metaphor of the tree growing in Brooklyn of the title, which in fact grows outside her window. 'An eleven-year-old girl sitting on this fire escape could imagine that she was living in a tree. That's what Francie imagined every Saturday afternoon in summer.' Her mother, who is herself only twenty-nine, says: 'Look at that tree growing up there out of that grating. It gets no sun, and water only when it rains. It's growing out of sour earth. And it's strong because its hard struggle to live is making it strong. My children will be strong that way.' And Francie is strong that way. She loves, and thrives at school, and particularly loves her school supplies: 'a notebook and tablet and a pencil box with a sliding top filled with new pencils, an eraser, a little tin pencil sharpener made in the shape of a cannon, a pen wiper and a six inch, softwood, yellow ruler.' In a long flashback to when Francie is younger and just starting school, the magic of the discovery of reading and the worlds to which it gives even the poorest girl access, is beautifully captured.

> Oh, magic hour when a child first knows it can read printed words!
>
> For quite a while, Francie had been spelling out letters, sounding them and then putting the sounds together to mean a word. But one day, she looked at a page and the word 'mouse' had instantaneous meaning. She looked at the word and the picture of a grey mouse scampered through her mind... She read a few pages rapidly and almost became ill with excitement. She wanted to shout it out. She could read! She could read!
>
> From that time on, the world was hers for the reading. She would never be lonely again, never miss the lack of intimate friends. Books became her friends and there was one for every mood. There was poetry for quiet companionship. There was adventure when she tired of quiet hours. There would be love stories when she came into adolescence and when she wanted to feel a closeness to someone she could read a biography. On that day when she first knew she could read, she made a vow to read one book a day as long as she lived.

Francie keeps a diary, like many of the girls in this genre. One day, when she is thirteen she writes: 'Today, I am a woman.' It's not clear whether this is because her periods have started. 'She looked down on her long thin and as yet formless legs. She crossed out the sentence and started over. "Soon, I shall become a woman." She looked down on her chest which was as flat as a wash board and ripped the page out of the book. She started fresh on a new page.' That same Saturday she sees her name in print for the first time, a story of hers having been printed in the school magazine as the best story in her composition class. But her composition teacher looks down on her family and her way of life and consequently looks down on the stories that Francie writes about them. 'I honestly believe that you have promise. Now that we've talked things out, I'm sure you will stop writing those sordid little stories.' Francie is appalled to be called sordid: she loves her mother and father, who do their best for her and her brother. She uncharacteristically lashes out at her teacher. 'Don't you *ever* dare use that word about us!'

> Walking home from school, Francie tried to figure the whole thing out. She knew Mrs Garnder wasn't mean. She had spoken for Francie's good. Only it didn't seem good to Francie. She began to understand that her life might seem revolting to some educated people. She wondered, when she got educated, whether she'd be ashamed of her background. Would she be ashamed of her people; ashamed of handsome papa who had been so light-hearted, kind and understanding; ashamed of brave and truthful mama who was so proud of her own mother, even though granma couldn't read or write; ashamed of Neely [her brother] who was such a good honest boy? No! No! If being educated would make her ashamed of what she was, she wanted none of it. 'But I'll show that Miss Garnder,' she vowed. 'I'll show her I got an imagination I certainly will show her.'
>
> She started her novel that day. Its heroine was Sherry Nola, a girl conceived, born and brought up in sweltering luxury. The story was called THIS IS I and it was the untrue story of Francie's life.

Francie has plans to publish the book when it is finished and has even worked out in her mind a fantasy of the dialogue she will have with her delighted teacher when she sees it. 'It was such a rosy dream that Francie started the next chapter in a fever of excitement. She'd write and write and get it done quickly so the dream could come true.' But there is no food in the apartment, just some stale bread and she can hardly write for hunger. Reading what she has written, she realises that she has been simply inverting her own poverty: she is writing about a heroine spoilt by a surfeit of rich food because her own hunger has made her obsessed. 'Furious with the novel, she ripped the copy-book apart and stuffed it into the stove. When the flames began licking on it, her fury increased and she ran and got her box of manuscripts from under her bed... She was burning all her pretty "A" compositions.'

After her father dies, Francie's mother cannot afford for both her and her brother to go to school and favours the boy. Francie starts working in a factory at the age of fourteen, lying about her age to make herself older so that she can get a job. Soon though she improves her situation enormously, working as a reader in a newspaper office and earning what by her family's standards is enormous amount of money while reading for a living. Even after she loses this job, she falls on her feet and gets a job working a teletype. 'She thought it a wonderful miracle that she could sit at that machine and type and have the words come out hundreds of miles away.' She works the night shift which takes care of her 'lonely evenings,' and allows her to sit outside in the sun during the day. Francie is still only fifteen. Her mother suggests that she could go to college while working the night shift.

> But what in the world could I learn in high school now? Oh, I'm not conceited or anything, but after all, I read eight hours a day for almost a year and I learned things. I got my own ideas about history and government and geography and writing and poetry. I read too much about people – what they do and how they live. I've read about crimes and about heroic things. Mama, I've read about *everything*. I couldn't sit still now in a classroom with a bunch of baby kids and listen to an old maid teacher drool away about this and that. I'd be jumping up and correcting her all the time. Or else, I'd be good and swallow it all down and then I'd hate myself for . . . well, . . . eating mush instead of bread. So I will not go to high school. But I *will* go to college some day.

When Francie is sixteen she meets Lee, a soldier who is about to go off to the war – this is 1917. He admits she means nothing to him but tries to persuade Francie to spend the night with him. She resists but promises to write to him every day while he is away and marry him when he comes back. And if he doesn't come back she promises never to marry, or even kiss anyone else. 'And he asked for her whole life as simply as he'd ask for a date. And she promised away her whole life as simply as she'd offer a hand in greeting or farewell.' Soon afterwards Francie gets a letter from Lee's mother thanking her for being a good friend to him while he was in New York and telling her that Lee has got married. 'I read the letter you sent Lee. It was mean of him to pretend to be in love with you and I told him so. He said to tell you he's dreadfully sorry.' Francie confides in her mother, Katie.

'Mother, he asked me to be with him for the night. Should I have gone?'

Katie's mind darted around looking for works.

'Don't make up a lie, Mother. Tell me the truth.'

Katie couldn't find the right words.

'I promise you that I'll never go with a man without being married first – if I ever marry. And if I feel that I must – without being married, I'll tell you first. That's a solemn promise. So you can tell me the truth without worrying that I'll go wrong if I know it.'

'There are two truths,' said Katie finally.

'As a mother, I say it would have been a terrible thing for a girl to sleep with the stranger – a man she had known less than forty-eight hours. Horrible things might have happened to you. Your whole life might have been ruined. As a mother, I tell you the truth.'

'But as a mother . . .' she hesitated. 'I will tell you the truth as a woman. It would have been a very beautiful thing. Because there is only once that you love that way.'

Francie thought, 'I should have gone with him then. I'll never love anyone as much again. I wanted to go and I didn't go and now I don't want him that way anymore because *she* owns him now. But I wanted to and I didn't and now it's too late.' She put her head down on the table and wept.

FRANCIE WITHERS: *OWLS DO CRY* BY JANET FRAME, 1957

Francie Withers is dirty. Francie Withers is poor. The Withers haven't a weekend bach nor do they live on the South Hill nor have they got a vacuum cleaner nor do they learn dancing or the piano nor have birthday parties nor their photos taken at the Dainty Studio to be put in the window on a Friday... Francie hasn't any shoes for changing to at drill time, and her pants are not *real* black Italian cloth.

She hasn't a school blazer with a monogram.

But Francie Withers is Joan of Arc, and she sang at the garden party –

Where the bee sucks there suck I

In a cowslip's bell I lie
There I couch when owls do cry.

Here we have another novel about a girl called Francie growing up in poverty with several siblings, of whom she is the eldest – the others are Toby, Daphne and Chicks, all of whom have to scour rubbish dumps like the children in *A Tree Grows in Brooklyn* to supplement their father's meagre income. It is by the New Zealander Janet Frame (1924-2004), a prolific and multi award-winning novelist whose autobiography inspired Jane Campion's film *An Angel at My Table*. In this private world of their own, this 'brave new world that has such people in't!' (the of the novel is from *The Tempest*) the children find some things which to them seem magical:

the children found, first and happiest, fairy tales.
And a small green eaten book by Ernest Dowson who said, in confidence, to Cynara,
– Last night ah yesternight betwixt her lips and mine.
Which was love, and suitable only for Francie who had *come*, that was the word their mother used when she whispered about it in the bathroom, and not the Daphne who didn't know what it felt like or how she could wear them without they showed and people said, Look.
– You will drop blood when you walk, Francie said.
And not knowing how to answer, Daphne said
– Rapunsel, Rapunsel, let down your hair;
quoting from the prince who climbed the gold silk rope to the top of the tower, it was all in the fairy tales they found at the rubbish dump.

Francie, who has obviously started her periods, is still only twelve but has to leave school to help support the family; her father, who seems to work in the local coal mine, wants her to work in the mill, though she and Daphne have heard terrible tales of girls being locked in there surrounded by dusty, dyed wool with no light and no escape. 'Some of the girls choked with the colours and died.' Frame provides us with a poetic and wonderful description of an adolescent girl at the crossroads, perhaps the most lyrical and beautiful evocation of that moment in *Girls in Bloom,* though many of the things Francie knows would be more appropriate to a more middle-class teenager.

It was the last day at school though she was only twelve, thirteen at Christmas. She could count up to thirty in French. She could make puff pastry, dabbing the butter carefully before each fold. She could cook sago, lemon or pink with cochineal, that swelled in cooking from dirty little grains, same, same, dusty and bagged in paper, to lemon or pink pearls. She knew that a drop of iodine on a slice of banana will blacken the fruit, and prove starch; that water is H_2O; that a man called Shakespeare, in a wood near Athens, contrived a moonlit dream.

But in all the knowing, she had not learned of the time of living, the unseen always, when people are like the marbles in the fun alley at the show; and a gaudy circumstance will squeeze payment from the cringing and poverty-stricken fate, to give him the privilege of rolling them into the bright or dark box, till they drop into one of the little painted holes, their niche, it is called, and there roll their lives round and round in a frustrating circle.

And Francie was taken, on the afternoon of the play, like one of the marbles, though still in her silver helmet and breastplate and waiting to be burned; and rolled to a new place beyond Frère Jacques and participles and science and Bunsen burners and Shakespeare, there I couch when owls do cry,

when owls do cry, when owls do cry,

To a new place of bright or dark, of home again, and Mum and Dad and Toby and Chicks; an all-day Mum and Dad, as if she were small again, not quite five, with no school, no school ever, and her world, like a tooth, under her pillow with a promise of sixpence and no school ever any more.

Having left school and started her periods, Francie is a worry to her parents: 'a young woman ready to take her place in the world,' who might 'get into trouble and be a disgrace to her parents and have to go away for a holiday up north while the baby came and everything was fixed up.' It is not clear whether Francie is having sex with her boyfriend Tim, but when she is with Daphne and they see the next-door neighbour sunbathing in the nude, Francie does not look because, she tells her sister, 'she didn't need to look,' she has 'plenty of opportunity, my dear Daphne, for looking at things like that.' Francie is very concerned to show Daphne how much more grown-up she is: trying on a dress that her aunt has made her, she looks at herself in the mirror: 'I am grown-up,' she says to Daphne. 'She had pink bulges where Daphne had mere tittie dots.'

Francie does not in the end have to go work in the mill, but finds a place as a servant with a local family; it is too close for her even to ride her new bicycle, which had seemed to her like pure magic. Before her first day in her new job she puts on a lipstick she has found in the grass and an old coat her aunt has given her. This is the day she comes of age.

– Goodbye, Daphne sang out after her.
– Goodbye, Francie said.
And she added, in the same voice that women in films use when they dismiss their lovers for the last time,
– Goodbye, *schoolgirl.*
Daphne did not know Francie after that. Francie was secret.

The new grown-up, modern-woman Francie shocks her father by wearing slacks on a Sunday; 'the father was frightened, and every time he saw the slacks he got angry;' he is scared of his new, adult daughter, who goes to 'hops' with men. She moves into her own room in the house – she had previously shared a room with Daphne – and treats her bicycle 'as if it were ordinary.' Daphne of course wants to know what goes on at, and after, the hops; Francie says she would not understand but Daphne swears she would. 'All right, Daphne, as between women I'll tell you. You won't be shocked?' Francie does not tell her anything anyway, perhaps because there is nothing to tell and she does not want to admit it to her younger sister. They still conspire together though, and agree that 'grown-ups are silly;' Francie has not yet quite grown up, does not even want to. And when she does it pulls her away from her family and into herself.

– But you have to grow up. It's today and tomorrow and the next day.
And it came with Francie – today and tomorrow and the next day. She grew more and more silent about what really mattered. She curled inside herself like one of those black chimney brushes, little

shellfish you see on the beach, and you touch them, and they go inside and come out.

And every day when Francie went to work, walking the few yards down the road to Mawhinney's, she seemed to be going miles away. And Daphne thought, one time when she peeped through the hedge at Francie going, If only she had some kind of treasure with her, inside, to help her; if only grown-ups could tell what is treasure and not treasure

if only

like the bicycle made magic and the gold and green clouds of birds to help her fight the armies of tangled wool, oh it was all tangled, being alive was tangled, and there was Francie going by herself every day to face it and fight it.

What if she were caught and choked and never came back?

Shockingly, she is and she doesn't: going back to the rubbish dump with her siblings one day Francie falls down the slope and into the fire at the bottom; she does not recover and neither does the novel: Frame has killed off her sympathetic heroine less than a quarter of the way through what looked as if it was going to become her book, just as Francie was about to fully come of age.

MATILDA POUND: *LINDEN RISE* BY RICHMAL CROMPTON, 1952

The English author Richmal Crompton (1890-1969) is most well known for her children's series of *Just William* books, concerning an incorrigible schoolboy, of which she published over forty from 1922 to 1970. But she also published over fifty non-William, adult novels during a similar period, which range from the innocent and charming to the slightly more serious comedy of manners. Several of Crompton's novels concern young women at the end of the teenage years or girls who are below teen age and members of large families: the eponymous *Millicent Dorrington*, 1927, is one of eight children; *Felicity Stands By*, 1928, is on the innocent and charming end, too frothy to be considered a coming of age novel, though it does concern the feisty, upper-class and wonderfully-named

Norma Felicity Montague Harborough, who has '(within the last hour) attained the age of sixteen' and left school as the novel opens.

> 'I've just entered into another stage. A new chapter of my life opens today. I have put away childish things, as Shakespeare says.'
> 'Not Shakespeare,' said the young man. 'St. Paul.'
> 'Well, St Paul then,' said Felicity impatiently. 'I knew it was some-one beginning with an S.'

In *Marriage of Hermione*, 1932, Hermione Pennistone has already come of age and is 'now Grown Up,' which 'was a sudden and rather bewildering affair, less enjoyable in many ways than she had thought it would be.'

> She did not realise at first how completely it meant the end of the old life. For now she was a Young Lady. No longer must she range the countryside, paddling in the river, wandering unaccompanied through the woods, living in a world peopled by her own invention, avoiding contact with the real world around her. Too long already had she been allowed to 'run wild', said the gossips of Little Barnwell. Janet Martin said that she had come upon her one afternoon in the woods talking to a tree. *Talking* to a *tree*. Without even a hat on.

Crompton's *The Holiday*, 1933 concerns a vicar's four children, mainly concentrating on the eleven-year-old Rachel and her thirteen-year-old sister Thea who, everyone says, plays the piano exceptionally well for her age. 'Thirteen . . . It was for that, after all, that Rachel envied her most. To have an age for the first time in the family . . . By the time thirteen reached Rachel – eighteen months later – it would be spoilt and familiarised by Thea's long use of it, like the frocks that came down to Rachel when Thea had outgrown them.' *Quartet*, 1935, also concerns four children and *Frost at Morning*, 1950, is also centred around four children living at a vicarage. In *Caroline*, 1936, after the death of her stepmother, the eponymous, nineteen-year-old Caroline 'who had just won a scholarship to Modern Languages at Girton, had quickly shown the stuff she was made of. She had resigned her scholarship and set to work at once to earn money for the young family.' In *There Are Four Seasons*, 1937, Vicky Carothers is educated and brought up by her governess, while in

Narcissa, 1941, Stella Markham is educated and brought up by her aunt, both novels following their heroines from childhood to womanhood.

Unlike all these upper- and middle-class girls, who are very typical of English women's novels of the time, Matilda (Tilly) Pound in Crompton's *Linden Rise* works as a servant from the age of fifteen. The novel follows her through adulthood and into old age but also follows the fortunes of the upper-middle-class family – what their housekeeper calls The Quality – that she spends her life serving. At the beginning of the novel they have – as one would expect from a Crompton novel – four children: two boys roughly Tilly's age and two younger girls. Both girls in their way come of age but Tilly herself, who seems to have almost no personality, no depth and is always totally subservient, hardly changes at all as she grows up. 'She had always been a docile, biddable child, accepting philosophically the ups and downs of life.' Tilly never questions her place in life from the day she is forced to leave home to become a domestic servant. As far as she and her family are concerned she is now 'grown-up, fifteen years old, and starting out into the world with a trunk full of sensible clothes and a head full of sensible advice.' She never has any further contact with her family.

Matilda Pound was going out to service for the first time. She was fifteen years old, solidly and somewhat clumsily built, with a smooth, round face on which the features seemed to have been fashioned by a hasty and inexpert hand. Her cheeks were crudely red, her nose shapeless, a mouth too large, her eyes black and bright and staring.

If this is what her author thinks of her, it is hard for the reader to have any sympathy for Tilly, or indeed any of the children of the household, none of whom have any redeeming qualities. Tilly's new situation appears to be far from ideal, but for her it has one overwhelming advantage.

Against the wall a scarred chest of drawers supported a discoloured mirror. Her tin trunk stood at the foot of her bed. There was no change of expression in the round, plain face, but something behind it seemed to glow and sparkle as the bright eyes moved around. At home she had always slept with her aunt, while her uncle slept on a camp-bed in his work-room, and she had never even considered the possibility of having a room of her own.

This, then, seems to be all Tilly needs to come of age: a room of her own, though not in the Virginia Woolf sense; Tilly is by no means the angel of the house. When she is a little older, Tilly has what would then have been called an 'understanding' with the local milkman, with whom she enjoys regular friendly banter, giving him as good she gets while rebuffing his advances; this form of social intercourse is also a form of social coming of age for her, though it never turns into sexual intercourse. 'She turned back into the kitchen, well pleased by the passage-at-arms. It was a language she had picked up since coming to the village and her progress in it give her much secret satisfaction.' The older housekeeper, who acts in an affectionate kind of *loco parentis*, watches all this going on with approval.

> 'That's right, Tilly,' she said. 'Hold your own with them. Always hold your own.'
> 'I'll hold it with *him*,' said Tilly, putting the milk-jug into the larder. 'Saucebox!'
> 'But don't go meeting him, now.'
> 'Not likely!' said Tilly.
> 'You're too young for that sort of thing, but not too young to learn to hold your own with them. Keep them at arm's length. That's the only way. Once you start giving into them – well, one thing leads to another till, before you know where you are – well, there you are!'
> 'Yes ma'am,' said Tilly.
> 'I could tell you some things about men,' said Mrs Horseferry, compressing her lips and beating the eggs as vigorously as if they represented the whole male sex, 'that'd make you so's you could never look at a man without shuddering for the rest of your life, but they aren't things I could tell to a young girl like you. Wolves in sheep's clothing, all of them, and some of them not even in sheep's clothing. Give them an inch and they'll take an ell. Hold your own and keep them at arm's length.'
> 'Yes, ma'am,' said Tilly.

The relationship with the milkman comes to nothing and eventually Tilly is the sole servant in the house, the fixed point around which everything revolves as the couple she serves divorce, their children grow up, move away, enter society, have children of their own and variously travel the world, stand for parliament, divorce and die themselves while Tilly, unnoticed, stays constant throughout.

ODD GIRL OUT: LESBIAN COMING OF AGE

We have already looked at an early lesbian coming of age novel in Rosamond Lehmann's *Dusty Answer* of 1927. For obvious reasons there are very few overt lesbians in literature before the 1950s apart from Radclyffe Hall's *The Well of Loneliness* in 1928, though the outrageous, cross-dressing Quaint Irene in EF Benson's Mapp and Lucia novels is a rare exception: when one of her male friends is afraid that she is about to kiss him, Irene says: 'Don't be alarmed dear lamb, your sex protects you from any forwardness on my part'. The lesbian coming of age genre was very sparsely populated until the advent of lesbian pulp fiction in the early 1950s, though I will consider in this chapter one American example which was first published in hardback in 1939 – though only became well-known when it was republished in paperback in 1952 at the beginning of the lesbian pulp fiction movement – and two English examples of the 1940s.

The history of lesbian literature in the 1950s and 60s is well beyond the scope of *Girls in Bloom* but restricting it to stories of adolescent girls coming of age as lesbian or bisexual makes it rather more manageable; in the case of these novels, the adolescent comes of age in terms of understanding their own sexuality, a very difficult understanding to arrive at given that homosexuality was illegal and suppressed at that time. Although they were very few of these novels, they had a huge impact: many adolescent girls who read them finally knew for the first time that they were not the only girl in the world to have romantic thoughts about women.

DIANA: A STRANGE AUTOBIOGRAPHY BY 'DIANA FREDERICS' (FRANCES V RUMMELL), 1939

This is the unusual and compelling story of Diana, a tantalizingly beautiful woman who sought love in the strange by-paths of Lesbos. Fearless and outspoken, it dares to reveal that hidden world where perfumed caresses and half-whispered endearments constitute the forbidden fruits in a Garden of Eden where men are never accepted.

This was the blurb for the 1952 paperback edition – republished right at the beginning of what we will soon see was the lesbian pulp fiction movement – of *Diana: A Strange Autobiography* by the pseudonymous Diana Frederics who kept her identity secret until it was finally revealed on a PBS documentary in 2010, long after her death, that the author was Frances V Rummell (1907-1969), a teacher of French at Stevens College, a women-only college in Columbia, Missouri, the second-oldest college in America to have remained all-female. At the time *Diana* was published the chairwoman of Stevens' Drama Department was the well-known actress Maude Adams, who is famous for being James M. Barrie's first Peter Pan in 1905 on Broadway and for popularising the Peter Pan collar. Rummell's only novel under her own name was *Aunt Jane McPhipps and Her Baby Blue Chips*, 1960.

Diana was originally published by Dial Press in 1939 and republished in hardback by City Press of New York in 1948. Both editions contained an introduction by the sexologist Victor Robinson, explaining that lesbianism was 'ancient in the days of Sappho of Lesbos. Yet such is our immunity to information, that when Havelock Ellis collected his various studies on *Sexual Inversion* (1897), he states that before his first cases were published, not a single British case, unconnected with the asylum or the prison, had ever been recorded.' Robinson added: 'I welcome any book which adds to the understanding of the lesbians in our midst. Among these books I definitely place the present autobiography.' Unlike *Dusty Answer* and *Well of Loneliness*, both the introduction and the main text use the word 'lesbian,' quite astonishing for 1939; it would not be used in a published novel again for years.

Although it purports to be an autobiography and may well reflect the author's own experiences, *Diana* is structured much like a novel. In fact, it is similar in many ways to *Dusty Answer* and to Vin Packer's *Spring Fire*, which we shall look at shortly. Here also the heroine is unsure of her sexuality until she falls in love with a girl at college, but unlike Judith in *Dusty Answer* she does not subsequently try to revert to heterosexuality and end up alone and miserable.

Diana has always been a tomboy: 'I had always played with boys instead of girls, and growing older make no difference; I still did. Girls frankly bored me.' Note that they did not attract her sexually at that time. 'I was scarcely conscious of being a girl. The boys accepted me as one of them as tacitly as I assumed that position.' No one, not even her parents, considers her to be a problem, she is just a regular tomboy to them.

> My mother and father had always taken my antics as they came, hopeful that time and age would season my tomboyish nature. Of course, they were indulgent with me; I was their only girl. I was a healthy young animal, full of energy and devilry, and tomboys were common enough. They mature into just as feminine young women as did the little girls who preferred dolls to BB guns.

Like Carson McCullers' tomboy Frankie Addams, but unlike most other tomboys, Diana is very musical; her mother is not sure that her daughter should be attending music theory classes with boys but the music teacher convinces her to let Diana go; he says rightly that age and gender have nothing to do with musical ability, though by the time she is in her senior year her teacher is telling her that her very 'clean touch' on the keyboard is 'masculine'.

In these classes, as well at home, Diana, like many tomboys, is surrounded by boys – including her brothers and young men from the college who rent rooms in her house – from the age of twelve to sixteen, when she goes to college. All these boys are of course protective of her and she is of course not the slightest bit seductive or provocative but one day, when she is 'a hopelessly naïve child of thirteen,' it becomes obvious to her that she is not in fact just one of the boys.

> One boy, a newcomer to our home, called me into his room one rainy Sunday afternoon to admire some snapshots. I hesitated a moment, since I never entered the guest rooms, but, reluctant to appear rude, I went. Ignorant as I was, his intentions were too abrupt to be misunderstood. I recall only my fury; in spite of my years, it was enough to upset a blundering collegian. Like many people who manage to keep their heads in a tight predicament, I suffered repercussions. For weeks afterward I felt the full impact of sordidness. Despite the sudden exit of the collegian from our home, with no more explanation to my mother on my part than on his, this scene remained indelible.
>
> It is almost incredible to me now to recall the extent of the effects of this assault on my innocence. I was made too abruptly aware that life amounted to something more than front yard games and school

and camp. My would-be seducer had said something to me which made me think more than I had ever honestly thought in my young life. I even got out my dictionary to find out what he'd meant by saying I was 'seductive-looking.' What a disturbing thought to one who until that very moment was completely unconscious of her body, despite a maturing physique.

I spent days brooding over the fact that I had been born a girl. I didn't want to grow up. I didn't want to be 'seductive -looking.' I hated the expression, I hated the vague meaning. Oh, the horror of becoming an adult!

Shocked into the realisation that I was growing up in spite of myself, I turned suddenly into an antisocial, introspective, melancholy bookworm. Life took on the proportions of a pitiless hoax. In the diary I kept at this time is entered, in the handwriting of a fourteen-year-old, such a penetrating observation as this: 'It is cruel of parents to read fairy tales to children. The transition from the delicate fantasy of the fairy tale real-life is painful. Life bumps into children as they grow up.'

This coming of age moment turns her against boys, 'for no reason except that they were growing up too. And some of them wrote notes to me in school that seemed silly and embarrassed me.' Diana retreats into her reading and music, though she does attend the school prom with the older boy Gil, whom she allows to kiss her, but that is far as it goes. Gil is swept aside when Ruth enters the school; Diana is smitten with her. 'She was too thin and her mouth was too large, but she had lovely titian hair, worn in braids around her head, solemn blue eyes, and such a sweet smile that I wondered if anyone could possibly be as angelic as she seemed.' Ruth and Diana, among others, are invited to a Christmas house party. 'I knew I would contrive in every way possible to share a room with her.' She manages it.

That night when we went to bed alone, tired and happy with the day, Ruth's thoughtless intimacy and good-night embrace almost took my breath away. I had been surprised to feel curious sensations of longing the few times I had ever touched her, but I could never have imagined the exquisite thrill of feeling her body close to mine. Now I was amazed. Then, before I knew it, I realised I wanted to caress her. Then

I became terrified by a nameless something that froze my impulse. The pain of resisting was torture, but the touch of her hand holding mine against her side was so infinitely sweet that I tensed for fear my slightest movement would make her turn away from me. Long hours I lay awake after she had gone to sleep, scarcely daring to breathe for fear she might move, not daring to hope that I might kiss her lips without startling her.

That night is set apart in my memory, supreme and forever. My longing for Ruth was the most exquisite pain I had ever known.

It made a very great difference in my affection. Where I had been gay with Ruth, I now felt shy, self-conscious, too fond. Where I had been willing to share her with friends, I became jealous and morose, though I made every effort not to show my feelings. I began to brood about my growing desire to touch, and the fear I felt at my impulse. At night when I got to my desk to study I would eventually push my books aside to write interminable letters I never did send her...

I never spoke to Ruth of my feelings. Fear restrained me. I had enough sense of proportion to realise that what I felt was extraordinary. I was afraid she would not understand my affection. I did not understand myself.

Diane later goes to college, to study French, and meets Grace, with whom we are expecting her to have an affair; 'I had been rather awed by her cool charm and by her oft-repeated refusals to go out on dates with the boys who invited her.' They read Baudelaire and Verlaine together – very heavy, decadent stuff for two college girls at that time; Baudelaire of course wrote *The Flowers of Evil* and Verlaine, one of his followers, was the lover of Rimbaud. 'Suddenly, inspired no doubt by Verlaine, she began to talk about homosexuality. Obviously, she was trying to sound out my reactions to the subject, and my self-consciously evasive replies made me blush with embarrassment.' Diana is unprepared for this line of questioning; 'As it was, my confusion was my defense. Extremely sensitive, Grace interpreted my awkwardness for reluctance, and, humiliated for having "misunderstood," she left.'

Before things with Grace have a chance to go anywhere, Diane meets Carl, an older man, who falls in love with her and asks her to marry him. 'My first feeling was one of dismay.' She is flattered but confused, thinking she must accept, but 'I could not force myself suddenly to end the

happiest friendship I had ever known' – with, presumably, Grace. Nevertheless, when he gives her his fraternity pin and kisses her she feels a
'pale emotion – the first I had ever felt for a man.' But even this pale
shadow of a feeling is enough to make her feel that perhaps she is after all
normal. When I left him I ran to my room giddily happy. Oh, dear God, it
had happened. It was going to be all right.' When Grace sees her, Diane
is:

> so radiant she guessed what had happened. Impulsively I told her I
> loved him. Then, embracing her with so much tenderness that I sur-
> prised her, I was reminded that my feelings were too jubilant to be en-
> tirely personal. My great joy was that my emotion portended the nor-
> malcy which I wanted more than anything else in the world.

But then of course the thought of having to have physical sex with Carl
enters her head. 'I have every possible reason but one to be convinced
that Carl and I would be happily married – I did not know whether I
loved him physically.' She has heard women talk and has read books on
sexology which lead her to believe that, even if she does not like having
sex with him at first, she will come round. Diane tells Carl that she will
live with him but not marry him. At first all goes well.

> Some indescribable emotion pulled at me as I looked at him, and all I
> could think of was something I had read – of a woman happy that her
> lover need no longer sigh with unrest; she would give him ecstasy. I
> understood that now. Suddenly I gloried in an unexpected sense of
> possession. It seemed to me that I had never been so happy. There
> was no need to question. My place was with Carl.
>   It did not matter that first physical intimacy had been disappoint-
> ing. I could not expect a miracle of chemistry to follow the mere act
> defloration; I understood that it frequently took some little time for a
> woman to become adjusted, for her to learn rhythm, to grow together.
> At least I had managed the first pain. Now I could look forward.

For some time, Diana feels as though she is becoming 'normal,' though
never in their time together had 'physical intimacy meant anything to me
but the giving of pleasure to Carl... the very words "desire," "passion,"
"ecstasy," were but fugitive words to me, symbols of unscented experi-

ence.' She has become 'a slave to dissimulation,' as she knows many married women are, whether or not they have lesbian tendencies. Diana definitely does, and when she goes to a women's college in Massachusetts to take a Masters in German, the 'number of lesbians I met there impressed me not only because my consciousness of them was sharpened, but because they were unmistakably frequent.' But even in this environment she decides to hide her own feelings: she learns 'the grace of a lie and a new admiration for hypocrisy;' she vows that 'no one would ever have such an easy clue to my own lesbianism.'

This self-imposed isolation of course makes her lonely. 'I was approaching a future whose peculiar loneliness I could already understand.' What Diana cannot understand is what it would be like to indulge her preferences. 'What was lesbian love like? Its intellectual pleasures were easy enough to guess at, but what physical pleasure did women achieve of one another... Vaguely I wondered how I would learn to know all the things I needed to know.' Then she meets Elise and has her first physical experience with another woman. But Elise is already spoken for.

Her fingers were on my breast, caressing, soft as warm water. Her hand went to my throat and then swiftly she lay full length beside me, and kissed me again. Suddenly an overwhelming tide of passion dragged at me and I threw my arms around her and held her body closer, wanting her but not knowing how...

Then suddenly there was a terrible, convulsing pleasure when she touched me. Miraculously, all past and present left me. I knew nothing but the touch of Elise, until I could stand no more and roughly pushed her away.

I was released of all feeling, submerged in a glorious lethargy, timeless and in a dream. I could make no effort to open my eyes. I hadn't expected it to be something like dying...

I told her a little wildly that she had been my first; that she could not leave me, could not. Very gently she told me she had known, and that she had known all the while that Katherine was coming so soon. Now I knew why she had left me. For Elise that had been a gesture of fidelity – lesbian fidelity. I had made no difference.

Diana reacts to these twin experiences – her first physical experience with a woman and her first emotional experience of betrayal – by leaving

212

that night for Paris, wiser if not much older. 'I realised that the incident with Elise had, for all its humiliation, given me a kind of assurance that I had needed desperately. Before Elise I had not known whether women could have sexual gratification of one another... Elise had completed my knowledge.' She has come of age physically and emotionally and her next relationship, with Jane, is much more straightforward. 'We wanted a normal domestic life and we wanted our happiness together. We asked nothing of anyone. We hurt no one. We were mature, free and perfectly sure of ourselves.' Diana now realises that to accept her 'lesbianism and my circumstances without fear, without distaste, would be my ultimate freedom.'

Unfortunately, even though she is free within herself and she and Jane are free within their relationship, the outside world intrudes. After her first term teaching, her relationship with Jane is remarked upon and she is offered the choice between moving by herself into the single women's accommodation or leaving the college. She chooses to leave. But Jane is not her final lover; she meets Leslie and leaves Jane – physically, though not emotionally, until the end of the book, when Leslie finally replaces Jane totally.

> I knew that Jane had been swept into time, into the forgotten. Even the thought of her seemed obscure. Leslie and I extricated ourselves; no longer need there be anything at all to remind us of Jane.
>
> I could feel how it had happened, but I could not have foreseen. Slowly, half-prayerful, half-exultant, it had come to me – the testimony of her patience was enough – I could turn toward Leslie and know that her loyalty was no less than my own.

ELSIE LANE: *THE FRIENDLY YOUNG LADIES* BY MARY RENAULT, 1944

Unlike some of the English novelists we have been looking at, Mary Renault (1905-1982, real name Eileen Mary Challans) was not brought up in the countryside by wealthy parents and educated by a governess. She was born in the East End of London, the child of an unhappy marriage between parents who did not see any point in educating a daughter. Fortunately for her, her godmother, who was also her aunt, had been university educated herself and sent Mary to boarding school and then subsidised her at Saint Hugh's College, Oxford, a women-only college for a hundred years after its founding in 1886. Renault has always been most well-known for her novels set in ancient Greece, where homoeroticism may be a subtext but is never explicit, but before she started that series she had published five contemporary novels, of which the third was *The Friendly Young Ladies*. The title is a subtle reference to lesbianism, though there is no explicit portrayal or even mention of lesbian relationships; the fact that two of the main female characters share a bed is never dwelt upon. Renault herself had a single, female partner from her early twenties until her death; they met while they were both doing nursing training.

When Virago republished the novel shortly before her death in 1983, Renault ask if she could change the ending, which she had come to regard as a compromise. Virago would not agree but did allow her to write an afterword. In this she says that the origin of the novel was in Radclyffe Hall's *The Well of Loneliness*, which she had first read in France in 1938 – it was banned in England at the time and Renault had to leave the book in France when she came home. She wrote her novel in reaction to Hall's po-faced and self-indulgent portrayal of lesbianism which she could never take seriously: 'it does, I still think, carry an impermissible allowance of self-pity, and its burnished humourlessness invites irreverence.' Writing during the war as a nurse and seeing 'terribly ill and dying and bereaved people,' she thought it 'becoming in people whose only problem was a slight deviation of the sex urge – not necessarily an unmixed tribulation – to refrain from needless bellyaching and fuss.' Certainly the two main lesbian characters appear to have entirely satisfactory and well-adjusted lives with not a trace of self-pity or shame.

Mousy, timid Elsie Lane – on the very first page we are told: 'Her calculations were instinctive, like those of a mouse –' is no lesbian and seems completely unaware of the actual nature of the relationship of the two women, one of whom is her much older sister, whom she comes to share a houseboat with, even though they share a bed in the room next to hers. This is in its way Elsie's coming of age story, but she never does come to maturity and hold her own; she cannot even hold onto her own novel, which starts with her as its central focus but moves away to other characters, leaving Elsie out of focus in the background. She exits the novel not with a bang but with a whimper, crawling in humiliation back to her parents in the penultimate chapter, irrelevant now to the story, leaving the other, more interesting characters around her – the grown-ups – to get on with their complicated relationships.

Elsie's parents, and especially her father, have repressed her personality completely, following the departure years earlier of Elsie's older sister Leonora. 'We already have one daughter outside the pale of decent society. If a second finds her way into the *demi-monde*, believe me, it won't astonish *me*.' The two sisters' very names point to the difference in their personalities: Leonora sounds free-spirited, romantic, almost – to Elsie at least – mythic, while Elsie sounds dull and mundane. Leonora is never mentioned in the household and Elsie has no idea what happened to her; she assumes her sister is 'living in sin' and has therefore been rejected by her parents, though she likes to think that Leonora is an artist, something Elsie herself will never be. This is another example of something we have seen several times in *Girls in Bloom*: two sisters being two sides of the same coin and perhaps representing two aspects of their author's personality. Elsie seems to have no trouble living up to the ordinariness of her name. Unlike other examples we have seen of one mousy, introverted sister and one popular extrovert, Elsie is not even bookish and intelligent.

> She was a dim, unobtrusive girl. One might conjecture that she had been afraid to grow up, lest the change should attract attention to her. She had acquired protective colouring which amounted almost to invisibility; almost, but not quite... Elsie had left school year ago, after failing in the School Certificate Examination. The mistresses, one after another, had told her that her homework was thoughtless and showed no signs of concentration at all, and had pointed out what a disappointment this must be to her parents; a prophecy regularly fulfilled when her reports came through. All this accumulated guilt formed a steady reserve, ready to add itself to the guilt of any given moment. Where would she be, indeed? Hypnotised, she pictured herself trudging through the rain into the gates of a large, dark factory, wearing a man's a cloth cap, or maybe a shawl. The factory was drawn from imagination; her travels had been few.

Although it is several years since Leonora has left, Elsie remembers her rebellion. The father had been shouting that if he had a son he would not be 'subjected day by day to this petty conspiracy of women.' Leo seems to have snapped into a coming of age moment.

> Elsie herself, small enough then to hide sometimes, had crawled just in time under the table; but Leo had been standing in exactly the same spot where her sister stood now. She had been about Elsie's own age; but suddenly, as Elsie peaked, her familiar thin brown face and dark tumbled hair had looked different, and one had had the feeling that a third grown-up, more frightening than either of the others, had come into the room. With her feet apart, and her fists pushed down into her shabby tweed pockets, she had said, unbelievably, 'If I were a man I wouldn't be here. And I bloody well wish I were.' A silence had followed, beside which the preceding storm had seemed like child's play; and in the silence, Leo had walked out, without even slamming the door.

Now the worm is about to turn, the mouse is about come out of her wainscoting. Elsie has not only left school but has learned about the facts of life, which were 'revealed to her behind a stand of Macintoshes in the school cloakroom' by a school friend. She believes them because 'they had been so much too frightful' for even the school friend to invent. The thought of her parents having 'once been involved in them,' had been 'so appalling that she had gone about like a hunted creature, weighed down by the horrible secret.' Even her mother notices something is wrong with Elsie and she makes up a story about having trouble with her arithmetic homework to explain it. The guilt about her lie haunts her. 'And she had only been confirmed a month before! The little red book which the bishop had given her, its exhortations against impure thought suddenly and awfully explained, accused her every time she opened her dressing-table drawer... Sometimes she found it hard to believe that anyone in the world was as wicked as she.' This of course is not the kind of wickedness that her parents are obsessively trying to prevent: she has become as paranoid as her mother could wish about 'stranger danger,' even in the remote and peaceful part of Cornwall where they live.

> It never for a moment occurred to Elsie to reflect whether her pale melancholy face, her brown eyes like an anxious retriever's, her gawky sharp-kneed legs in their ribbed stockings, made up exactly the kind

of quarry after which purveyors of vice might range. She lived under the threat of rape and seduction, and once, losing her mother in Truro, had wandered for nearly an hour sooner than ask anyone but a policeman the way.

The fact that she went nowhere, met nobody but her mother's friends, and lived in a world of her own imagination, had suspended her in the most awkward stage of adolescence for quite three superfluous years. At seventeen her mind was still like Madame Tussaud's Exhibition, with Love, represented by kings and queens in velvet, on the upper floors, and Sex, like the Chamber of Horrors, tucked away underground.

Elsie can see no end to this way of life. 'There seemed no reason why it should not all be the same ten, or even twenty years from now.' She tried to imagine how Leo's life has turned out since she left nine years ago. She would now be 'twenty-six or twenty-seven, almost middle-aged. By now she must be walking the streets at night, speaking to strange men,' because this was how, according to Elsie's mother, women 'who were led astray' ended up. She imagines Leo with her hair dyed a vivid colour, in the manner of fallen women everywhere but finds this hard to square with her memory of Leo as a tomboy who had 'spent her pocket-money, not on powder and rouge, but on telescopes, pocket compasses, knives fitted with screwdrivers and tools for attending to horses' feet.' Even when she was old enough for a dress allowance Leo did not spend the money on 'pretty lace collars and artificial silk stockings,' but on a 'plain tweed suit,' which she wore for 'almost everything, bulging the pockets with apples and bits of string.' A tweed suit on a woman is almost universal code in fiction for a lesbian but Elsie and, presumably, her parents would not recognise it.

Like many of the adolescents in *Girls in Bloom*, Elsie starts to keep a diary, her second attempt, which she titles 'IMPRESSIONS OF LIFE – ELSA LANE'. It is not obvious whether Elsa is her given name and Elsie a nickname. She looks through her first diary from two years ago and sees an entry consisting just of 'a row of five asterisks, with another row of five exclamation marks below.' She has 'presently remembered what the five asterisks had celebrated,' and decides to burn the diary. 'She jumped out of the bed, and, moving the fireguard, stood for a moment in her pink crochet bedjacket and winceyette pyjamas, holding a sombre Byronic pose with the book poised over the flames.' This is as delightful an image of an awkward adolescent and her self-image as you will find anywhere.

As readers we of course assume we know what the asterisks and exclamation marks represent but later it turns out we may be wrong as, when Leo asks her if she is pregnant, she says she has never done anything like that. Thinking about her earlier diary, she says: 'Now I am older I realise how foolish it is to imagine that something one was writing down would happen to one every day (at least to an *ordinary* person, particularly a girl)'. Nothing of course very much happens in Elsie's life until a young doctor, Peter, takes over temporarily from the doctor in the village and appears to show an interest in her. She writes in her diary:

> 'There is something very touching to the heart about a Doctor who is young. One thinks of the years before him, with his eyes bent on sad and sordid things, doing good all around him, but missing romance in his own life, like Sir Galahad.' She re-read the last two words doubtfully, altered them to 'St Francis,' crossed this out, and decided to end the sentence with 'life' after all. 'You would need to marry someone with a great love of Beauty to keep him from becoming lonely and disillusioned in middle age. Someone younger than himself would probably be best for this.'

Elsie holds on to the fantasy that Peter will be interested in her right up until the end: 'Some time, she supposed – perhaps not for years, as he had seemed to imply, what did it matter? – she and Peter would be married.' However it quickly becomes clear to us, though not Elsie, that he simply likes to toy with women, including, later, Leo and her partner Helen who both reject him, less for his gender than for his patronising attitude, which is shown early on, in a letter to a fellow doctor in which he talks about her, referring to her as 'the child'.

> An interesting case, psychologically I mean, and rather a pitiful one. The child is nearly eighteen, but what with the stone rabbits and the Atlantic and the fact that her parents live like cat and dog and she knows the whole village knows it, she has taken refuge between the covers of a Girls' Annual and, unless someone snaps the poor little brat out of it, is in a fair way to going through her adult life in a sort of fifth-form daydream. Which would be a pity, as she obviously has the

makings of emotion and intelligence, combined with the kind of painful plainness which in a year or two, with sexual animation, might suddenly become attractive, and without it will get more dismal from year to year.

Peter talks to Elsie about her problems with her parents, and the lacuna of Leo. 'Don't you think, knowing your parents as you do, that perhaps the reason they don't talk about is that they haven't got a word for love?' This mention of the L word – in this case standing for love rather than lesbian – transforms Elsie. 'The word had never been spoken, until his voice articulated it. She thought that she would hear it every moment, now, for the rest of her life.' This is a coming of age moment for Elsie, though it is based on fantasy, and she decides to leave home to find Leo who, as we saw, is living happily and contentedly on a houseboat with her female partner Helen; it turns out that, rather than being an artist, Leo writes pulp Western novels to order, though even this is impossibly romantic to Elsie. At this point the novel's focus shifts rapidly away from Elsie to Leo and Helen and to Peter who meets them through Elsie and tries to romance both of them, though without much success; like Elsie he seems blissfully unaware of their sexuality – this is the early 1940s and he can perhaps be forgiven. Seeing Peter with Leo, it eventually occurs to Elsie – correctly – that he is not interested in her and – incorrectly – that he and Leo are in love; her self-realisation comes in the middle of the night as she gets up for a glass of water. It is another coming of age moment but it is a retrogressive one; having briefly bloomed in the sun she has returned to the earth, she has come up and been cut down like a flower.

Standing there to drink it, she saw taking shape out of the dazzle, in the glass before her, her own face, its plainness underlined by weeping and strain, her limp hair, her awkward schoolgirl's body. For the first time they were real; she believed in them; they were not a disguise in which a lovely future hid, ready to break forth like winged creatures in the spring; there were herself, and would always be, for now she had accepted them. Her life would be lived within their boundaries...

As long as I live, I shall be a person whom someone made love to because he was sorry for her. But I know, now, that it wasn't even really making love. Just being sorry: nothing else...

I thought I hated her but I don't. To hate people you have to feel they've robbed you, that they've kept you down. I was down from the beginning. If he hadn't loved Leo, he would have loved someone else. He'd never have loved me. How could he? I shall never be able to make anyone love me now. You have to believe, first, that you're a person who can be loved...

I must go back to Mother and Father now, and make it up to them. Nobody else wants me, anyway.

OLIVIA: *OLIVIA* BY DOROTHY STRACHEY, 1949

Dorothy Strachey (1865-1960) was a member of the Bloomsbury group, sister of Lytton Strachey, the author of *Eminent Victorians*, and James Strachey, the first English translator of Freud. She was a friend and the English translator of André Gide under her married name: Dorothy Bussy; she was married late, at thirty-seven, to Simon Bussy, a painter who knew Matisse. Although they were famously liberal, her parents Lieutenant-General Sir Richard and Lady Jane Strachey found Bussy unsuitable: he was five years younger than Dorothy and the son of a French shoemaker with table manners that appalled her parents. One possible reason for choosing Bussy as a husband was that Dorothy was bisexual and they perhaps had an understanding. She had an affair with Lady Ottoline Morell, also bisexual, who herself had affairs with many artistic people, including Bertrand Russel, Augustus John and Dora Carrington. *Olivia* was published anonymously by Virginia and Leonard Woolf's Hogarth Press, with a cover by Duncan Grant, Virginia Woolf's brother in law, an admirer of Bussy's who had lived with the Strachey family as a child. *Olivia* is inscribed 'to the beloved memory of V.W.' (Virginia Woolf had died in 1941).

Dorothy Strachey's only novel, *Olivia* is a brief and avowedly autobiographical account of her short time as an atheist from a family of atheists in a Methodist school in England and then as a pupil in a small French boarding school. Strachey herself later taught at the school in Fontainebleau, near Paris that she had attended; it later moved to England, where one of Strachey's pupils was Eleanor Roosevelt. In the novel, Olivia nurtures a passion for the co-owner of the school, Mlle Julie, who is the partner of the other co-owner, Mlle Cara. They 'had lived together for about fifteen years. They were both young, beautiful and gifted when they first met and decided to become partners in starting a girls' school... They were a model couple, deeply attached, tenderly devoted, the gifts of each supplementing the deficiencies of the other. They were admired and loved. They were happy.' A model, indeed, for a teenage girl unsure of her sexuality, of a happy, well-adjusted mature lesbian couple, like Leo and Helen in *The Friendly Young Ladies*.

In her later introduction to a reprint of the book, after she had admitted to being its author, Strachey talks about the 'poison of passion,' and the impossibility of an antidote; the reader only realises later that this is a reference to the death of Mlle Cara, jealous of Mlle Julie's possible affairs with the pupils, from an overdose – whether accidental or deliberate is never clear.

But the poison that works in a girl of sixteen – at any rate in the romantic, sentimental girl I then was – has no such antidote, and no previous inoculation mitigates the severity of the disease. Virgin soil, she takes it as the South Sea islanders took measles – a matter of life and death.

How could I have known indeed, what was the matter with me? There was no instruction anywhere. The poets, it is true (for even then I frequented the poets), had a way of talking sometimes which seemed strangely to illuminate the situation. But this, I thought, must be an illusion or an accident. What could these grown-up men and women with their mutual love-affairs have in common with a little girl like me? My case was so different, so unheard of. Really no one had ever heard of such a thing, except as a joke. Yes, people used to make joking allusions to 'schoolgirl crushes'. But I knew well enough that my 'crush' was not a joke. And yet I had an uneasy feeling that, if not a joke, it was something to be ashamed of, something to hide desperately. This, I suppose, was not so much a matter of reflection (I did not think my passion was reprehensible, I was far too ignorant for that) as of instinct – the deep-rooted instinct, which all my life has kept me from any form of unveiling, which has forbidden me many of the purest physical pleasures and all literary expression. How can one bathe without undressing, or write without laying bare one's soul?

But now, after many years, the urgency of confession is upon me. Let me indulge it. Let me make my offering to the altar of – absence. The eyes that would have understood are closed. And besides, it is not my soul but that of a far away little girl of sixteen.

Nothing very much happens in this short novel except that Olivia (neither she nor any of the other characters have surnames) and her schoolmates read and quote a lot of high classic French and Italian literature; in this almost literally cloistered environment all their passion comes from books and it is Olivia's first passionate encounter with great literature that triggers a coming of age revelation of sorts: it is with Racine's *Andromaque*, which

> gave me my first conception of tragedy, of the terror and complication and pity of human lives... I went to bed that night in a kind of daze, slept as if I had been drugged and in the morning awoke to a new world – a world of excitement – a world in which everything was fierce and piercing, everything charged with strange emotions, clothed with extraordinary mysteries, and in which I myself seemed to exist only as an inner core of palpitating fire... 'I understand,' I cried to myself, 'I understand at last. Life, life, life, this is life, full to overflowing with every ecstasy and every agony. It is mine, mine to hug, to exhaust, to drain... Now, now, I must grow strong. I must feed on beauty and rapture in order to grow strong.

Olivia's passion for Mlle Julie seems to be unrequited, though she does seem interested in some of her other pupils, especially Laura. One of the teachers says to Olivia, 'Mlle Julie had only cared for Laura's intelligence. But hadn't I seen with my own eyes their affection manifested in fifty different ways, the obvious ease and happiness of their relationship?' Olivia sees Laura as superior to her in every way, 'a sublime, unconscious saint... Nobody could say that Mlle Julie cared for my intellect. Oh, my intellect couldn't compare with Laura's. I have none of her gifts, I was totally unable to carry on a conversation with Mlle Julie on a footing of equality.' Olivia sometimes goes into the library when she knows Mlle

Julie will be alone there; on one occasion, inspired by Vigny's *Moïse*, she is thinking about the exaltation of loneliness:

> To live above the crowd in loneliness. To be condemned to loneliness by the greatness of one's qualities. To be condemned to live apart, however much one wanted the contact of warm human companionship... I forgot where I was as I thought of it. At last I raised my head and saw her eyes fixed upon me. Without knowing what I was doing, without reflection, as if moved by some independent spring of whose existence I was unaware, and whose violence I was totally unable to resist, I suddenly found myself kneeling before her, kissing her hands, crying out over and over again, 'I love you!' – sobbing, 'I love you!'
>
> Can I remember what she said, what she did? No. Nothing. I can only remember myself kneeling beside her – the feel of her woollen dress on my cheeks, the feel of her hands, the softness and warmth of her hands under my lips, the hardness of her rings. I don't know how I left the room. The rest of the day I lived in a kind of maze, dreaming of those hands, of those kisses.

Olivia, whatever Strachey said later, is at the mercy of a schoolgirl crush, whipped up into a frenzy by the intense fervour of classic literature unchecked by the realities of normal life in the outside world, dreaming 'the foolish dreams of adolescence: how I should save her life at the cost of my own by some heroic deed, of how she would kiss me on my deathbed... Of how I should become famous by writing poems which no one would know were inspired by her, of how one day she would get it, and so on and so on.' Whether she is doing it deliberately to make Olivia jealous or is unaware of the consequences, at a ball Mlle Julie kisses the beautiful and beautifully dressed Cécile. 'A long deliberate kiss on the naked creamy shoulder. An unknown pang of astonishing violence stabbed me. I hated Cécile. I hated Mlle Julie.' Julie seems to mock Olivia's jealousy. 'Is Olivia jealous of so much beauty?' She is. Mlle Julie twists the knife: 'No, Olivia, you will never be beautiful, but you have your points.' Angrily, Olivia feels as if she is being appraised like 'an animal at cattle show,' as Mlle Julie praises her for her 'pretty hands, pretty feet, a pretty figure.' Then Mlle Julie pulls Olivia towards her and whispers in her ear, her lips almost touching Olivia. 'I'll come tonight and bring you a sweet.' Soon afterwards, Olivia is in raptures back in her room.

A pretty body. Mine, the pretty body. I had never thought of my body till that minute. A body! I had a body – and it was pretty. What was it like? I must look at it. There was still time. She wouldn't be coming yet. I lighted the candle, sprang out of bed and slipped off my chemise. The looking-glass – a small one – was over the wash-hand-stand. I could only see my face and shoulders in it. I climbed onto a chair. Then I could see more. I looked at the figure in the glass, queerly lighted, without legs, strangely attractive, strangely repulsive. And then I slowly passed my hands down this queer creature's body from neck to waist – Ah! That was more than I could bear – but an excruciating thrill I had never felt before. In a second my chemise was on again, I was back in bed.

But Mlle Julie does not come, despite Olivia's yearning and lying awake all night listening. 'Hope rose and died a dozen times that night. Even when I knew it was impossible – even when the late winter dawn was beginning to glimmer in the room, I still lay, tossing and listening... And yet I was to know other, bitterer vigils, during which I looked back on this one as happy – during which I realized she had never loved me, never would love me as well as on that night.' After that, Mlle Julie is 'kind to me, but distant.' Olivia listens to footsteps at night, but 'no longer with the beating heart of hope.' By that time, though, 'the signs of approaching change, of approaching catastrophe even, were becoming more and more visible.' The catastrophe, when it comes is the unexplained death of Mlle Cara.

Just before Mlle Cara dies of the overdose, the couple have agreed to split up and Mlle Julie has made over half of everything to her. In her will, Mlle Cara has left everything to someone else and Mlle Julie decides to move to Canada with one of the other teachers. The last time Olivia sees Mlle Julie is when she is saying goodbye to all the pupils. 'There's to be no scene, if you please, Olivia,' she says, coldly. 'I don't want to make a scene,' Olivia answers, equally coldly. Mlle Julie dismisses her but then calls her back. 'Ah! she has relented! Ah! now I shall be gathered to her heart, and impatient as the wind, I turned to fly towards her.' But Mlle Julie is still behind her desk and merely wants to give Olivia a parting present; she says she had a book for Olivia but she does not know where it is and distractedly gives her an ivory paper-cutter instead, saying curtly, 'now send me the next girl.' Olivia is devastated. 'Those were the last words I ever heard her speak.'

Against all the evidence, Olivia still has hope that Mlle Julie will come to her that night. 'How hard it is to kill hope! Time after time, one thinks one has trodden it down, stamped it to death. Time after time, like a noxious insect, it begins to stir again, it shivers back again into a faint tremulous life.' But then Olivia finds that Julie is in Paris and will not return that night.

Ha! That was better. The noxious creature was dead now. It would undermine me no longer. I was free at last from its insidious burrowings. I could be calm now and braced myself to endure.

I went to the window and looked out. I should never see that sky, those trees, that road again. The road along which I used to hear her carriage driving back at night. Good-bye! Good-bye! *Pour jamais adieu! Pour jamais!*

I knelt down by my bed and burst into tears.

THERESE BELIVET: *THE PRICE OF SALT* BY 'CLAIRE MORGAN' (PATRICIA HIGHSMITH), 1952

L's was on a little side street in Greenwich village, a dark, cosy lesbian bar.

It was the beginning of graciousness in the lesbian bar world. There was no evidence of Mafia ownership, no men in baggy double-breasted suits sporting pinkie rings guarding the door. In fact, no men were allowed. The bathroom was clean. The customers didn't seem to be divided so much into butch and femme. Most looked like young college girls, well-dressed and without the heavy make up some habituées wore...

A handsome, dark-haired woman in a trench coat, drinking gin, stood at the bar, while around her there was the buzz that she was Claire Morgan!

She was better known in the outside world as Patricia Highsmith, author of *Strangers on a Train*, which had become an Alfred Hitchcock thriller in 1951.

But in L's, Pat was revered for her pseudonymous novel, *The Price of Salt*, which had been published in 1952 by Coward McCann. It was for many years the only lesbian novel, in either hard or soft cover, with a happy ending.

It stood on every lesbian bookshelf, along with classics like *The Well of Loneliness*; *We, Too, Are Drifting* [by Gale Wilhelm, 1935]; *Diana*; and *Olivia*.

Marijane Meaker, *Highsmith: A Romance of the 1950s*

This quote is from an intimate portrait of Patricia Highsmith (1921-1995) by her one-time lover Marijane Meaker, about whom much more shortly. As well as *Strangers on a Train*, Highsmith is most well-known for her Ripley novels, featuring the 'suave, agreeable and utterly amoral' Tom Ripley. There are some indications that Ripley may be gay but this is certainly not a feature of the books; Highsmith was only known to be a lesbian by a selected few and only once wrote a lesbian novel, hiding herself behind a pseudonym also known only by a few insiders. *The Price of Salt* (the title may be a reference to Lot's wife) was rescued from its cult status when it was made into the 2015 film *Carol* directed by Todd Haynes and starring Rooney Mara and Cate Blanchett; the novel had been reissued with the title *Carol* under Highsmith's own name by the respected Bloomsbury publishing group in 1990. It interesting that Carol is not the main focus of the novel, which shows the sexual and emotional coming of age of the younger character Therese, who had come, according to Highsmith herself, 'from her own bones,' and whom a friend of Highsmith's described as her 'alter ego'.

The rather unlikely premise of the novel – that a young sales assistant in a New York department store is so taken with an older female customer that she takes note of her address and sends her a Christmas card, then meets, becomes obsessed and enters into an affair with her – was in fact a fantasy based on Highsmith's own experience. In a 2015 interview with the *Daily Telegraph* she said:

Perhaps I noticed her because she was alone, or because a mink coat was a rarity, and because she was blondish and seemed to give off light. With the same thoughtful air, she purchased a doll, one of two or three I had shown her, and I wrote her name and address on the receipt, because the doll was to be delivered to an adjacent state. It was a routine transaction, the woman paid and departed. But I felt odd and swimmy in the head, near to fainting, yet at the same time uplifted, as if I had seen a vision.

As usual, I went home after work to my apartment, where I lived alone. That evening I wrote out an idea, a plot, a story about the blondish and elegant woman in the fur coat. I wrote some eight pages in longhand in my then-current notebook or cahier.

Therese is a perfectly normal nineteen-year-old at the beginning of the novel, working in a department store but aiming to make a career out of designing stage sets for the theatre. She has a boyfriend, Richard, though she 'still wasn't in love with him, not after ten months, and maybe she never could be, though the fact remained that she liked him better than any one person she had ever known, certainly any man.' She sees 'his face shining with affection for her because of some gesture of affection on her part,' but her feeling 'bore no resemblance to what she had read about love. Love was supposed to be a kind of blissful insanity.' Richard is clearly unsuitable for her, as he is trying to make her read Joyce's *Portrait of the Artist as a Young Man*; she has already read Gertrude Stein, whose works were, surprisingly, in the library of the Episcopalian school she has recently left. Richard is of course patronising towards her regarding literature; we have already seen this with Olivia Curtis and Cassandra Mortmain: a man unable to take a woman's literary tastes seriously and browbeating her into a feeling of inferiority. Therese does indeed feel 'a bit inferior when Richard talked with her about books,' as he no doubt means she should.

Like her author, Therese serves a woman in the department store and is so impressed with her that she decides to send her a Christmas card. The woman, Carol, makes contact and they meet. Carol is, Therese thinks, about thirty or thirty-two, is obviously married and presumably has a daughter aged about six or eight, since she bought a doll in the store. Carol, obviously enjoying toying with the younger woman, invites her out to her house. It is not obvious whether Carol fully understands the implications but Therese clearly does not: walking out with Richard, he swings her hand. 'As if they were lovers, Therese thought. It would be almost like love, what she fell for Carol, except that Carol was a woman. It was not quite insanity, but it was certainly blissful.'

Bliss is definitely not what she feels for Richard. They are due to go together on a trip to Europe; Richard wishes that they could share a room on the boat. Therese does not want to, indeed she does not want to go at all, or ever to share a bed with Richard again; as in some of the other lesbian coming of age novels we are looking at, Therese has already had an unsatisfactory sexual relationship with a man before finding her true sexuality.

> She remembered the first night she had let him stay, and she writhed again inwardly. It had been anything but pleasant, and she had asked right in the middle of it, 'Is this right?' How could it be right and so unpleasant, she had thought. And Richard had laughed, long and loud and with a heartiness that had made her angry. And the second time had been even worse, probably because Richard had thought all the difficulties had been gotten over. It was painful enough to make her weep, and Richard had been very apologetic and had said she made him feel like a brute. And then she protested that he wasn't.

To any young women unsure of her sexuality reading this novel at the time, with no one to confide in, no available source of advice and afraid of sex with men, this negative paragraph is surely as important as the positive scene where Therese and Carol first sleep together: sex with men can indeed be painful and unpleasant and sex with women can be beautiful. But it is not her lukewarm feelings for Richard, nor the unpleasantness of sex with him that drives her towards Carol; she is far more attracted to Carol than she is repulsed by Richard. 'She had never loved anyone before Carol,' nor even, it seems completely relaxed with anyone before; with Carol she can 'be herself, relax and laugh. But one could laugh at anything with Carol.' Therese comes of age with the realisation that it really is possible to share one's life with another person, to love that person, to be one with that person, even if that person is a woman.

> Therese longed for the store again, longed for Monday, because Carol might come in again on Monday. But it wasn't likely. Tuesday was Christmas Eve. Certainly she could telephone Carol by Tuesday, if only to wish her a merry Christmas.
> But there was not a moment when she did not see Carol in her mind, and all she saw, she seemed to see through Carol. That evening,

the dark flat streets of New York, the tomorrow of work, the milk bottle dropped and broken in her sink, became unimportant. She flung herself on her bed and drew a line with a pencil on a piece of paper. And another line, carefully, and another. A world was born around her, like a bright forest with a million shimmering leaves.

But all this is of course confusing: being from New York, she is not completely naive, she has 'heard about girls falling in love, and she knew what kind of people they were and what they looked like. Neither she nor Carol looked like that. Yet the way she felt about Carol passed all the tests for love and fitted all the descriptions.' Therese realises she does not love Richard, though she admires his certainty, his secure place in the world as a man. 'She envied him his faith. There would always be a place, a home, a job, someone else for him.'

Instead of going to Europe with Richard, Therese goes on a road trip west with Carol – perhaps this is a metaphor for exploring the unknown. Inevitably they end up sleeping in the same bed, though up to then they have slept in the same room but separately. Carol makes no moves towards her; Therese is willing but neither of them seems to want to make the first move. 'If she simply asked, she thought, Carol would let her sleep tonight in the same bed with her. She wanted more than that, to kiss her, to feel their bodies next to each other's.' She gets her wish eventually.

It was dawn now. Carol's fingers tightened in her hair, Carol kissed her on the lips, and pleasure leapt in Therese again as if it were only a continuation of the moment when Carol had slipped her arm under her neck last night. I love you, Therese wanted to say again, and then the words were raised by the tingling and terrifying pleasure, the spreading waves from Carol's lips over her neck, her shoulders, that rushed suddenly, the length of her body. Her arms were tight around Carol, and she was conscious of Carol and nothing else... While a thousand memories and moments, words, the first darling, the second time Carol had met her at the store, a thousand memories of Carol's face, her voice, moments of anger and laughter flashed like the tail of a comet across her brain. And now it was pale-blue distance and space, an expanding space in which she took flight suddenly like a long arrow. The arrow seemed to cross an impossibly wide abyss with ease, seemed to arc on and on in space, and not quite to stop. Then she realised that she still clung to Carol, that she trembled violently and the arrow was herself. She saw Carrol's pale hair across her eyes, and now Carol's head was close against hers. And she did not have to ask if this were right, no one had to tell her, because this could not have been more right or perfect...

'My angel,' Carol said. 'Flung out of space.'

Therese looked up at the corners of the room that were much brighter now, at the bureau with the bulging front and the shield-shaped drawer pulls, at the frameless mirror with the bevelled edge, at the green patterned curtains that hung straight at the windows, and the two great tips of buildings that showed just above the cell. She would remember every detail of this room forever.

This is another coming of age moment for Therese but it is also the moment when their relationship falls apart: it turns out later that Carol's husband has had a private detective following them and has recorded them making love. He threatens Carol that if she does not give up her relationship with Therese, he will take the divorce to court and insist on full custody of their daughter which of course, at the time, the courts would have granted. This theme is apparently also taken from Highsmith's own personal experience: one of her lovers, Virginia Catherwood, had lost custody of her daughter this way. Carol tries to explain to Therese that they must stop seeing each other; Therese says 'what she had only sensed before, that the whole world was ready to be their enemy, and suddenly what she and Carol had together seemed no longer love or anything happy but a monster between them, with each of them caught in a fist.' In Carol's absence, Therese has another coming of age epiphany. In a library she sees a picture, a picture that she knows from a reproduction in her own childhood home, of a 'smiling woman in the ornate dress of some court.'

She knew the short, firmly modelled cheeks, the full coral lips that smiled at one corner, the mockingly narrow lids, the strong, not very high forehead that even in the picture seemed to project a little over the living eyes that knew everything beforehand, and sympathised and laughed at once. It was Carol. Now in the long moment while she could not look away from it, the mouth smiled and the eyes regarded her with nothing but mockery, the last veil lifted and revealing nothing but mockery and gloating, the splendid satisfaction of the betrayal accomplished.

Therese is on her own now, on her own and grown-up, fully come of age, matured and hardened by the betrayal. She decides to move back to New York and look up all the people she used to know, make new friends and go to night school. 'And she wanted to change her wardrobe completely. Everything she had now, the clothes she remembered in her closet in New York, seemed juvenile, like clothes that had belonged to her years ago.'

It looks as though we may be in for the unhappy ending we expect from lesbian novels of this era (because, as we shall see later, publishers demanded them, though *Diana*, republished in paperback the same year as *The Price of Salt* and *Spring Fire* were first published, also has a happy ending). Perhaps Carol will slink back to her husband and Therese, who has already lost Richard, will end up in a life of meaningless drudgery back at the department store, die of some wasting disease or perhaps even kill herself. Or maybe she will become a strong independent woman, free but alone, with no need of sexual relations with either gender.

But no: in another unlikely twist at the very end, Carol repents and returns to Therese. It is such a surprisingly happy ending that, in another era it might have ended: 'Reader, she married her.'

Carol raised her hand slowly and brushed her hair back, once on either side, and Therese smiled because the gesture was Carol, and it was Carol she loved and would always love. Oh, in a different way now, because she was a different person, and it was like meeting Carol all over again, but it was still Carol and no one else. It would be Carol, in a thousand cities, a thousand houses, in foreign lands where they would go together, in heaven and in hell. Therese waited. Then as she was about to go to her, Carol saw her, seemed to stare at her incredulously a moment while Therese watched the slow smile growing, before her arm lifted suddenly, her hand waved a quick, eager greeting that Therese had never seen before. Therese walked toward her.

SUSAN MITCHELL: *SPRING FIRE* BY 'VIN PACKER' (MARIJANE MEAKER), 1952

1952 was something of an *annus mirabilis* for the lesbian coming of age novel, seeing the paperback republication of *Diana*, the original publication of both Patricia Highsmith's *The Price of Salt* and *Spring Fire*, written by Marijane Meaker under the pseudonym Vin Packer. As we just saw, Meaker wrote about Highsmith in her late memoir *Highsmith* of 2003; they were on and off lovers in a stormy relationship for many years; Highsmith was much older and more established when Meaker finally plucked up courage to walk up to her in L's bar. 'Pat had become my idol. Although we were both reviewed in Anthony Boucher's mystery column in the *New York Times*, she was published in hardcover by Harper Brothers. As Vin Packer, I was one of Gold Medal Books' mystery/suspense paperback "tough guys," and, as Ann Aldrich, a softcover reporter on lesbian life.'

Meaker's *Spring Fire*, published under the Vin Packer pseudonym, has the distinction of being the first lesbian paperback-original novel (*The Price of Salt* was issued as a Bantam paperback in 1953, but this was after the release of the hardback). 'Serious' books had mostly been published in hardback and quite expensive; if they were likely to be popular they would later be republished in a cheaper paperback version. This idea held in the publishing world for a very long time. But in the early 1950s Fawcett Publications had the idea of publishing good books in original paperbacks under an imprint called Gold Medal Books, edited by Dick Carroll. The difference was that paperbacks were affordable by almost anyone.

As far as the censors were concerned, anything that happened between the covers of a relatively expensive, limited-run, hardback book was only likely to be read by the mature, educated middle-classes – people like themselves indeed. The censors were therefore quite relaxed about them; high-priced hardbacks would not be likely to deprave or corrupt the pillars of society who would be the only people to read them. But when books were so cheap as to be disposable, cheap enough to be bought in large quantities by the impressionable, undereducated working classes, or even – heaven forbid – by young people, the censors got much more twitchy. As Anne Weldy, Meaker's protégée, whose lesbian pulp novel *Odd Girl Out*, published under the pseudonym Anne Bannon we will look at, put it:

> They were sold on the shelves of news stands, available in train stations and airports. Anywhere that you could buy magazines, pulp fiction was available as well. It was kind of an ephemeral literature. People would pick up a paperback novel to read on the train, on their way to work, keep it for a day or two until they finished it and then throw it away...
>
> Readers who weren't likely to go into bookstores or didn't have one in their hometown could walk into their drug store and pick up a lesbian novel... Anybody could find them, so you didn't have to go into the library and request access to the rare and naughty books they held in the back.

A lot of people did pick up *Spring Fire*: it sold 1,463,917 million copies in its first year of publication; even a well-reviewed, popular hardback might only sell in the low thousands. Publishers were prepared to take a risk with censorship when the costs were relatively low; they knew that if the censors were to seize a book it would be pulped – the origin of the term pulp fiction: fiction published knowing that it might end up being pulped. At the same time, these cheap paperbacks did not attract the attention of serious reviewers and therefore often escaped the attention of the censors. Anne Weldy said:

> How did we get away with it, those of us writing these books? No doubt it had a lot to do with the fact that we were not even a blip on the radar screens of the literary critics. Not one ever reviewed a lesbian pulp paperback for the *New York Times Review of Books*, the *Saturday Review*, *The Atlantic Monthly*. We were lavishly ignored, except by the customers in the drugstores, airports, train stations, and new stands who bought our books of the kiosk by the millions.

Marijane Meaker had been one of Dick Carroll's secretaries at Gold Medal Books; she read books on his behalf and gave him notes. 'I very often finished reading a new manuscript thinking: *I could do that.*' Meaker showed Carroll a novel she had been writing about a girls' boarding school.

'You might have a good story there,' Dick said, 'but you have to do two things. The girls would have to be in college, not boarding school. And, you cannot make homosexuality attractive. No happy ending... your main character can't decide she's not strong enough to live that life,' Dick said. 'She has to reject it knowing that it's wrong. You see, our books go through the mails. They have to pass inspection. If one book is considered censurable, the whole shipment is sent back to the publisher. If your book appears to proselytise for homosexuality, all the books sent with it to distributors are returned. You have to understand that. I don't care about anybody's sexual preference. But I do care about making this line successful.'

In those days, authors had very little say in the matter of titles or covers. Meaker had wanted to call it *Sorority Girl* but Carroll thought that was not racy enough. 'I don't want it to have an unhappy title like *The Well of Loneliness*,' Meaker said, referring to the only explicitly lesbian novel to have been published by a mainstream publisher, in 1928. Carroll called it *Spring Fire* because there was a big seller at the time by James Michener called *The Fires of Spring* and he was hoping to make sales to people who were confused. He got his wish regarding the ending too: as Meaker says, 'at the end one young woman goes mad, while the other realises she had never really loved her in the first place. While that may have satisfied the post office inspectors, the homosexual audience would not have believed that for a minute.'

Meaker subsequently kept the Vin Packer pseudonym but used it for a line of thrillers with no lesbian content – she said she wanted to write books that the papers could review. She later wrote young adult novels under the pseudonym ME Kerr, and, as Ann Aldrich – Carroll told her she needed a 'soft, all-American name' – published two non-fiction books: documentary dispatches reporting on lesbian life from the frontline in Greenwich Village, New York City meant to be read by her sisters in the sticks; these were also hugely successful and influential. Anne Weldy was one of those whose life was transformed by Meaker/Aldrich's *We Walk Alone*, 1955 and *We, Too, Must Love*, 1958. In her introduction to a reissue of both books, Weldy praised Meaker as a founding sister.

If you were a lesbian in the 1950s, you were probably married, with children. Or solitarily drudging in the hinterlands . . . Could you be the only woman on the planet with tender feelings for other women? Were you evil? Cursed? Or merely sick? . . . And then a miracle happened. In the drugstore, the train station, the bus stop, the newsstand, you came across a rack of pulp paperbacks. Among the cowboy tales, the cops-and-robbers, and the science fiction, there began to be books about lesbians. Suddenly, you had a name, an identity, and a community of unknown sisters.

The central character of *Spring Fire*, Susan (Mitch) Mitchell is rich but 'not pretty. She was not lovely and dainty and pretty, but there was a comeliness about her that suggested some inbred strength and grace.' She has been to several different boarding schools over a period of six years with no apparent romantic or any other kind of interest in or from other girls. But because of her wealth, her wardrobe and her cool car, the Tri Epsilon sorority is very keen to have her when she first goes to college.

> An absolute *must* for Tri Epsilon. The Mitchell girl is 17. Her father is a widower and millionaire. There are no other children. The Mitchell girl owns a brilliant red convertible, Buick, latest model... Susan has been educated in the best private schools. She is not beautiful, but she is wholesome and a fine athlete... Edward Mitchell's reputation is above reproach. They are definitely nouveaux riches, but their social prestige in Seedmore is tiptop. Susan has a fabulous wardrobe.

Obviously, the sorority has a very shallow view of its members but Mitch is keen to join anyway; as one of the senior member says: 'The purpose of a sorority is to help a girl grow, and if Susan needs our help, it will be our privilege to give it to her.' Susan does in fact have more than one coming of age moment with the sorority, the first of which is meeting and sharing a room with the beautiful Leda, to whom Mitch is attracted at first sight; this seems to be her first same-sex attraction. However, before the relationship has time to go anywhere, she is assigned a date by her sorority with the appalling Bud. Left alone with Mitch by Leda and her date Jake, Bud does not waste time in preliminaries. 'His mouth came on hers and she could feel the roughness of his beard. At first she tried to push him back and she struggled desperately. Then she let him kiss her. *Ever been kissed – hard?*' Mitch makes it very clear that she does not want him to go any further, but Bud does not listen.

> Fighting desperately with him, she could not stop his hands from pulling her skirt up. A thin wail escaped from her mouth and she began to heighten it into a loud moaning sound.
> 'Shut up,' he snapped. 'Shut up!'
> Her moaning increased and some of the lost strength returned so that she kicked him and sent him back away from her. He stood up and glared down. 'Mamma tell you not to?' he said angrily. 'Mamma tell you sex is dirty?'

Mitch has no Mamma and a very liberal father but has never had sex before, either with a boy or with a girl. The next time he tries it with her she resists but he grabs her arms. 'Damn you and your damn innocence!' He shouts drunkenly. Mitch fights back; 'grabbing the china vase on the table, she brought it down on his head, and left him staggering back against the wall.' This public humiliation of a senior fraternity member has to be put right: the fraternity threaten the sorority that unless Mitch invites Bud to their next party and makes it up with him, the sorority will be ostracised. Reluctantly, Mitch agrees, if only because Leda is so unsympathetic: her mother had her when she was very young and did not let the young Leda stand in the way of her seeing men; it is implied that some of her mother's boyfriends were more interested in the daughter than the mother. In Greek mythology of course, Leda is raped by Zeus in the form of a swan; Meaker may have had in mind Yeats' poem about that rape, which emphasises its brutality and the power men hold so casually over women.

> A sudden blow: the great wings beating still
> Above the staggering girl, her thighs caressed
> By the dark webs, her nape caught in his bill,
> He holds her helpless breast upon his breast.

But, at the end of the poem, Yeats implies that a woman may gain in knowledge from this brutality.

Did she put on his knowledge with his power
Before the indifferent beak could let her drop?

Leda certainly has gained in knowledge from her experiences, as well as
in cynicism and bitterness. When Mitch tells Leda that everything seems
'so dirty and nasty,' Leda is incensed. 'I bet you still think babies grow
under cabbage leaves. Well, they don't. I've got news, Mitch, they don't
grow under any goddam cabbage leaves. I had to learn it! I had to learn it
the hard way!' Getting her into the basement at the party, Bud appears to
drug Mitch. She comes close to passing out and Bud starts to undress
her.

> Very softly, almost too softly for her to hear her own words, she said,
> 'No,' but her eyes saw the circles and there was a new feeling in her
> body when he touched her and she could feel her clothes being pulled.
> 'No,' she said. 'No, please, no!'
> Then swiftly, suddenly, and with terrific pain, she felt pressure and
> her eyes opened wide and she would have screamed but his hand cov-
> ered her mouth and he struck her hard.
> 'Shut up,' he said. 'You wanted to know. You wanted this, Miss
> Virgin.'

She cannot move as he rapes her while she is 'down in the mire of pitch
black and the quicksand sucking her in and her whole head dizzy and the
pain.' Afterwards, he tells her to get dressed, but she tells him to go to
hell. He has no remorse. 'Look, take a hot bath. You're not hurt. Go up
and take a hot bath and keep your mouth shut.' She manages to get back
to her room; when Leda comes in she realises something has happened,
and this time she is sympathetic and sleeps in Mitch's bed with her. But
when they both wake up at five o'clock in the morning, sympathy turns to
something else.

> Leda moved her hand forward and ran her fingers lightly over the but-
> tons on Mitch's pajama top. Then, gently, she slipped the round, plas-
> tic buttons from their loops, leaving the coat open. Almost as if Mitch
> knew what would follow, she held the top of the sheet back while Leda
> moved down and lightly kissed Mitch's breasts. A soft sigh broke free
> from Mitch's throat and evolved into a plaintive cry. Leda pulled her-

self up and her lips found Mitch's and crushed them, burning and moist.

'Mitch,' Leda whispered, and they held each other fast and hard. 'Mitch.'

Mitch has her first experience of heterosexual sex – bad, very bad – and lesbian sex – good, very good – on the same night. Quite some coming of age. Like Therese Belivet, Mitch can directly compare one experience with the other and come to the obvious conclusion. But things with Leda do not go unequivocally well. Leda tells Mitch that she is not a lesbian – 'I've got bisexual tendencies, but by God, I'm no damn Lesbian' – and could not could not love Mitch if she were. Meanwhile, Leda continues to see Jake, of whom Mitch becomes very jealous. 'I may be a little uncertain about it, but men come first with me. What do you think we are – engaged to be married?' Mitch protests. 'You said you loved me. Maybe I don't understand –' Leda tells Mitch that she had 'better get to know men too,' to hide her true sexuality.

Mitch does in fact get to know a man: Charlie, a nice, kind and nerdy young man, the opposite of Bud. He is too shy to initiate sex with her, so she starts things off; although 'it still was not the way it was with Leda,' and she feels 'empty and aimless,' she goes ahead anyway. 'He was sweet and shy and he loved her. If it was not now, then when?' But Charlie cannot do it, even though he has come prepared. 'Listen, Susan, I've never touched a girl. Honestly, never once in my life. I – I have something in my wallet.' But in the end, he feels Mitch's coldness. 'Mitch felt the chill through her whole body. "Hurry," she said. "Please hurry."' In the circumstances, Charlie can't do it; she offers to put on her sweater and let him take his time but he still cannot do it and she drives him back to town in the Buick, the normal roles of driver and passenger reversed, with him crouching, embarrassed in the back seat. That is the end of Charlie, and indeed any further attempts at relationships with men.

We already know that we are going to be in for an unhappy ending; the publisher demanded it. The setup for the fall is a letter that Mitch writes to Leda, a Dear Jane letter telling Leda that she loves her, but is calling it off. Reading the letter, Leda decides she cannot be without Mitch and they make love; unfortunately two of their sorority cohorts open the door and see them. Leda attempts to blame Mitch for forcing her into it, showing the sorority mother the letter. Things then appropriately take on the mythic dimensions of a Greek tragedy; in the Greek myth Leda is associated with the goddess Nemesis; in this story she nearly becomes Mitch's nemesis. Leda is involved in a car accident and appears to have brain damage. The truth about the letter then comes out and Leda is seen as the real villain, following which she has a complete mental breakdown; Mitch forgives her but does not attempt to go back to her. As if this is not unhappy enough to satisfy the publishers, the last sentence of the book is: 'she didn't hate her at all, and she knew then that she had never really loved her.'

LAURA LANDON: *ODD GIRL OUT* BY 'ANN BANNON' (ANN WELDY), 1957

In the introduction to her anthology *Lesbian Pulp Fiction*, the author Katherine V Forrest remembers how a book she found in a bookshop in Detroit in 1957 changed not only her writing but her life.

> Overwhelming need led me to walk a gauntlet of fear up to the cash register. Fear so intense that I remembered nothing more, only that I stumbled out of the store in possession of what I knew I must have, a book as necessary to me as air.
>
> The book was *Odd Girl Out* by Ann Bannon. I found it when I was eighteen years old. It opened the door to my soul and told me who I was. It led me to other books that told me who some of us were, and how some of us lived.
>
> Finding this book back then, and what it meant to me, is my touchstone to our literature, to its value and meaning. Yet no matter how many times I try to write or talk about that day in Detroit, I cannot convey the power of what it was like. You had to be there. I write my books out of the profound wish that no one will ever have to be there again.

Bannon was really Anne Weldy; she had the same editor, Dick Carroll, and the same publisher, Gold Medal Books, as Vin Packer/Marijane Meaker. As Bannon had changed Forrest's life, so Meaker had changed Bannon/Weldy's. Weldy had been in a sorority at college like the characters in *Spring Fire* and thought she could write a similar kind of novel. She wrote Meaker 'a kind of a fan letter.' Even though Meaker had been getting hundreds of fan letters she responded, inviting Bannon to meet her and Carroll, who looked at her novel and saw both problems and promise in it.

> In the view of Dick Carroll, the twinkly old Irishman who was running that show, the manuscript was twice as long as they wanted. He also felt that I hadn't recognised my story. I had told a kind of straightforward coming of age type novel, and rather cautiously and timidly put a small romance between two young women in the corners of the background. He said cut the length by half and tell the story of the two young women, Beth and Laura, and then maybe we'll have something.

Unlike Meaker, Weldy was allowed to write the ending she wanted. In a later interview she said that Meaker 'was constrained very heavily in having to end her book on a very negative note. Writing five years later, I found things had loosened up. I was able to, in a sense, have a happy ending.' Weldy told the same interviewer how difficult life was for homosexuals and lesbians in the early 1950s, in the middle of the Cold War, the McCarthyite anti-communist witch hunts and the paranoia that surrounded them.

> It was a very repressed and frightening time. After World War Two ended, the country had made a frightening turn and embraced the most conservative and traditional roles. All the girls were supposed to be home having babies and making soup and casseroles. Everyone was supposed to be as conventional as is possible to imagine. People whose nature led them to a same-sex attraction were forced to put up a conventional façade. The danger was very severe, and gay attraction was frankly illegal in a lot of places. You could be jailed, you could certainly be publicly humiliated and everything could be thrown into jeopardy in terms of your job and your family. You were treated almost as if you had a disease, and if you were known to be gay then your friends had to abandon you because they might catch it too.

Marijane Meaker put it in a very similar way in a later introduction to a reprint of *We Walk Alone.*

In the 50s, we felt no entitlement, and most of us were wary of any organisations. The 50s was famous for its witch-hunts and congressional investigations. In the eyes of the law we were illegal, and religions viewed us as anathema. I wanted to write about what it was like to live in one of the most sophisticated cities in the world, and find yourself unacceptable because of your sexual orientation.

Odd Girl Out was the first of what became *The Beebo Brinker Chronicles*: five linked novels from 1957 to 1962, of which the second, *I Am a Woman*, 1959, follows the same character, Laura into maturity. But Weldy was a very unlikely pioneer of lesbian fiction.

I must have been the most naïve kid who ever sat down at the age of 22 to write a novel. It was the mid-1950s. Not only was I fresh from a sheltered upbringing in a small town, I had chosen a topic of which I had literally no practical experience. I was a young housewife living in the suburbs of Philadelphia, college graduation just behind me, and utterly unschooled in the ways of the world... To my continuing astonishment, the books have developed a life of their own. They were born in the hostile era of McCarthyism and rigid male/female sex roles, yet still speak to readers in the twenty-first century.

Originally introduced to it by Marijane Meaker, Weldy spent time in New York's Greenwich Village. 'It was love at first sight. Every pair of women sauntering along with arms around waists or holding hands was an inspiration.' Weldy's debt to Meaker extends to the plot of *Odd Girl Out*, which, like *Spring Fire*, concerns an inexperienced girl, Laura, going to college and falling in love with an older member of her sorority, Beth, but being unsure what her feelings mean and what to do about them. 'There was a vague, strange feeling in the younger girl that to get too close to Beth was to worship her, and to worship was to get hurt.' Beth is a larger-than-life character; Laura 'had never met or read or dreamed a Beth before.' One of Beth's eccentricities is that she never wears underwear. Laura's 'whole upbringing revolted at this... Nobody was a more rigid conformist, farther from a character, than Laura Landon.' Sharing a room together, Laura is very shy about getting undressed in front of another person, feeling that 'Beth's bright eyes were doting on every button.' Beth makes up the bed for her.

> She helped Laura under the covers and tucked her in, and it was so lovely to let herself be cared for that Laura lay still, enjoying it like a child. When Beth was about to leave her, Laura reached for her naturally, like a little girl expecting a good-night kiss. Beth bent over and said, 'what is it, honey?'
>
> With a hard shock of realisation, Laura stopped herself. She pulled her hands away from Beth and clutched the covers with them.
>
> 'Nothing.' It was a small voice.
>
> Beth pushed Laura's hair back and gazed at her and for a heart-stopping moment Laura thought she would lean down and kiss her forehead. But she only said, 'Okay. Sleep tight, honey.' And climbed down.

Laura knows nothing of lesbianism and is simply 'fuzzily aware of certain extraordinary emotions that were generally frowned upon and so she frowned upon them too, with no very good notion of what they were or how they happened, and not the remotest thought that they could happen to her.' She had had crushes on girls in high school but 'they were all short and uncertain and secret feelings and she would have been profoundly shocked to hear them called homosexual.' Laura of course considers herself normal even though she 'wasn't attracted to men. She thought simply that men were unnecessary to her. That wasn't unusual; lots of women live without men.' Like Mitch in *Spring Fire*, Laura has to fight off the unwanted attentions of a boy from college who will not take no for an answer; in this case he does not go so far as to rape her, but still, like Mitch, her first experience with a boy is very bad.

> Laura looked at him wide-eyed, held so hard that she felt she could count his ribs with her own. She hated him. She wanted to spit at him, hurt him, run. But she was afraid.
>
> 'Oh, yes,' he said. 'You and I are gonna get along just fine, Laura. Just fine.' And he kissed her. 'Just fine. Hey, open your mouth honey. Hey, come on, Laura.'
>
> Laura turned away from him and whispered, 'Jim, this is our first date. I mean – please, Jim.'

'I know, baby. You're just a kid, you want to do everything right.' He tickled her neck. 'Well, believe me, Laura, this *is* right.'

Laura's nails bit cruelly into the heels of her hands in a frenzy of revolt. Oh God, stop! she thought.

Also like Mitch, Laura's love object Beth has a boyfriend; Laura, as she begins to understand her true nature – as she comes of age – knows she has to give Beth up to him; 'you need a man, you always did.'

I'm not wrong about myself, not any more. And not about you, either.'

'Oh, Laura, my dear –'

'We haven't time for tears now, Beth. I've grown up emotionally as far as I can. But you can go farther, you can be better than that. And you must, Beth, if you can. I've no right to hold you back.' Her heart shrank inside her at her own words...

'You taught me what I am, Beth. I know now, I didn't before. I understand what I am, finally.'

MAUDE HUTCHINS' MISCHIEVOUS ANGELS

Maude Hutchins... is one of our few erotic writers, and by erotic I mean something quite different from sexual. We have many direct anatomical sexual writers. Very few erotic. By erotic I mean the totality of sexual experience, its atmosphere, mood, sensual flavours, mystery, vibrations, the state of ecstasy into which it may plunge us, the full range of the senses and emotions which accompany, surround it, and which the explicit flat clinical descriptions destroy. She deals with unusual relationships, adolescents who discover their bodies, the hypocrisy of adults. *A Diary of Love* is as subtle an exploration of the senses as Colette's books. She has wit and intelligence. The lesser published short stories are highly surrealistic. She makes use of subtle physical images to describe sensual feelings, experiences, relationships. She can say startling things with elegance, and they carry further.

Anaïs Nin, *The Future of the Novel*

Maude Hutchins writes like a lascivious Ivy Compton-Burnett.

Time Magazine

Maude Hutchins writes like a mischievous angel

Maxwell Geismar

Maude Phelps McVeigh Hutchins (1899-1991) was raised in an upper-class environment, born to wealthy parents in New York City but, like Jane Eyre, orphaned at a young age and brought up by relatives, in this case her grandparents, prominent members Long Island society. A 1935 article about Hutchins (in her then role as a sculptor in Chicago) makes it clear just how aristocratic her family were. 'Mrs Hutchins' mother was a Phelps, of a New England family that made their advent in Massachusetts in 1632. It was her Phelps grandparents who brought her up after her parents died.' Critic Maxwell Geismar, in his 1962 introduction to Hutchins' collection of stories *The Elevator*, called her 'this country-bred, inherently "upper-class," and off-beat virtuoso (for Maude Hutchins is certainly that; while like most native aristocrats, she is profoundly democratic in her instincts).' Women of Hutchins' class had to contend with expectations as to what they could and could not do, though being artistic was not necessarily a problem.

It was nice for young ladies of fashion in her girlhood circles on Long Island to paint and draw. So Maude Phelps Hutchins had no traditional background of stern family objections thrown into her way of following her instincts to be an artist. Painting or drawing was one of the 'accomplishments,' like playing the piano and doing needlework (as distinguished from sewing).

Her only problem when trying to be taken seriously as an artist was 'the suspicion of being a dilettante,' even though she did have an art degree from Yale University. But even there, women were treated differently. The main focus of the degree course was to get students on the Prix de Rome, but women were not allowed to apply for that so 'the girls are allowed to develop pretty much as they please.'

Women in her own circles are proud of 'dear Maude' as being a little above themselves in artistic judgement, helping to elevate by that much the whole level of her caste. The artists 'from the people' – well, you know how they are apt to feel and talk if you ever had occasion to associate with 'the people,' whether in art, letters, politics, or working in a factory.

The back cover blurb for Hutchins' penultimate novel, *Blood on the Doves*, 1965 – an untypical, multi-voiced, Faulkneresque narrative – describes her background very nicely, underneath a photograph of Hutchins smiling broadly, sitting at the controls of the plane that she flew solo across America and looking nowhere near her age, which was then sixty-six. The logo on the side of the plane reads Super Cat, perhaps appropriately.

Although Maude Hutchins was born in New York and brought up on Long Island, she is half Virginian and half New Englander. Tutored, as she says, by a Connecticut Yankee, her grandfather, and a Virginian great aunt, she realised early that 'I was always wrong.' This bringing up accounted also for her formal education ending at sixteen (grandfather said ladies do not go to college), and for her matriculation in the Yale School of Fine Arts after her marriage. She received a B.F.A. from Yale University, but 'piling clay on an armature in the basement of that University was not exactly an intellectual pursuit. I learned how to read, however,' she adds, 'and had read most of "The Great Books" before that term was invented.' She also learned to fly, and pilots her own plane.

For Hutchins' family, being an artist was just about respectable – though she did cause a stir in Chicago by exhibiting life-size nude male statues – but being a writer was something else. Long before she thought about writing novels Hutchins collaborated on an illustrated 1932 book called *Diagrammatics*, for which she provided lightly erotic, neoclassical line drawings of young, nude women – they are rather like more minimal versions of Picasso's *Vollard Suite*, the first of which appeared in 1930 or his illustrations for Ovid's *Metamorphoses*, published in 1931. They also resemble the erotic, Beardsleyesque illustrations of young girls that Willy Pogány, by then a well-known illustrator and set designer living in New York, provided for a 1926 English-language translation of Pierre Louÿs' *Songs of Bilitis*, which Louÿs had originally claimed were his French translations of Greek manuscripts from the same era and sexual orientation as Sappho.

It seems that Hutchins herself initiated this project and, not yet herself a writer, asked Mortimer J. Adler, a professor from Chicago University, of which her husband was then president, to write the words. Adler provided a truly terrible sub-Gertrude Stein text; it is not obvious whether the text is a spoof and the whole thing was a joke. The volume was privately published in a luxurious, limited edition. Although it was not widely distributed, Hutchins' family were not amused.

'When I was fourteen and visiting a great-aunt, I was late to luncheon,' Mrs Hutchins relates, 'and I said, "But I beat Sylvia at tennis." My aunt looked at me coldly and said, "We have never had an athlete in the family before." Three years ago, I sent a copy of *Diagrammatics* to an elderly cousin. In a letter to me, he said, "We have never had an author in the family before."'

Much worse, from her family's, and her then ex-husband's point of view, was to come when she started to write novels; though Hutchins did not publish anything until after her divorce, she wrote under her married name. Hutchins' first novel was published in 1948, when she was forty-nine, the age at which Shirley Jackson was when she died and around ten years older than Carson McCullers, Grace Metalious and Flannery O'Connor were when they died. Elizabeth Bowen, born the same year as Hutchins, and Rosamond Lehmann, born two years later, both published their first novels in 1927. So although, like Jackson, Hutchins had daughters, they were much older when she was writing about teenage girls: the eldest of the three, Mary Frances (known as Franja) was born in 1926 and in her twenties when her mother's first novel was published, though the youngest, Clarissa, was not born until 1942; she (or a character with her name) starred in her mother's last novel, published when Clarissa was also in her twenties. The middle daughter, Joanna Blessing, born in 1935, was known as Jo-Jo. The respective ages of their daughters when they were writing their novels may partly explain why Shirley Jackson's teenagers are almost entirely sex-free – except Natalie Waite, whose one experience of sex is so awful she erases it from her mind and Jackson erases it from the novel – while Hutchins' teen girls embrace sex and sensuality with great joy and a total lack of inhibition.

Another explanation might be that, though Jackson and Hutchins published their first novels in the same year – 1948 – Hutchins was literally old enough to be Jackson's mother; this is belied by their respective appearance in publicity photographs: Jackson always looks overweight, bespectacled, mature and maternal while Hutchins, though seventeen years older, looks like a young, glamorous society figure; as we have seen, in one publicity shot she is about to take off in her own plane – one can hardly imagine Shirley Jackson being on a plane, let alone piloting one solo across America, as Hutchins frequently did. (What better metaphor for a newly-divorced woman's freedom? Especially in a plane called a Super Cat.) And, to prove that Hutchins was no stuffy, old-money New Englander, but was in tune with her teenage daughters, she had a cartoon by Marty Links – the artist who drew 'Bobby Sox' and 'Emmy Lou' – installed in her husband's office.

But despite the aloof toughness her upbringing had given her, Hutchins is an example of a creative woman overshadowed – temporarily at least – by a dominant, alpha male. In 1921 she had married Robert

Maynard Hutchins, who was to become the youngest dean of Yale Law School and then the youngest president of the University of Chicago. He was called Golden Boy even at the time. Maude already had a moderately successful career as an artist and sculptor and was a rather glamorous figure: beautiful and striking, she was almost as tall as him. They were a golden couple and were compared to Scott and Zelda Fitzgerald; later they might have been compared to JFK and Jackie: it was at one time assumed that Robert Hutchins would either end up in the Supreme Court or running for president, though in fact he did neither, partly at least because of the 'trouble' he had with his wife.

In a memoir about Robert Hutchins, his former colleague Milton Mayer called Maude the 'multifariously talented daughter of the editor of the *New York Sun*,' and said of her that, 'her schooling was fashionable and her artistic talents were encouraged. She meant to have her own career – not her husband's – and she had it. If he was shy, or stand-offish, she was genuinely aloof. She wasn't meant to be a schoolteacher's wife. (Perhaps she wasn't meant to be anyone's wife.)'

In a story published long after their divorce, 'The Man Next Door,' published in her story collection *The Elevator*, 1962, Hutchins writes a description of a man who seems to be a dead ringer for her ex-husband; it is by no means an unkind or unflattering portrait.

> I am a country girl born and bred but my husband lives and thinks in a tiny city that he carries around inside his head. His handsome skull encloses very tall buildings and subways and elevators, and the buildings and subways and elevators are full of tiny cell-like people, each with his franchise, his exemption and his problem. My husband is emperor, prince, chancellor, and his influence is like the handwriting on the wall.

In another story, 'Innocents', in *Love is a Pie*, 1952, a collection of stories and playlets, Hutchins describes the relationship of a nameless couple that might possibly be a portrait of herself and Bob.

> His outbursts of anger against her, which she feared, but which she preserved her strength for and which she made every effort to meet with the community, failing always, with the only 'conclusions' he ever made. She was always fresh and he was always fatigued because it was

her idea, not his; she was the artist. Unrequited love only comes to those who want it and even then it is not simple.

Artistic, creative, off-beat Maude never fit into her husband's stuffy social milieu, and caused him endless headaches. To 'keep Maude quiet' and keep her busy, 'poor old Bob' encouraged his wealthy friends to commission sculpted heads and busts from her – for enormous fees which many of his friends seriously resented – but this was never enough. Maude scandalously paid undergraduates from her husband's university, male and female, to model nude for her. She also produced family Christmas cards based on her own mildly erotic drawings that were sent to faculty and trustees; as one friend of Bob's said about them in a memoir:

On at least one occasion with the nude figure of a going-on nubile girl holding a Christmas candle – the model was sensationally reported around town and gown to be the Hutchinses' fourteen-year-old daughter Franja.

It was even rumoured that Maude was having an affair with Bobsy Goodspeed, an old friend of Gertrude Stein's partner Alice Toklas (which might explain the sub-Steinian text of *Diagrammatics*); she was President of the Arts Club of Chicago and wife of Charls, a trustee and the son of the founder of Chicago University while Bob was the university's president. Two friends of the Goodspeeds and the Hutchins – three-time Pulitzer winner Thornton Wilder and the historian Bernard Faÿ – mention meeting Bobsy and Maude and their families in Chicago in their letters to Stein, Faÿ stating as a fact in 1934 that the two women were lovers.

In the end, Bob got tired of keeping Maude quiet; after twenty-seven years of marriage, he left her in 1948 and she divorced him. He never spoke to her again. To make things worse, within a year he had married his secretary; worse still, she was called Vesta – for a wife to be left for a secretary twenty years younger and apparently considerably shorter than herself is one thing but if the other woman is called Vesta the horror is unimaginable. Maude moved with her two younger daughters to the backwaters of Southport, Connecticut and stayed there, never remarrying and never – at least publicly – having any other serious relationship with a man; despite their differences, Bob must have been a tough act for any man to follow. And Maude didn't need to work: Bob, whose salary was $25,000 a year, paid her $18,000.

Still, Maude was something of an alpha female herself, and thrived as an independent woman: she soon got her pilot's licence, as we have seen. Being left without a husband also seems to have encouraged Maude to write novels rather than concentrating on her visual art. She published nine novels between 1948 – the year of her divorce, so she must have been writing this while she was still married – and 1967, plus two collections of her short stories, many of which had been published in leading magazines and printed in anthologies, including *New Directions*. None of them are the kind of thing that the wife – even the ex-wife – of a highly respected member of Chicago society would be expected to produce, and she probably delighted in that fact.

Robert Hutchins published around twenty books of educational and political theory from 1936, when he was thirty-seven, to 1972, but Maude Hutchins was forty-nine when her first novel was published, sixty in 1959 when *Victorine* was released and sixty-eight when her final novel was published. It is not of course unheard of, nor indeed anything to be ashamed of, for a mature woman to write about adolescent female sexuality: Marguerite Duras was seventy when she wrote *The Lover*; Violette Leduc was sixty-three when *Mad in Pursuit* appeared, the autobiographical novel in which as an older woman she masturbates while writing about herself as a younger woman masturbating while writing about her adolescent sexual experience. And that most patrician of New Englanders, Edith Wharton, was in her seventies when she wrote a highly explicit scene of father/daughter incest called *Palmato*, though she never published it. But older women writing about sex makes middle-aged, male critics squirm; as we shall see, Hutchins suffered at their hands for daring to suggest that the mature woman – indeed any woman – might have lascivious thoughts.

The *New York Times* said of her: 'the sensuous is her window on the world; sexuality is the sea for all her voyages'. Unlike Nin, most critics saw the sexual rather than the sensual; there was far too much sex in Hutchins' novels for many people. At this time of course, censorship was still very much the norm: Hutchins' second novel, *A Diary of Love* was nearly prosecuted for obscenity; even the title seems designed to upset the prurient. Other risqué titles – in the prudish atmosphere of 1950s America at least – included *Love is a Pie, Honey on the Moon, Blood on* the Doves, Victorine and The Memoirs of Maisie, all of which sound like they ought to be Victorian pornography.

Some of Hutchins' novels were in fact republished in sleazy, pulp-fiction covers: A Diary of Love was issued in at least three different pulp covers, all of which had above the title the teaser: 'the sexual awakening of a teen-age girl.' At the bottom of the book's cover, readers were assured that this was 'complete and unabridged:' it had been previously issued in a censored version. Victorine was reissued as The Hands of Love, with the blurb, 'a strange love transforms a young girl into womanhood,' and Maisie was issued by the Paris-based, erotic-novel specialist Olympia Press with the quote 'the shockeroo of the literary season;' the cover featured a woman in bed who looked like she might be a prostitute in the saloon of a Western movie.

'Poor Bob' must have felt each of these as an arrow in the back; her family were probably not amused either. Maude could have used a pseudonym, but where would have been the fun in that. These trashy covers and blurbs are entirely misleading and readers would have been seriously disappointed. It is not obvious whether Hutchins approved the lurid covers for these reprints of her books – as we saw in the section on lesbian pulp novels, authors at that time had little to no control over titles and covers – though Maxwell Geismar implies that she would not have:

Mrs Hutchins would resent, I know, any description of her work as 'erotic.' The curious thing about her writing, so remarkably open about all forms of personal behaviour, was the prevailing tone of candor. If nothing human was foreign to her, everything human was a constant source of delight, of pleasure and gaiety.

When her book was banned by those sagacious guardians of the public morals, the Chicago police, Mrs Hutchins was quite naturally bewildered. 'I can assure you that I have no desire to shock, disrupt the morals or undermine the conventions of the general public,' she wrote at the time. 'My defence for A Diary of Love is that having written it, I published it; and that I would not willingly withdraw any of it. My intention was purely artistic, and the subject matter innocence.'

The police were finally routed in Chicago; but in England eight thousand copies of this book were ordered to be burned by a local magistrate... Maud Hutchins' 'innocence,' as in the present volume, is highly sophisticated, sometimes ribald and always entertaining. It is really a devilish kind of innocence.

Still, as I said above, some of Hutchins' books are still in the list of the prestigious literary house New Directions with far more sober covers, though *A Diary of Love* has a very slightly naughty line drawing by Hutchins and *Love is a Pie* still has its original 1952 Andy Warhol line drawing of a woman as a cover. Surely no twentieth-century writer except Nabokov has been represented by such a range of cover art. *Victorine* has even been reissued recently as a New York Review of Books Classic, part of an eclectic list that ranges from Balzac to Leonora Carrington, and includes Colette's *The Pure and the Impure*. Hutchins is now becoming part of the American literary canon and moving slowly out of the ghetto of sex-obsessed writers, where she had been closeted, but the critics of the time were generally not kind to her, variously accusing her of being too experimental/literary on the one hand and of being too raunchy on the other. A review of the short story collection *Love is a Pie* in the *Saturday Review*, for January 3, 1953 took the former line.

> The stories, written in a prolix and often impenetrable prose, have the self-conscious literary stamp of the little magazines which first published several of them... For a book devoted to the tender human emotion, *Love is a Pie* seems curiously aloof and unemotional. It consists largely of strained and wearisome cerebral exercises.

Nine years later, a review of *Honey on the Moon* in the same magazine for February 29, 1964, slung at her the second kind of criticism.

> According to all traditional criteria, the book is almost a complete failure. It has no core of moral significance; it takes place in no recognisable social context; most of the characters never come alive, and 90 percent of Mrs Hutchins's dialogue could never have been spoken by a human being.
>
> But, although she never distinguishes between love and lovemaking, Hutchins writes about pure, animal sex with a genuine lyrical passion unmatched by any other contemporary American woman. And the blurry, schizoid interior monologues are almost as good – and hard to read – as those in *Tender Is the Night*.

If you are willing to endure a banal, pointless novel just for a few first-rate passages of good old you-know-what and a brief close-up of a personality tearing itself apart, you will like *Honey on the Moon*.

Even as late as 1964, the year after sexual intercourse had begun for Philip Larkin, critic Stanley Kaufmann was advising the then-sixty-five-year-old Hutchins to grow up and stop being so obsessed with sex; male critics have always tended to treat female novelists like naughty children – perhaps Hutchins was old enough to be his mother, and perhaps that was his problem with her. (Male novelists, of course, never grow up and are allowed, even expected, to hang on to their obsession with sex their whole life.)

> Many novelists pass through such a period, but there comes a time when 'then they went to bed' suffices; or when the bed is to society what war was to von Clausewitz, a continuation of politics by other means. To remain as interested in sex as Colette was all her life long, and as Mrs Hutchins continues to be, requires an almost monastic single-mindedness.

To be compared with Colette may be considered no insult: Anaïs Nin certainly meant it as a compliment; Colette wrote a series of novels that show the coming of age of her heroine Claudine, begun in 1900 with *Claudine at School*. Hutchins and Colette are probably the best exemplars of Nin's ideal of an author who can write erotically without having any – or at least not very much – actual sex in her work. *The Memoirs of Maisie* is a good example: despite the lurid picture on the cover the pulp edition, which misleadingly shows a woman lying seductively on a bed in her underwear and despite the 'shockeroo' quote in the blurb, Maisie is in fact a grandmother on the verge of dementia, surrounded by her daughters and granddaughters (men are rarely at the centre of Hutchins' novels and here they are pushed way out to the periphery). Maisie does however have reveries of her younger, passionate self, apparently masturbating, almost like an older Molly Bloom.

> The old lady was incapable now of blushing for the girl who blushed that night in her maiden's bed for the bold little slut she had been in the afternoon in her father's woods with her handsome groom. But

253

the pleasure of his wild embraces when he finally succumbed to her blandishments and teasing, his seeking hands, his hot mouth and flaming eyes, his dense brown locks that smelled of the stables, and hard thighs, the little Maisie could not censor but only wanted again and lay awake living it over until the swallows in the ivy announced it was daylight, and her newly aroused passion, unused to the energy it took, the calories it burned, sent her into a deep short nap.

Maisie's eldest daughter Bessie had died at sixteen, without ever coming of age, and still a virgin despite everything.

Bessie, affectionate, naughty, impudent and sensuous, at sixteen had soberly passed away of meningitis, unaided by science, which was sleeping, but tenderly administered to by an old doctor with a colorful variety of pills and an occasional mustard plaster. Her precocious soft body that had already burned under the caresses of her brothers and her cousins and had so tempted every male that visited the house, was taken away to the dusty cemetery on the hill dressed in a modest jumper, its sweetness lost, its virginity intact, its desires stifled under a handful of earth.

The nearest *Maisie* gets to a sex scene is written very erotically, but no actual sex happens – because of the man's temporary impotence. Colin and Sissy are both married, but not to each other; she agrees to meet him.

'Sissy.'
'Colin.'
He knew better than to wait a split second. The pomegranate that had gleamed on a limb too high for him to reach, shivered and fell away from its meager branch and fell into his outstretched hands. The sensualist, the carpet knight, the crapulous, held in his arms the woman he had not dared even dream of possessing and, lazy, had not planned to seduce. He moved his big hands over her responsive body gently, so gently, as if she might break, and waited for her to lift up her mouth... He felt his knees as weak as water and it was Sissy whose loins supported his. The moment, that was after all a moment only, disengaged itself from time and stood still. Neither spoke, neither ad-

vanced or retreated, the intimate pose of love looked like a white statue in the park, a bent and tender head, a raised and rapturous face.

Colin returns to his wife, knowing that he 'had been fooled. He felt as if
he had been lifted out of a magician's hat by the ears and exposed to ridicule, wet and slinky, pink-eyed rabbit.'

Some of the short stories collected in Hutchins' *The Elevator* also
contain wonderful examples of erotic but sex-free writing. This passage
could almost be by Anaïs Nin herself, with its focus on a woman's mirror
image of herself about to come of age; it is from the story 'Tonight My
Love is Coming', which perhaps did not at that time carry the *double entendre* it does today. Or perhaps it did. It is from *The Elevator and Other
Stories*.

It grew dark and I stood perfectly still, the moon came in the window
and touched me but I did not acknowledge it. I saw the reflection of
myself in the big mirror at the end of the room, I seemed a long way
off. I moved. I saw the girl in the mirror likewise move. The girl put
her hand up to her hair and pushed it aside and so did I. The girl's
white dress shimmered in the moonlight. Soon I would be standing
naked in this same spot and in the mirror I would see the man come
up behind me still in the shadows. He would never come out of the
shadows, the moon would not shine on his naked body. I could not
imagine his naked body and so I compelled him to stand there close to
me but unseen. The moon dropped like a comet, it went down into the
chimney of the big barn, the girl in the mirror disappeared. The stars
that were following the moon were too pale, too far away, to come in
the window and sit in the hair of the girl who had gone away out of the
mirror.

I too left and went downstairs.

Hutchins can even make a description of a bride's bouquet at her wedding crackle with an erotic charge. This is from 'The Wedding,' also in
The Elevator.

The bride looked at the bouquet and saw that it was beginning to
droop. One of the topaz roses turned brown, Violette began to shrink
and a pink carnation trembled as if in a convulsion. A number of pet-

255

als detached themselves and floated aimlessly in the still air and a
hatch of yellow pollen, riding some tiny updraft, shone like powdered
gold. She felt the stems grow feverish and then cold. A pair of stamens
detached themselves and floated downward, a pistil was bathed in
perspiration, and the Shasta daisies, as if they were guillotined, lost
their heads. She felt what remained of the bouquet struggling to be
free of her hands, the flowers were delirious and the pulses in her own
wrists began to beat like drums.

In *The Future of the Novel,* Nin points out perceptively that Hutchins
tends to centre her works around and see the world through the eyes of
young people, especially adolescent girls, who are set against their awful
parents while we see them coming of age.

Some of her parents resemble the parents of Cocteau's *Les parents
terrible.* It is the adolescents in her book who carry the burden of
clairvoyance. They see, they know. It is not a battle between innocence and evil but between awareness and hypocrisy. Her adults are
hypocritical. The novels are requests for truth, and this truth is usually uttered by those at the beginning of their lives. The work is unique,
rich, animated by a sprightly intelligence and verve.

GEORGIANA LORD: *GEORGIANA,* 1948

Maude Hutchins' first published novel is a strange affair: the first and
third parts are in a kind of modernist, stream of consciousness third person that Virginia Woolf would have recognised and is even slightly reminiscent of early Gertrude Stein, whose 'Melanctha' in *Three Lives,* 1909,
is a kind of coming of age story . Like Jane Eyre and like Hutchins herself, Georgiana is an orphan brought up by relatives.

Georgiana dreamed at night of falling into the waterless pond and as
she fell, no longer safe but suddenly fearless in the sense of 'What's
the use,' saying clearly last apart audibly as she awakened 'Is that all?'
and each time this happened it seemed an effort to find herself in bed
again and it an imperative thing to get up, brush your teeth, and face a

256

milky, tasteless egg for breakfast after such an important, climactic, sacrificial decision about life and death it was not these dreams alone that made her unafraid to die in later life, there were other things as well, but it was a sub-early-conscious knowledge which made her sweetly and courageously precocious but not arrogant, on the contrary sympathetic, if a little contemptuous of others.

Georgiana sustained an image, sought something or someone here and there, gave the impression oddly enough of fickleness, steadfast as she was. The fact that she was an orphan, brought up with cousins, aunts, great aunts, grandparents and even her one sister blue-eyed, anglo-saxon, with only the hearsay much-beloved in her imagination father as dark-eyed as herself, and with a reputation as wicked as she felt her own to be making him twice loved, added, I feel sure, to her lack of attachment, at least for any length of time, to anyone. As all these places and things are forming this girl as if they were food and drink for her body's growth; all these stable smells, divine barns, lanky dog-attractions, leaping, pawing horses, waterless ponds, kitchen palaver and 'drawing room regulations; so the boy cousins her future antagonists and lovers; the small, erect, blue-eyed, arrogant grandparent fight for possession as the prototype of her profoundest love against the hearsay picture but closer blood-bond and incestuous drive of her dead father; these little men will trouble her in the future differently incarnated but recognisable; frightening.

Rather than anything in Virginia Woolf or Anaïs Nin, this in a way resembles Joyce's *Ulysses*, which, among many other things, contains a kind of coming of age story of Gerty MacDowell.

For Gerty had her dreams that no-one knew of. She loved to read poetry and when she got a keepsake from Bertha Supple of that lovely confession album with the coralpink cover to write her thoughts in she laid it in the drawer of her toilettable which, though it did not err on the side of luxury, was scrupulously neat and clean. It was there she kept her girlish treasure trove, the tortoiseshell combs, her child of Mary badge, the whiterose scent, the eyebrowleine, her alabaster pouncetbox and the ribbons to change when her things came home from the wash and there were some beautiful thoughts written in it in violet ink that she bought in Hely's of Dame Street for she felt that she too could write poetry if she could only express herself like that poem that appealed to her so deeply that she had copied out of the newspaper she found one evening round the potherbs.

It is not clear to us what is the status of the narrator in *Georgiana*: she (or he) does not have the detached, authorial voice of Jane Austen or any of the English female novelists we have been looking at, but neither does she seem to be a character in the story; she is more the knowing, ironic narrator of later post-modernist fiction. The narrator has not up to now given us any description of Georgiana. 'About now, at least by now, the reader, if he has not already formed in his mind a nostalgic or literary picture of our heroine, must be demanding one.' But then she does not exactly give us one. 'The difficulty in describing Georgiana however is the feeling of loss when Georgiana went away, left you, said good night, was more like having your leg cut off, your glasses taken away, or a dream lobster changed into rose-quartz.' And this is all we have. We do know that Georgiana is very innocent as regards sexual matters: when their maid has a baby Georgiana has no idea where it came from or how it was created; 'the only evil and therefore guilt that a child knows is that which is, in various guises, sex – am I right?' But Georgiana at this age knows nothing about sex, and thoughts of it do not enter her mind; her thoughts about the gypsies who have moved nearby are 'pictorial rather than sensational and at least consciously she was not aware of any sexual impulse. The continued consciousness was more like a rogue story, picaresque, appealing to the adventurous, than a substitute of any more obvious kind.'

Part two of the novel consists of extracts from Georgiana's adolescent journal, which the narrator gives us and then invites us to ignore; this is a nice irony: this is the coming of age novel in which the narrator informs us that adolescence is of no interest.

Several years have passed. Our heroine is thirteen and I give you part of her journal. I am amazed at its objectivity until I remember that she had from the beginning a literary ability (a way of talking to herself) as well as the power of observation. That is all you will find here but it is not important that the reader pry into the life of an adolescent, because, as I have said elsewhere, it is of no consequence. Unless you find the journal amusing you may skip it.

The narrator is of course right, and the diary is deliberately uninteresting, consisting almost entirely of trivial gossip about girls at school of whom we are not told anything; unlike most of the adolescent diaries we have seen so far, this is not a teenage girl having a conversation with her other self, her future self, her confidante. Here Georgiana merely records day by day what is happening, which is not very much and into which she does not read any significance. She seems to have no awareness of the world around her, nor of her own maturing. Georgiana certainly appears to have no sexual awareness or longings of any kind, surrounded though she is by adolescent girls in her girls-only boarding school. 'Fredericka gives me a hug, keeps her arms around me as the music stops. "No wonder the boys love you. You are so thin at the waist." Her eyes are shining and she's pretty. She is sixteen. I don't know what she means. There are no boys.' There is page after page of this and the reader begins to wonder whether it might have been wise to skip it after all.

Eventually the narrator takes over again but now Georgiana is older and the narration passes over her coming of age as if it were a trivial thing, of no great importance.

And so this long quotation has taken your mind off the girl I am writing about. In her journal she has told you nothing of herself; something about others. She simply seems to have been there. No one saw anything odd in a girl who seemed to be having fun and was; but it was a kind of neuter fun, an excitement of almost a literary kind... Please note that she did not enter into the passionate bisexual adolescent love of her companions. That love life seems to be mostly confusion, a compelling sporadic interest in both sexes and all ages: little boys, old men, schoolteachers, contemporaries; as if the body hadn't decided yet what it was going to be: male or female; whether it was young or old; mythologically uncertain, Hermaphroditic this strange love life keeps the adolescent continuously attached to this and that, incontinent; an absurd polygamy, unable to concentrate on the Great Books that concentrating on something, learning to pay attention, perhaps. It is not important. Neither was Georgiana's slightly offside growing-up important. It is true she walked straight through it thinking of something else, a little scared by the confusion around her but not very, a little curious about what was going on but not enough to ask questions. She kept her head. Only her walking straight through it as if she were taking the 7:45 in the Grand Central Station was characteristic and besides, her successful, if unconscious, avoidance of sex.... The interim of her adolescence is over; not so difficult for her as for most because she didn't notice it; and now, in her maturity, she will return to her childhood. It will be a continued story, as it were. She will behave in her grown-up life as she was surely conditioned to behave in her childhood, and if there was such an idiom as *raison de faire* that is what I would have called this fatalistic story of Georgiana.

NOEL: A DIARY OF LOVE, 1953

Maud Hutchins first came into prominence – brilliant writer, painter, sculptor that she is – with *A Diary of Love*, in 1953. This was a charming story of a young girl's coming of age, told with a kind of eighteenth century aristocratic, or agrarian, frankness of tone, filled with a delicate sensuality which was at once touching and witty – which was on the side of the pagan gods, as I said once, and written with the pen of a mischievous angel. The book is still, and is likely to remain, a minor classic, which, now that we have been able to digest the erotic writings of DH Lawrence and Henry Miller without apparent harm to our moral sensibility, should have its own revival.

Maxwell Geismar.

Not everyone in 1953 thought *A Diary of Love* was charming; not everyone had in fact digested the erotic writings of DH Lawrence and Henry Miller, which were then still widely banned. The precocious central character, Noel (she has no last name) is completely unlike her naive predecessor Georgiana. The Chicago police tried to ban the novel; the very title must have been designed – whatever the author or publisher said later – to attract the attention of the authorities and it did. Capt Harry Fuller, who was the Chicago police censor – many sophisticated Chicagoites were shocked just to find out that there was such a post – said it was 'so candidly filthy in parts as to constitute a menace to public morals.' The ban elicited much local outrage, principally because it was arbitrary and had not been imposed by a court or decided by a jury. The protests included a printed and widely distributed open letter to the mayor of Chicago by the Chicago Civil Liberties committee, part of which was gleefully printed at the front of the pulp paperback edition, which was subtitled *The Sexual Awakening of a Teen-Age Girl*. 'Censors are notoriously behind the times. Let average jurors, who reflect average public morals, judge books, dramas and movies.' This edition also published Hutchins' rather disingenuous rebuttal of the accusations of sexual exploitation:

> I can assure you that I have no desire to shock, disrupt the morals or undermine the conventions of the general public. My defence for *A Diary of Love* is that having written it, I published it; and that I will not willingly withdraw any of it. My intention was purely artistic, and the subject matter innocence.

Early on in *Diary of Love* there is a sly little authorial aside about censorship, as if Hutchins was in fact well aware in advance of the reaction the book would provoke. The children have been studying Macauley's *History of England*, but Noel feels it has been 'extensively blue-penciled.' She wonders 'if all history has not been similarly censored into a kind of bedtime story so that we may sleep without dreaming.' Noel, like her author, doesn't like censorship: when a neighbour's baby is born, her aunt tells Noel that the stork has been. 'I am inspired with anger, the stork for gosh sakes! There it is again! That degrading censorship!'

Although innocence is hardly the subject matter, *A Diary of Love* is a true coming of age story, a proper female *bildungsroman*, unlike the earlier *Georgiana*, but like the later *Victorine*. Like the eponymous Georgiana and Victorine, Noel is a young teenager (she does not tell us her age) for whom everything is new and exotic. Like Georgiana and like many of the girls in English novels, she lives in a sheltered, almost claustrophobic world in an aloof, tightly knit, eccentric, New England family. Also like some of her English counterparts, Noel does not even go to school, she is tutored at home with family friend Dominick and Eugenie, the gardener's daughter. Noel, again like Georgiana and like Hutchins herself, does not seem to have a mother or father; she lives with her grandfather and her 'maiden' aunt, who apparently had one chance at love when she was younger, but he was put off by her independence, her 'unfeminine' intellect and outspokenness: 'I was wittier than he, I frightened him.' Perhaps Maude might have said the same about Bob.

> We all recognise a tragedy when we see one, even a small one, and Aunt had said something profound besides, something almost basic about the sexes. And so she had indeed, if you wanted to think about it, raised her skirts. Hadn't she regretted her virginity? Didn't she say in a sentence, 'if I had my life to live over again I would sleep with him and keep my mouth shut?'
>
> If I am speaking harshly of a delicate matter it is because I am angry that Aunt should know the facts of life better than I do and that those facts are so simple, without poetry. As Henny once said when CK Ogden started a fashion for Basic English, 'I've always used basic English,' he said, 'the facts of life can be stated in four letter words; what's new about it? All the other words in the language were invented to conceal the fact... It's getting harder and harder to find out where the toilet is and if a woman will sleep with you.'

This was written in 1953 but could well have been said yesterday by a man complaining about political correctness. Of course, Hutchins herself never used any four letter words nor indeed any explicit references to the sexual, not to mention the lavatorial. As we have seen, her writing is implicit rather than explicit, it is sensuous and erotic even when sex is not being described. We saw earlier how she could make even a bride's bouquet seem erotic; here is what she makes of Noel eating raspberries. Even today this might make a Chicago police captain blush, especially if he had a teenage daughter of his own. It might even have made Humbert Humbert himself blush: Noel is the classic nymphet, even though this was published two years before the word first appeared in *Lolita*.

> It is like the smell of perfume in my mouth. I want more of this but not too fast, a little variety: I pull ten more, lovely and plum colored, away from the small penis-like excrescence of each and the naked immodesty of the little scene settles in my brain. Already, thinking ahead about something else, I carry out my sensuous plan of a moment ago, losing a little of the pleasure. I trundle the ten in my tongue, covering it up at the edges, and then I slowly raise the lovely load to the vault, the red vault, and crush them softly, all of us the

same color, the same, even the fog is pink . . . It is a kind of sweet disintegration, a lack of tension: no bones. But what about this curious identification with genitalia? I feel the pressure of blood (is it the juice of the raspberries?) enter up into my throat, my ears; the soft tenuous fog, the smoky, loving mist outlines gently the uncovered parts of my body with a mild pressure, making me whole again; and I want to undress and feel how sweet it would be all over; compassionately moulded, how I would fit into this pink fog!

Noel eating grapes is hardly less sensuous. 'I pluck out one grape at a time and gently, suavissima, force the grape out of its skin into my mouth, suck the sweetest part from the skin at last and toss it away.' It is interesting to compare Hutchins' sensuous, erotic use of fruit to Keats' language in *The Eve of St Agnes*.

And still she slept an azure-lidded sleep,
In blanched linen, smooth, and lavender'd,
While he forth from the closet brought a heap
Of candied apple, quince, and plum, and gourd;
With jellies soother than the creamy curd,
And lucent syrops, tinct with cinnamon;
Manna and dates, in argosy transferr'd
From Fez; and spiced dainties, every one,
From silken Samarcand to cedar'd Lebanon.

These passages even bear comparison with the *Song of Solomon*:

Let him kiss me with the kisses of his mouth: for thy love is better
than wine.
Because of the savour of thy good ointments thy name is as ointment
poured forth, therefore do the virgins love thee.
I am the rose of Sharon, and the lily of the valleys. . .
While the king sitteth at his table, my spikenard sendeth forth the
smell thereof.
A bundle of myrrh is my wellbeloved unto me; he shall lie all night betwixt my breasts.
My beloved is unto me as a cluster of camphire in the vineyards of Engedi. . .

As the lily among thorns, so is my love among the daughters.

As the apple tree among the trees of the wood, so is my beloved among the sons.

I sat down under his shadow with great delight, and his fruit was sweet to my taste.

How many writers can be compared to Colette, Nabokov, Keats and the King James Bible?

Noel's first actual experience of actual sexual activity, though only as a voyeur, comes when she stumbles upon Frieda (the Swedish maid) and Brady (her grandfather's young music pupil) in the Playhouse.

Brady's beautiful young face had a stricken look as he faced her; his eyes were closed so tightly he did not see me at all. They were the same height and they were clasped and yet not clasped together. Brady's hands gripped her slight, strong shoulders and she was speaking so soothingly, but with a deep undertone of compassion, in a thrilling contralto like someone singing, and she was saying, 'it will not hurt, it does not hurt, sweet little love, there, my darling, isn't it wonderful? It does not hurt does it? This is the way.' I stepped back in fear from this terrible loneness, this complete unawareness of others, this loss of orientation that love gave them, this almost bravado, this fearless temerity of lovers.

It was the first time I had witnessed the act of love. The variety that Frieda gave it, guiding him as she did with her into a secret microcosm did not detract from the perfect mystical beauty of the whole scene and at the same time it gave me a terrific impulse for action. I felt desire. All the diffuse sensations I had had became one specific pain, as if a powerful astringent had been poured over my body.

Almost all the girls in *Girls in Bloom*, on finding out about the facts of life (or whatever version of them their school friend or older sister gives her) are either horrified or disappointed. Noel is inspired. 'I am waiting for love. It is all around, disguised it is true as this and that, but I feel it and I too love. But what? Not *what*, but *whom!*' She realises that she has to 'love some *one*.' Love must be directed towards a person, 'this love without content no longer anaesthetizes me. From raspberries (soft roses) to Frieda and Brady was quite a leap. My education seems elementary, very, to me. (Elemental?) Where is my love? And who?' Noel talks to Frieda about what she has seen (though her snobbish aunt tells her not to 'fraternize with the servants. It only confuses them'): Frieda puts her hands on Noel's breasts and, 'breathing a little hard, slid her cheek down mine. "Baby, let him do it," she said in a low, tense voice, "let him, it won't hurt."'

The only 'some *one*' she is interested in is Dominick. 'Dominick Vanderdock is interesting: he is carnal, lascivious, sensual, saucy, but he is, also, in a kind of opposition to these characteristics without cancelling them: bookish, scholarly, almost erudite, indolent, innocent.' One night, as she is lying in bed awake, Dominick enters:

'Noel?'
I lay still.
'Noel?'
I did not stir. I felt him lean over and stare at my eyelids.
'Noel?' he whispered.
He turned down the sheet and waited. I did not move. He carefully, gently, undid me completely and looked at me. In the half light I felt my body shine, he saw all of me, only my eyes were dark. Then I sensed, chillingly, hesitance, a listening: I opened my eyes and looked and he was listening, his head turned to one side. (What was that!) Stillness, so complete that it was frightening. Dominick was as still, as motionless, as a rabbit that a dog smells but cannot see.

What happened was: I could not stand it forever: Dominick motionless and unidentified like that, like one of the Marys on an empty tomb, and I pretended to sigh in my sleep. I moaned and turned on my side, still absolutely naked. Dominick quickly and dexterously covered me to the chin but he did not go away; with his hands he molded the sheet to my body.

'Wake up, Noel, I am making a statue of you,' and he did not miss an inch of me; his fingers went into my armpits, gently separated and rounded my knees, designed my thighs that were tense, expectant; they went up close, so close, between my legs, into the two halves of me, behind.

Noel gets TB and spends three years in a sanitarium; her diary is very sketchy throughout this period. Eventually Mr Vanderdock collects her. He says she must have been bored after all that time.

> I thought of the stimuli that I have tried to describe, of love and lust in a sanitarium, of vendetta and trauma, principles based on whimsical notions, fantasy and credo; I thought of morphine, burning mesquite, valerian, Vichy water, oxide of zinc and assafoetida; of opium, digitalis, belladonna and quinine; I thought of cadmium yellow, alizarine red, cobalt blue and rose madder, jumping cacti, inverted nipples; I saw the glittering urine in the bottle that the nurse clutched as she came running just too late to save the old bank president from sudden death, and I smiled.

After she gets back from the sanitarium, Noel reconnects with Dominick, though at first she hardly recognises him. She asks what he is going to do when he grows up. 'Dominick stared at me a long time thoughtfully. "I am going to translate Baudelaire's translation of Poe," he said quietly but I felt his hands tremble on my body.' Neither of them has ever been to a formal school, and it is decided that Noel should not go to college, but both of them read voraciously, especially in the realms of history and literature. They challenge each other mentally, crossing intellectual swords, keeping each other as sharp as blades.

> No one, not even Dominick and I, quite realised that my education has been going on for a long time as he and I, like Héloïse and Abelard, defend our theses, in the study, on the pond, in the swamp and in the groves, orchards, and footpaths and overgrown gardens, feeding on the minds of poets and philosophers almost to excess but saved, Dominick from impotence and me from frigidity by our own burning *motif*.

Their engagement to each other 'is as taken for granted as I took Dominick's proposal and he my silent acceptance. No special kiss sealed any excessive promise and no trousseau is being prepared for me, no plans being laid.' In fact, there is no wedding, but the two leave on a kind of honeymoon anyway. On the train she sleeps in Dominick's arms, 'warm and dark, a dozen times last night hoping each time to wake up sooner so that I could do it again.'

We are analogous, twins, the Gemini. Dominick, who has loved me ever since I can remember, who undressed me when I was six and taught me all he knew not much later, did not think, I felt, that the night was long enough.

Perhaps Hutchins did indeed see herself as Héloïse and perhaps, when she first met him, her husband did seem like Abelard to her; perhaps at first Maude and Bob did joust intellectually. But Abelard of course ended up being castrated.

VICTORINE L'HOMMEDIEU: *VICTORINE*, 1959, REPUBLISHED AS *THE HANDS OF LOVE*, 1960

The New York Review of Books Classics series website describes its recent republication of *Victorine* thus:

Victorine is thirteen, and she can't get the unwanted surprise of her newly sexual body, in all its polymorphous and perverse insistence, out of her mind: it is a trap lying in wait for her at every turn (and nowhere, for some reason, more than in church). Meanwhile, Victorine's older brother Costello is struggling to hold his own against the overbearing, mean-spirited, utterly ghastly Hector L'Hommedieu, a paterfamilias who collects and discards mistresses with scheming abandon even as Allison, his wife, drifts through life in a narcotic daze.

And Maude Hutchins's *Victorine*? It's a sly, shocking, one-of-a-kind novel that explores sex and society with wayward and unabashedly weird inspiration, a drive-by snapshot of the great abject American family in its suburban haunts by a literary maverick whose work looks forward to – and sometimes outstrips – David Lynch's *Blue Velvet* and the contemporary paintings of Lisa Yuskavage and John Currin.

This is from a respected and serious publisher but it is hardly less salacious than the pulp-fiction reissue cover blurbs; it is inaccurate and illit-
erate – Victorine is twelve rather than thirteen at the start of the book
and the father is called Homer rather than Hector – hardly befitting a
Classic book reissue. And it is really hard to see any connection between
Victorine and *Blue Velvet*. The blurb on the back of the earlier, 1960 pulp
reissue, retitled *The Hands of Love*, is even more salacious.

> A young girl, on the threshold of womanhood, is consumed by her
> rapidly weakening desire for love. Many are ready to initiate her into
> the ways of sex . . .
> . . . her brother Costello, teased by her beauty and scarred by an abor-
> tive encounter with his father's mistress.
> . . . Lydia, a too-wise adolescent, whose rejection by Costello prompts
> her to seduce his sister.
> . . . Joe, frustrated by his frail wife.
> . . . and finally, Fool Fred, the outcast, discovers how to satisfy Victo-
> rine – if he dares.
> THE HANDS OF LOVE is a fascinating novel about a highly sensitised
> young nymph – too innocent to fully understand her desires, to
> undeserved to tame them.

The eponymous Victorine L'Hommedieu (which, if it means anything,
means 'The Man of God') is twelve and looks much like her mother had at
sixteen: 'a dreamy intensity about her, a withdrawal in her eyes, a sensuous, almost teasing, curved to her mouth.'

She has a pompous and ridiculous father named Homer (pre-
Simpsons of course), who never 'looked into himself or asked questions
about why things happened,' a practically invisible mother Allison, 'who
kept the pretty chintz-covered chaise-longue warm, was a woman of vi-
sions but, one might say no vision. To reality she was blind.' Allison had
lived with Homer for twenty years, 'and didn't know anything about him
at all.' For Victorine, 'Allison was beyond her, too beautiful to touch, too
good to be true; Homer? She felt no carnal interest in him, no curious
incestuous drag, he neither irritated her nerves nor gave her confidence
or any sweet security at all.'

Victorine has a sixteen-year-old brother called Costello and a much
younger, almost baby, brother called Dennis who, like his older brother

has 'inherited his father's tools and even at his age seemed proud of his appendages, and did not hesitate to exhibit himself to the family and friends.' She also has an imaginary (boy)friend called Misael and some real, outsider friends with whom she has taboo, erotic – but never sexual – relationships: there is no sex in this book, but, like Noel's in *A Diary of Love*, Victorine's consciousness is filtered through Hutchins' erotic prism. The first paragraph starts:

> Victorine felt a lovely thrill in her very bones, a sweet taste in her mouth and along the edges of her teeth, and her thighs felt soft and warm and pneumatic to the touch of her palms, even through her gloves, as she walked to church alone.

The only 'person' with whom she can share her feelings is Misael, 'the make-believe boy who had shared her sorrows and divided her joys since she had first found out that it was impossible to live alone amongst savages and Indians and paper dolls and adults, and holding onto his hand that she really felt, warm and smooth around, she turned her face towards him and kissed him, "Misael."' Coming home from church, Victorine goes into the kitchen, where the maid Elsie is preparing a meal. She is fascinated and horrified by the 'thick scarlet steak that leaned against a hatchet-shaped knife and draped itself over the edges of a bloody board ("Take, eat, this is my Body").' She goes up to her room feeling 'a terrible hunger that nothing could satisfy.' (Note here another *double entendre* on the verb to come.)

> Victorine looked at herself in the mirror, her dark eyes were hot, the lobes of her ears were pink as coral, but her smooth heart-shaped face was pale as Elsie had said, as white as a sheet. At the base of her throat she could see her pulse beating, slower now, but hard and even
> . . .
> 'Victorine!'
> Suddenly she opened her legs and placed her hand between them; through her gingham dress she felt the heat of desire without subject-matter, the swelling of her virgin mount. She smiled with surprise as if she had come upon something that had been lost for a long time. She gave herself a little slap and felt a stinging pleasure that sent the colour at last into her cheeks.

'Victorine!'
'Yes, Mother,' her voice was husky.
'Luncheon, dear, do come.'
'I am.'

Victorine has a complex relationship with her older brother Costello: 'she had loved him dearly, almost to idolatry – perhaps the only real person she would ever love.' His relationship with her is complex too: his 'sister's beauty teased him. He longed to find her weakness and put his finger on it.' (Yet more *double entendres*.) When they were younger they had played at wrestling. 'How she had fought back! And then how suddenly she had become limp in his arms, her eyes darkening, her wet mouth shining and he would let go of her, frightened.'

Costello felt a terrible longing for his sister that he could not help, that he did not even know was desire; taking a hold of one of her fingers, he bent it at the first knuckle hard and slow until his sister moaned in pain.

'Say uncle,' he whispered, and it was as if he had asked her to repeat a dirty word. He was pressing her thighs with his knees. His beauty was the beauty of a faun, his expression of lust suited him. 'it,' he insisted.

'Oooh,' moaned Victorine, 'please!'

'Say it, say it.' He pressed harder. His lips parted over even white teeth, a little silvery saliva formed at the side of his mouth.

Victorine sank to her knees; it was as if she were surrendering her virginity. 'Uncle,' she said and her tone was caressing, sweet as honey, and the little conqueror felt as if he had possessed her. He let her go and went off on his bike, the bell tingling, the dry leaves crackling.

Now that Costello is 'mostly away at school or in camp something had happened to their queer relationship and it was queerer than ever. The mystery of his sister deepened. It hampered his growing up.' He wonders: 'Does she know about *it* yet?' She doesn't; she hasn't yet come of age.

But Victorine had not forgotten all the fun and the excitement, she just, being woman, all of a sudden knew better, was that it? How did she know that the time had come for them to separate? It is hard to say, but like a pretty genie she changed herself into a little cloud and evaded him. Might he not have, if she hadn't, passionate as she was, slept in her bed at night, his mouth on hers, his legs supporting her loins, her chest, still flat and smooth as his, fitted to his own and their hands clasped, wouldn't it have been incest, the sweetest of all; and their punishment, what would it have been?

But despite their encroaching maturity, the childish, or rather childlike, brother and sister wrestling bouts continue, this time involving Lydia, a tomboy friend of Victorine who likes Costello, though not vice versa. This next long scene, full of eroticism, is written in the rhythms and steamy language of pornography, though nothing at all 'happens'. Everything is innocent but not, as the childhood playfulness teeters on the edge of adult sexuality.

'Let's tickle him!' she cried. 'Vicky, come on, you hold him.'
    Costello got lazily to his feet and stood with a slight slouch, his feet apart, and waited. He liked Lydia well enough. She was fun, but she was not woman; she had no niche in his hall of dreams, she was just that tomboy, Lydia Van Zandt... Soon the three of them lay struggling and laughing on the sofa as they had often before, Lydia, mad with excitement, pressed herself against Costello's legs, her head digging into his ribs. Victorine was straddling Lydia and with one hand grasped a fistful of her brother's hair. She drove her pointed chin into Costello's chest. Costello tried to hold onto them both and at the same time retaliate; freeing one hand he grabbed Lydia's shirt at the neck and tore it down the front. Lydia raised her head and bit his neck, and Victorine, suddenly free of Lydia, wrapped her long legs around one of her brother's and the two girls, almost dying of laughter and the excitement of promiscuous bodily contact, entangled with each other and the boy, hardly knew or cared whose arms and legs were whose. The wild attacks and counter-attacks were like violent caresses and they fought for breath to laugh with, and each untangle herself, to be preciously entangled again. Costello's elbow jabbed Lydia's soft breasts and she screamed, but it turned into a laugh and a gasp, and she tore open his shirt and fitted her fist into his armpit. Victorine felt her brother's round thigh flexing and unflexing between her legs and he,

271

succeeding in freeing himself of Lydia's octopus -like grasp for a second, forced Victorine's legs apart and closing his hand on her, he shoved her away from him along her back, but she quickly jumped his neck and ran her tongue into his ear, which felt so pleasant he threw back his head and laughed and tried to do the same thing to her, whereupon Lydia took hold of his other thigh, as Victorine had, and sliding down it she let go with her hands and hit the floor. 'Oh!'

'Cut it out!' yelled Costello, dodging up and away from both of them. As they struggled to their feet for more of the same he held each at arm's length, one palm flat between each pair of half-formed breasts; Lydia's shirt, nearly torn off, exposed her and his hand was on her their skin. She longed to hug his legs again and ducked; she fell to her knees; pinioning him, she hung with her loins to his hard leg like a leech to a blood-vessel.

'I'm pooped,' said Victorine and sat down on the sofa.

Said of course like a child. Costello does not seem to 'notice the sensual let-go in Lydia's face, or see the woman in her steady smile.' The three of them, all on the verge of coming of age, 'children, who were growing up, each at a different rate, and each a little behind his and her body, precocious, only chemically, one might say, rearranged the furniture and separated in silence.' Watching Lydia ride away on her bike is Costello.

Unconsciously, hands in pockets, he fondled himself. But he did not connect, I think, his body's responsiveness to the girl's mad caresses with any need for love or women. He certainly did not want to sleep with the little hoyden, Lydia, and his fraternal, even if sensual, love for his sister did not much trouble him.

Note here the narrator's postmodern 'I think,' and the lovely archaic word 'hoyden', meaning 'a boisterous girl,' a word from old Dutch which predates the word tomboy and might well have been current in the Phelps family, perhaps even to describe Maude herself. When Lydia and Victorine are alone they start to talk about having babies and other girl/woman-ish things.

They heard the front door close, Costello had gone out. Lydia looked straight at Victorine, who was praying to God that she would leave

(Dear God, make Lydia go away), and said, 'Did you ever do it to your-self?'

'Lydia!' whispered Victorine.

'What of it!' said Lydia, but her face turned rosy pink and she ran downstairs, marbles and jacks and lipstick jingling in her jeans, and outside, slamming the door behind her, leaving Victorine as if trying to balance herself over an abyss.

Victorine and Costello's father, Homer, has a mistress, Millie, who is also his wife's dressmaker. They first had an affair twenty years earlier, when he was about to be married and she was a great prize, the 'village queen.' They have recently taken up with each other again.

For a moment Homer saw naked plump blonde girl lying on his bed, on the side table under the lamp a big box of chocolates, and himself awkwardly pulling on his trousers. 'Aren't you even going to say good-bye,' she had said, choosing a big nougat. Even now, after twenty years, a little of the pride, if none of the passion, returned, and his having so easily slept with the village queen... Homer had seduced the prettiest girl in the village although she preferred Tony Hyde and was engaged to an electrician, and for ten years she had generously taken care of his, what are called, needs.

Within a week of the first seduction, Homer is 'back in Millie's room where the completion of the act that made such regular demands on him did not make him feel bad afterwards. So for ten years, oddly enough, he had eased his conscience with Millie whom he disliked and Millie put up with what she called his elementary-school lovemaking.'

As for Homer's wife: 'Allison's sex life is anybody's guess and her sin con-jectural. It is certainly no one's business whether Homer's attacks on her body at regular intervals pleased or displeased her.'

Now, twenty years after the beginning of her affair with his father, Millie tries to seduce the beautiful young sixteen-year-old Costello; she fails but helps him with his coming of age.

Millie wore something soft and pink that matched her skin and it was cut low showing of her breasts; and as he looked at them, stunned, drugged as if she had given him a Mickey Finn, she lifted them out and he saw the violet nipples. 'Come on', she said, 'how do you feel?' She gave him a slight push and there was only the bed to sit down on. He had lifted his eyes from her naked torso and he gave her a tentative, moony stair.

'Well?' she said, it irritated her, and her own preparations, her bath, her perfume, her silk pyjamas, the bed, had aroused her sexual appetite and she wanted him to begin. She had forgotten, if she had felt it seriously at all, the desire to get even with Homer. It was desire plain and simple. But her sense of timing was bad, the boy was too stunned to react normally, too much in love to dream of even touching her.

'Dearest,' he said, attempting to regain what already seemed lost.

'Take off your clothes,' she commanded, 'there, in the closet, if you're so shy.'

Costello stood up. He was struggling not to cry. The disillusionment had been too sudden and he couldn't keep up with his feelings. The semi-nude woman on the bed did not look to him like his dream of fair women.

'Goodbye,' he said softly.

One of the adult outsiders Victorine is drawn to is the 'hired man,' Joe, who has a hut rather like Mellors'; she visits it, rather like Lady Chatterley. But Joe is no educated, officer-class Mellors. He is not an adult to Victorine but a fellow child. Joe is probably unique in Hutchins' work: he is a Southern Gothic character and might have walked from a Carson McCullers or Flannery O'Connor story into Victorine's world, which is otherwise more like that of the girls in the gentle, upper-middle-class, home-schooled environment of the English novels we have looked at. The simple-minded Joe likes to line his hut with things that people have thrown out; he is adamant that he does not steal them. Although they are both emotionally children, they have a kind of sexual relationship.

What Joe said was true, the folks *had* thrown the things out, but he didn't believe it because, ignorant though he was and surely lacking a formal education, his reasoning had to find, well, a reason, a reason for the strange and passionate guilt he felt alone in his little ten-cent but priceless temple, and unerringly he invited into it only a child, a sensitive and passionate one, too, Victorine. It was sin at its purest, and basic metal, without adulteration or chicanery or prestidigitation, and to call it mutual masturbation would simply be calling it by another name that smelled sweet, but would not disclose its secret meaning or mystery. To delve too deeply into Victorine and Joe would be to destroy them. Let us say only that they were brother and sister under the skin, fastened together by an understanding that they did not understand and the crime they had not committed.

It is not clear if they have in fact committed that particular crime: Victorine remembers 'the specific thrill, the spot thrill, the sudden let-go tension after her big Sunday, upstairs in her room, her spontaneous find, and for a split second she understood but not really. It evaded her.' But still, something happens: she says to Joe, 'we are abominable sinners,' though he thinks she is referring to the 'stealing they had or had not done.' Despite his limited intellect and low status, Joe is married; he is 'kind to his distempered wife and used her no worse for his pleasure than the next man did his.' Joe does not 'look elsewhere for gratification when her head ached.' So it does not enter Joe's consciousness' to take advantage now of the pretty little girl with long legs and warm skin who stood so close to him. He did not calculate, or make a guess at how simple on this particular Sunday a quick and heaven-sent it would be.' It is not the sexual but 'the childish thrill of secret indulgence that so attracted Victorine to him, his dark brotherhood,' and she feels they have 'sinned together secretly and strangely.' "It's dark now, let's shoot rats."'

The second of the three outsiders Victorine is attracted to – outsiders both in the sense of being outside their fictional society and outside Hutchins' normal range – is another Southern ' though not the love of a woman, and certainly not the love of Victorine whom he sees as 'a quiet nice child, part of the landscape almost.' The following conversation is a bit like that between Sabbath Lily Hawkes and would-be preacher Hazel Motes, also a 'holy bum', in Flannery O'Connors' *Wise Blood*; Victorine is far less seductive than Sabbath Lily but in both cases the 'holy' man resists.

'I can see that you have lost interest,' he continued, 'but the love I so stupidly sacrificed for admiration has nothing whatever to do with sex. Neither do I mean by sex what you mean by sex.'

'I don't know about sex yet,' said Victorine a little primly.

'It is of no consequence what you know or don't know yet,' said the bum, 'you are guilty nevertheless. I saw your guilt when you leaned over the fire with me, I saw it as plainly as if you had lifted your skirt and open your legs, but I chose to ignore the invitation, I am not interested.'

Victorine was astonished.

'You look astonished,' said the bum, 'but you need not feel offended. It isn't that you aren't pretty or desirable but I simply refuse to share another's guilt. If you wish to be evil, be evil alone, sin is not divisible and the responsibility lies with the individual... You look so stupid sitting there with your big eyes, how many times must I say a thing, how many analogies must I make, for you to understand. *I will not sleep with you*, is that clear?'

'I'm not sleepy,' said Victorine...

'She sits quietly and says nothing,' he said.

'Love?' whispered Victorine.

The bum jerked back his head and narrowed his eyes. 'You sit there without breasts and dare to speak of love!' he said; he trembled.

'I . . . ' said Victorine, but the bum lost track of her again.

Without her knowing, the holy bum has instilled in Victorine a 'fear that would never leave her, a sexual fear, the real thing.' His 'passionate pantomime' was something different from the 'make-believe, so comparatively innocent, that had up to now made her feel guilty.' She feels as though her childhood is leaving her, along with Misael, though she has not yet come of age. 'The bum who would be Jesus had acted out by the tracks a sexual charade, a parable too hot to print.' Victorine does not realise that she has 'sat in a private box and watched the opera of sex,' which has 'left its imprint, the print of its heel, one might say and a tiny lesion formed, hardly visible to the naked eye, but one that would cause spiritual adhesions later on.' Victorine may have been watching the opera but the fat lady isn't ready to sing yet.

The third of Victorine's outsider friends – she has obviously never been taught about stranger danger – is Fool Fred, not a fool at all but, like the bum, sharp and philosophical, if decidedly weird; an idiot savant of sorts. He takes her to see a white stallion. 'His long white tail arched out behind him like a colourless rainbow and his big genitals were firm and rosy pink as peaches. It was the most beautiful apparition that Victorine had ever seen and she turned shining eyes on Fool Fred, "Lovely," she whispered when she could speak, "thank you."' Fred tells Victorine he loves her, '"I love *you*," said Victorine.' Fool Fred has an apartment over the garage, where, as in Joe's hut, he can meet Victorine. His rooms are 'thick with books, the shelves reached the ceiling, and they were piled up too in corners and under tables. He saw her looking at them all in amazement, and he said, "many answers are not there, but turning the pages amuses me."' Fred tells Victorine that he too is 'an outcast'. 'You and I are taboo. Perhaps you have been excluded from the house because you are menstruating... They will take you back again, but not I, not me. I am an idiot, and as such, although I am most respected, I am taboo. I am feared.' Victorine says she is not afraid but Fred says that they are both evil, 'because we are sick'.

'I would contaminate the dishes, you know. You must not mind, little one, I am not afraid to touch you, to take you in my arms, come! We cannot contaminate each other.'

Victorine put her arms around his neck and laid her cheek to his. 'I love you,' she said.

'Sweet,' he said in his clear voice, 'sweet and lovely and lonely. At last.'

She drew away a little, 'At last?'

'I have My-Girl,' he said and he smiled so adorably and so happily that Victorine trembled as if she saw, for the first time, a star.

He kissed her longingly and softly on the mouth. He kissed her neck and opened her blouse and looked at her small breasts like half oranges, he caressed her skin with soft fingers and looked at her, and undressed her as if she were a doll. He wrapped her in a Paisley shawl that his mother had given him because it was pretty and he lay her on pillows and stood over her, unable to take his eyes off her. Then he dressed her as gently and deftly as a woman might. He fastened her shoes and kissed her ankles. 'My-Girl,' he said again.

Victorine felt his tender love as if she tasted a cup of hot cocoa after skating, it nourished her. She said nothing, did nothing, but her body, her skin and muscles, responded, and he felt her love under his hands.

'I will come back.' said Victorine.

Again he kissed her, their two wet mouths clung together, their virgin bodies almost talked.

They separated, but he held her hand, he kissed the palm of it, 'You know,' he said seriously, 'little one?'

'I think so,' said Victorine, wondering. She felt that she did and that she didn't.

Later, she 'longed to be wholly taboo, to be linked, wedded, to Fool Fred.' She does go back; he tells her that he is a bastard, as was his father. (Remember how Sabbath Lily thought that being a bastard put her outside normal morality.)

'The children of sinners are abominable children... My father, the bastard,' said Fool Fred, 'slept with many women.'

Victorine was silent.

'I heard it said in the village that his over-indulgence in fornication resulted in idiocy for me. I do not regret it.'

'Fool Fred,' Victorine murmured.

'I have not been circumcised,' said Fool Fred.

'I love you just the same,' said Victorine.

If *Lolita* is *Little Red Riding Hood* told by the wolf, *Victorine* is a tale, not of 'sound and fury, told by an idiot,' though the relationship between Victorine and Fool Fred is a bit like Faulkner's Caddy and Benjy Compson's, but a sweet tale told by her grandma.

SIGOURNEY LOGAN: *HONEY ON THE MOON,* 1964

Sigourney Wagstaff, née Logan is not an adolescent, she is twenty years old when the novel opens and on honeymoon after her wedding to a man twice her age. But she does come of age, suddenly, on that night. Before marriage she had been an innocent country girl – something of hoyden indeed – and, we presume, a virgin, but now she has been brought to the sophisticated city by her sophisticated and experienced husband and become a woman, almost literally overnight, the night of their wedding, when she makes love for the first time. He has insisted on her going to bed naked but afterwards he allows her to put on her 'trousseau night-gown, diaphanous and fawn-colored.'

I slipped on the wisp of a nightie and tiptoed over the soft carpet to the mirror. I had scarlet polish on my toenails for the first time in my life and I admired my pretty narrow feet with five red candy-like shells on each. The nagging desire went away and the euphoria, the kind that follows physical fatigue, came over me. An electrical discharge in the stuff of the gown made it cling in parts to my skin and I plucked it away and looked at myself. Could it be Sigourney, the girl reflected there, Sigourney who had never worn anything but boy's pyjamas before and mismated socks to keep her cold toes warm? I saw a very slim, it is true, girl's body, but it was nicely rounded over the hips and the thighs were curved, the knees small with perceptibly full calves and very slight ankles like an antelope's. The breasts were the prettiest, round as two apples with pink tips the colour of strawberry jam.

Her new husband Derek tells her she looks very sweet, 'like a boy.' She replies, 'you don't like my hair short.' But perhaps Derek does: perhaps it is her boyishness and youth that attracts him. Sigourney soon meets Peter, a rather boyish and effeminate young man about the same age as her and strikingly like her; it has never been clear how Derek met Sigourney nor why he asked her to marry him but perhaps it is because of her resemblance to Peter. '*I* am Peter! It is *I* remind you of Peter! *I* look like Peter, *I* smell like Peter, *I* taste like Peter.' It turns out that Peter has had keys to Derek's New York apartment, where he and Sigourney are having their strange honeymoon. Have Derek and Peter been lovers? Sigourney seems to know very little about his life. She spends more time with Peter than with Derek, who is working and leaving her alone in the big city with nothing to do during the day. She kisses Peter one day and again the next; we already know that Derek has sadistic leanings and Peter seems to be something of a masochist.

I trembled, but I raised my chin for yesterday's kiss. His mouth was cold. I stepped out of his embrace and lifting my hand, I slapped him, the softness of his cheek infuriated me, I slapped him again, hard. Tears came into his brown eyes and into mine as well. I had lost my womanhood, I felt insulted. I raised my hand again but I couldn't bear to touch him. The mark of my slap painted his cheek crimson. He looked very beautiful like an angel.

'Punish me,' he said and he closed his eyes, his long lashes quivered, his lower lip protruded like a sullen child's. 'Punish me,' he said again. 'Call me a little beast.'

'Little beast!' I cried before I could stop myself.

'Strike me,' he said.

I wanted to say a dirty word... But I couldn't, I was neither child nor woman, all I could think of as a countdown was: He's crazy. And then I said, 'You little fairy!' I was astounded that I said it. Had I said it out loud? What did it mean?

Sigourney is 'neither child nor woman' now; perhaps she is closer to the boy that perhaps Derek prefers: he sometimes wants her to turn over before he can have sex with her, as if he cannot bear to see the proof that she is female and so she can be a boy in his mind. 'For Christ's sake turn over... or cover yourself up.' But later there are hints – Hutchins never reveals the truth – in the rather Tennessee Williams-like finale (*Suddenly Last Summer* comes to mind, with Sigourney as Catharine, and Derek as Sebastian) that Derek may be Peter's father and the 'other woman', Marie, who seems to be an old lover, and older possibly than Derek himself, may be his mother. There are gatherings of obviously homosexual men in the apartment and Marie mentions incest.

Either way, these experiences and all of these other people seem to drain Sigourney of her identity – she has lost her old one but not gained a new one, she has not come of age at all in fact and is in a kind of limbo. She seems to lose her mind slightly, starts referring to herself in the third person as 'the girl.' It starts when she notices that all the mail that comes to the apartment is addressed to him or to Occupant, but never to her, as if she doesn't exist; as was the case with married women then, she is now Mrs Derek Logan. 'I have lost my identity. Derek had taken away the girl's identity. Arson! Manslaughter! Rape!' Derek has a gun and Sigourney fantasises about shooting him when he is especially cold to her. One time after a row he slaps her then walks out of the apartment and slams the door on her; she screams at him.

If he had heard her, he would have killed her but the girl got the gun first. Click! In my face the door closed.

The girl, Sigourney looked at her in the mirror, her face was flushed, her eyes like wet stones, her hair hung over her eyes like tall grasses over the pond. Pretty, someone said.

CLARISSA: THE UNBELIEVERS DOWNSTAIRS, 1967

Anaïs Nin had said that Maude Hutchins' novels mostly set young women in opposition to their parents, but in some of her novels, including this, her last published novel, *The Unbelievers Downstairs*, the narrator Clarissa (she has no surname; Clarissa was the name of Hutchins' youngest daughter, born in 1942, presumably not named after Richardson's heroine) does not have parents, only grandparents, an aunt and an uncle. She is Hutchins' youngest female character, as the real Clarissa was her youngest daughter. She is no adolescent but a very precocious and pretentious eight-year-old who speaks French to her doctor and calls the servants bog-Irish, a less evil version of Shirley Jackson's Fancy O'Halloran. 'My teacher says I have a vocabulary of eighty-five hundred words which is unusual at my age.' Clarissa claims to be invisible – she means this literally; the unbelievers of the title are her family – though, like many children she also means it metaphorically in the sense that no one takes any notice of her.

She also points out there are no photographs of her, though later she finds photographs that may be of her mother, from which Clarissa appears to have been cut out. Clarissa has never seen her mother and does not even know her name (it turns out to be Isabella); she, and therefore we, do not know what happened to her mother, but it turns out that Clarissa is illegitimate, so the mother may have been sent away in disgrace to give birth. 'Some unseen hand had cut out the baby so you could see or *not see*, so carefully what it had cut away, the tiny turned up nose against the lady's breast and two little outstretched hands, you could count the fingers that weren't there.' This is what Clarissa has been looking for: 'It is my mother and me, me invisible! That is the explanation of everything. At last!'

The Irish servant Delia seems to know the story of Clarissa's birth; Clarissa overhears her talking to another servant but she hardly makes things any clearer. 'Better her unfortunate mama, God save us, should never have had her (who, me?), Delia said, the poor Missus a gamma so young and it bein' a sin and all and himself in a ragin' fit (ahh!), an' a good thing the Other (Auntie) could have any. God in His wisdom knows best.' Later Delia says, 'a *bastard*. It would have been better to flush her down the toilet and no harm at all, she'd never know it.'

Like Sabbath Lily Hawkes and Fool Fred, Clarissa believes that she is outside society and her family because of because of her bastardy, even though she – and we – do not really understand the circumstances. Like Frankie Addams, there is no 'we' of Clarissa's 'me.' 'I am alone in the world, a foundling. How sad. The tears streamed down my cheeks. I am a minority of one, I said. I've a good mind to disappear. They think I'm nuts. Maybe I am!'

> There are comings and goings. I am ignored, pushed aside, walked right through, the way I was when I was young and invisible. I am a minor, I don't exist, I am hearsay, I am not a witness, I am nuts, I am drunk; the Unbelievers downstairs are in majority. Perhaps I shall be liquidated.

Clarissa watches – as it were, invisibly – everything that happens in her bizarre family, including various sexual activities that she reports in the way that an eight-year-old would; what little she knows about sex she has learned from overhearing the servants talk. At one point she says to her grandmother: 'I think, I said approvingly, it would be healthier to get my sex information from my family than from the servants.' She certainly does not fully understand about her paedophile uncle, who is arrested for indecent exposure; Clarissa tells us this is impossible: he cannot expose himself since he is invisible; though being invisible too, she did see him out of the window. 'You didn't *feel* him anywhere?' asks her grandfather. 'No, I said, I must have been asleep too much.' Clarissa is very fond of her grandfather, though very confused about his relationship to her.

> I thought of how attractive grandfather really was and how I might marry him someday and comfort him and cure him. My relationship with him is very confusing. I am illegitimate which means my invisi-

ble mother is a virgin and I am fatherless. If I am fatherless, of course I am grandfatherless. Perhaps I am his sister. Nietzsche loved his sister very much and so did Byron. But they didn't marry them. I shall have to be content with a *liaison* (French) but then granny would be terribly jealous.

In this next scene the family doctor is 'examining' her aunt, who Clarissa suspects is also becoming invisible.

Marie. (He calls Auntie, Marie?)
    Yes, doctor.
    How are you, little one?
    I have a terrible sore throat, said Auntie feebly.
    Let me see, said the doctor. He pulled the sheet off Auntie to the bottom of the bed. Sit up, he said.
    He took Auntie's nightgown off up over her head and laid it neatly across a chair.
    That's better, he said, quite professionally. Now lie back and tell me all about it.
    He took out a little flashlight and looked into Auntie's throat. I must say I was perfectly amazed to see Auntie stark naked like that with absolutely nothing on, not a single stitch anywhere, and I mean anywhere. I suppose it is perfectly ethical because he is a doctor and she has to disrobe to be examined, like the time they thought I had appendicitis, I was terribly embarrassed, but Auntie only has a sore throat, and with nothing on she is very visible.
    The doctor put the flashlight on the table and sat down on the bed and ran his hand all the way down Auntie's body and then he did it again and up between her thighs. Auntie opened her legs and moaned. It must hurt her.
    Neither of them said anything and I was getting cold so I decided to leave.
    I had not been in bed very long when I heard him coming down the stairs. The examination must be over.

The doctor is not the only one to visit Auntie's room at night: at four o'clock one morning Clarissa is again listening outside Auntie's door.

Oh, please please, I heard Auntie say.

There was silence for a few minutes.

Then I heard the man's voice clear enough and I recognised it at once, Delia's boyfriend, the big enormous man with the red hair, the new hired man, the milkman.

I can't get it up.

Try, set Auntie.

Silence.

I can't.

Oh oh oh.

It's because you're a fine lady, it's no use ma'am.

I heard him coming toward the door. I fled.

Auntie kills herself with an overdose of pills she no doubt got from the doctor, but Clarissa does not believe she is dead, only that she has become invisible. Later, another aunt, Penelope, whom Clarissa has not seen since she was a baby, comes to stay, in Auntie's room. Clarissa tells her that Auntie has become very small and there will be room for both of them in the single bed. Clarissa notices a gun in Penelope's handbag.

What's it for? I asked. I was terribly interested.

To protect my virginity, she said.

You mean like a panty girdle?

I never wear a girdle, she said.

So you have the gun?

Well, not 'and so I have the gun,' I just have the gun. I don't wear a panty girdle and I have a gun, it's two sentences about two different things.

It looks as if I caught it from Granny, I said.

Caught what?

I seem to have said a *non sequitur*. Nevertheless, I went on, ladies used to wear chastity belts and their husbands kept the key.

I don't, she snapped.

Why?

Because I have a gun, she said.

Then I didn't make a *non sequitur*, I said, glad.

Unlike Auntie however, Penelope does not welcome Delia's boyfriend, the milkman, into her room, though she does seem to be expecting a male visitor. Not her husband tjough: Penelope's husband is 'queer', which explains her virginity. Clarissa knocks on her door later that night.

She had on fresh lipstick and blue eyeshadow and a violet chiffon negligee almost as sheer as Auntie's and high-heeled satin slippers.
Après ski? I said in French.
I sleep better in high heels, she said.
I looked at the bedside table and saw two glasses and a pint bottle of brandy...
You expected the milkman?
Of course not, really how absurd, I don't like milk.

Clarissa is too young to come of age in this novel but she does find herself, or at least names herself.

I had a name at last. I wrote it on the kitchen table in tomato juice, on all the doors in Crown, on the sideboard with a pin, on my underwear with indelible ink, on all the mirrors with soap; I wrote it a hundred times in my notebook and in school I wrote *Clarissa* in big letters diagonally across my lesson and themes. I made up notes and poems to make-believe people, signed them *Clarissa* and pushed them under people's doors. I signed about fifty checks in my grandfather's checkbook. I pricked my finger with a needle and traced my name in blood on my handkerchiefs. I longed to get myself tattooed and began saving my pennies and have Clarissa on my stomach in purple and blue. I began asking for an identification bracelet for Christmas and my birthday.
Did you write the editorial in this morning's *Times?* said my grandfather.
Which, I said.
Suppose It Were Con Ed?
No, I said truthfully.
You signed it.
I didn't have time to write it, I said.
Oh.
How about *Stocks Chalk Up Another Record Session?*

I shook my head.

It was a very well-written account, he said. Would you advise me to sell my Union Carbide?

I wouldn't advise it, I said.

By the very end of the novel, Clarissa has stopped writing her name everywhere; she feels like a real, visible person at last.

I don't need to be tattooed any more anyway, I said, I have established my identity. Je m'appelle . . .

Clarissa! yelled Granddaddy

POST ADOLESCENCE

Maude Hutchins' novels about teenage girls carried on to the mid-1960s but they were already something of an anachronism. The teen-ager, the bobby-soxer, the Sub-Deb all belonged to an earlier, more innocent age – America had not had its innocence destroyed in quite the same way as Europe by the Second World War but by the 1960s its innocence was fading too: America itself was coming of age and its teenagers becoming more cynical, were growing up faster than before and didn't want to become like their parents. Girls especially didn't want to become housewives like their mothers, despite the modern, labour-saving household devices still advertised alluringly in *Ladies Home Journal*. As late as July 1959, Richard Nixon, in the famous 'Kitchen Debate' with Russian President Nikita Khrushchev had been bragging about how the latest technology in American kitchens made the American housewife the envy of the world, not to mention the role model for American teenage girls.

> Nixon: I want to show you this kitchen. It is like those of our houses in California. [Nixon points to dishwasher.]
> Khrushchev: We have such things.
> Nixon: This is our newest model. This is the kind which is built in thousands of units for direct installations in the houses. In America, we like to make life easier for women...
> Khrushchev: Your capitalistic attitude toward women does not occur under Communism.
> Nixon: I think that this attitude towards women is universal. What we want to do, is make life more easy for our housewives...

But this smug self-satisfaction, this feeling of the superiority of American family values, was rapidly fading. The cosy image of the American family, watching innocuous TV shows about other cosy American families together in the evenings was breaking down. And some of those innocuous family TV shows had run their course: *Father Knows Best* ran from 1954 to 1960, *Leave It to Beaver* from 1957 to 1963 and *Ozzie and Harriet* from 1952 to 1966. As the Cold War and the Vietnam War both escalated, America's warm, cosy vision of itself had started to falter: the Bay of Pigs fiasco of 1961 showed the limits of America's power overseas and the Cuban missile crisis following it in 1962 made everyone afraid that the world was going to end; Bob Dylan's *Blowing in the Wind* and *Hard Rain's Gonna Fall* popularised fears about nuclear holocaust and teenagers began to think that perhaps there was no future, that they might not even live to come of age.

By 1963, American involvement in Vietnam was staring to emerge. In January *Life* magazine had the cover story 'We Wade Deeper Into Jungle War;' more than 12,000 American troops were already stationed in Vietnam but no one could adequately explain what they were doing there. On May 11, 1963 bombs in Birmingham, Alabama targeted at black leaders caused race riots; on Sunday, September 15 a Baptist Church in Birmingham was bombed by Ku Klux Klan members, killing four young girls. Then on November 22 President Kennedy was assassinated and the age of innocence in America was really over.

1963 was a coming of age year in the UK too, but in a completely different way. The death knell of the age of deference, which had begun its rapid decline in 1960 with the *Lady Chatterley* trial, was sounded by the satirical and irreverent television programme *That Was the Week That Was* which mercilessly mocked formerly taboo subjects. The Great Train Robbery made folk heroes of the daring robbers who showed no respect for authority and stole the unimaginable sum of £2.6m from the Royal Mail. The Profumo affair and the naming of Kim Philby as the 'Third Man' in the Burgess and Maclean spy ring revealed the moral and sexual corruption at the heart of the British upper class and the political establishment; for teenagers of the time, the people who were supposed to be their betters turned out to be no better at all. And in 1963 the Beatles reached number one in the singles chart for the first time, leading the first wave of a revolution in popular music that accompanied the new sexual revolution. The generation of classless, sexually-liberated teenage girls of the time had come of age into a radically new age and had no intention of becoming like their mothers, preferring to drive around in Minis wearing miniskirts; in 1963, Mary Quant, inventor of the miniskirt, was named Woman of the Year. English poet Philip Larkin described it perfectly in 'Annus Mirabilis':

Sexual intercourse began
In nineteen sixty-three
(which was rather late for me) –

Between the end of the 'Chatterley' ban
And the Beatles' first LP.

Up to then there'd only been
A sort of bargaining,
A wrangle for the ring,
A shame that started at sixteen
And spread to everything.

Then all at once the quarrel sank:
Everyone felt the same,
And every life became
A brilliant breaking of the bank,
A quite unlosable game.

So life was never better than
In nineteen sixty-three
(Though just too late for me) –
Between the end of the 'Chatterley' ban
And the Beatles' first LP.

In 1963, Betty Friedan's *The Feminine Mystique* was published and became the best-selling non-fiction book of 1964 in America; based on interviews Friedan conducted in the 1950s it showed the emptiness of the
American girl's consumerist dream of coming of age as a modern housewife with all the latest appliances – the very dream portrayed in the ads
surrounding the *Sub-Deb* column in their mother's *Ladies Home Journal*. Friedan showed how the leisure the appliances Nixon boasted about
simply led to alienation.

The problem lay buried, unspoken, for many years in the minds of
American women. It was a strange stirring, a sense of dissatisfaction,
a yearning that women suffered in the middle of the twentieth century
in the United States. Each suburban wife struggled with it alone. As
she made the beds, shopped for groceries, matched slipcover material,
ate peanut butter sandwiches with her children, chauffeured Cub
Scouts and Brownies, lay beside her husband at night – she was afraid
to ask even of herself the silent question – 'Is this all?'

Friedan noted that this problem had been identified even earlier in both the academic world and the popular press. *Newsweek*, March 7, 1960 ran an article about the unfulfilled American housewife. 'She is dissatisfied with a lot that women of other lands can only dream of. Her discontent is deep, pervasive, and impervious to the superficial remedies which are offered at every hand.' Some people blamed women's education, which was supposed to have made them unsuited to be housewives. *The New York Times* for June 28, 1960 said: 'Many young women – certainly not all – whose education plunged them into a world of ideas feel stifled in their homes. They find their routine lives out of joint with their training. Like shut-ins, they feel left out.' Friedan argued that some female writers and editors were exacerbating the problem by glorifying the role of housewife, specifically singling out Shirley Jackson, not as a bad writer but as a good one who should be a better role model for girls coming of age than what Friedan calls the 'Housewife Writer.'

> Coupled with the women editors who sold themselves their own bill of goods, a new breed of women writers began to write about themselves as if they were 'just housewives,' reveling in a comic
> world of children's pranks and eccentric washing machines and Parents' Night at the PTA. 'After making the bed of a twelve-year-old boy week after week, climbing Mount Everest would seem a
> laughable anticlimax,' writes Shirley Jackson (*McCall's*, April
> 1956). When Shirley Jackson, who all her adult life has been an extremely capable writer, pursuing a craft far more demanding than bedmaking, and Jean Kerr, who is a playwright, and Phyllis
> McGinley, who is a poet, picture themselves as housewives, they may or may not overlook the housekeeper or maid who really makes the beds. But they implicitly deny the vision, and the satisfying hard work involved in their stories, poems, and plays. They deny the lives they lead, not as housewives, but as individuals.

English novelist Elizabeth Taylor was also what Friedan would call a Housewife Writer. She said that she had given up writing when the children were born but had learned to write 'while answering questions, settling quarrels and cooking dinners. I write slowly and without enjoyment, and think it all out while I am doing the ironing.' She obviously had a very similar experience to Jackson, whose son Laurence said in a 2016 interview: 'She was always writing, or thinking about writing, and she did all the shopping and cooking, too. The meals were always on time'.

A completely different kind of 1950s Housewife Writer was the closet lesbian with husband and children, like 'Anne Bannon' (Anne Weldy), author of *Odd Girl Out* which we looked at, and other lesbian pulp novels. In an interview she talked about how, after World War II, 'the country had made a frightening turn and embraced the most conservative and traditional roles. All the girls were supposed to be home having babies and making soup and casseroles.' In the introduction to a much later reprint of her novels Bannon talks about what it was like at that time to be both housewife and writer, unable to let all but her closest friends in on her secret and hiding behind a pseudonym. (Shirley Jackson wrote under her maiden name; most of her neighbours and friends knew her simply as Mrs Stanley Hyman, housewife and mother of four children, so there was less need to hide.)

> Why didn't I break out of wedlock? Well, this was 1956. I was twenty-two and while I had a college education, it was ornamental; I had no marketable skills. I was also very much my mother's child. In our family there was a grand tradition of soldiering through in the traditional role, whatever the challenges. My mother had done it and her mother before her. They were both very much alive and I was not going to let them down. This was familiar territory; better the shackles of the known than the terrors of the new and unfathomable.

But by the mid-1960s things had changed enough for Weldy to feel she could pursue a real, academic career. 'I went back to graduate school. I earned a teaching credential, a master's degree, and ultimately, a doctorate. It was an undertaking that consumed a full decade from the mid-60s to the mid-70s.' Despite her criticism of Shirley Jackson and the other Housewife Writers, Friedan quotes interviews with teenagers whose case studies are miniatures of the coming of age novels Jackson wrote so well; this real-life seventeen-year-old girl could almost be Harriet Merriam or Natalie Waite.

> I used to write poetry. The guidance office says I have this creative ability and I should be at the top of the class and have a great future.

But things like that aren't what you need to be popular. The important thing for a girl is to be popular.

Now I go out with boy after boy, and it's such an effort because I'm not myself with them. It makes you feel even more alone. And besides, I'm afraid of where it's going to lead. Pretty soon, all my differences will be smoothed out, and I'll be the kind of girl that could be a housewife.

I don't want to think of growing up. If I had children, I'd want them to stay the same age. If I had to watch them grow up, I'd see myself growing older, and I wouldn't want to. My mother says she can't sleep at night, she's sick with worry over what I might do. When I was little, she wouldn't let me cross the street alone, long after the other kids did. I can't see myself as being married and having children. It's as if I wouldn't have any personality myself. My mother's like a rock that's been smoothed by the waves, like a void. She's put so much into her family that there's nothing left, and she resents us because she doesn't get enough in return. But sometimes it seems like there's nothing there. My mother doesn't serve any purpose except cleaning the house. She isn't happy, and she doesn't make my father happy...

Lately, I look into the mirror, and I'm so afraid I'm going to look like my mother. It frightens me, to catch myself being like her in gestures or speech or anything. I'm not like her in so many ways, but if I'm like her in this one way, perhaps I'll turn out like my mother after all. And that terrifies me.

In the same year as *The Feminine Mystique*, 1963, the cosy image of the American 1950s family received another body blow when Michael Leigh published *The Velvet Underground* – from which Andy Warhol's house band got their name – a study of sexual shenanigans in American suburbia, including reports of widespread orgies and wife-swapping among the 'respectable' middle-class. According to Leigh, for many suburban housewives the answer to 'is this all?' was, 'not by a long way'. The back cover blurb read:

'Come to the party – and bring your wife!' . . . An innocent-sounding invitation in any man's language. Except when 'party' spells 'sex orgy' – and 'bring the wife' means she's to be swapped for someone else for the night. Does this really happen?

It does.

The entertainment varies. From a heap of car keys a wife chooses a key – and its owner. Or blindfolded husbands just grab any wife who happens to be handy. And no one need worry, ever, about running out of parties. After all, it's a favorite parlor game – played all over America.

In literature the age of innocent adolescence was also coming to an end in the late 1950s. In the UK, the polite novel and play of manners was being replaced by a new breed of kitchen sink novel and drama where amoral, affectless young women with no parents or with bad parents moved through a world of casual sex in seedy flats with no thought for the future and fully intending to not end up like their mothers: *A Taste of Honey* by Shelagh Delaney, 1958, *The L-Shaped Room* by Lynne Reid Banks, 1960, which became the 1962 film and *Up the Junction* by Nell Dunn, 1962, which also became a film as well as a TV play. *Bonjour Tristesse* (*Hello Sadness*) by Françoise Sagan, published in French in 1954 when the author was only eighteen, was a bestseller in its English translation by 1955 and very influential – you may remember that even Gidget read it; the English-language film of it was released in 1958. The aimless and amoral seventeen-year-old narrator Cécile rails against the futility of the life of the housewife, a life she never wants to lead, while talking to her surrogate mother, Anne, about her boyfriend's mother.

'You don't realise how pleased with herself she is,' I cried. 'She congratulates herself on the life she has had because she feels she has done her duty and . . .'

'She has fulfilled the duties as a wife and mother, as the saying goes . . .'

'And what about her duty as a whore?' I said. . . 'She got married just as everyone gets married, either because they want to or because it's the done thing. She had a child. Do you know how children come about?'

'I'm probably less well-informed than you,' said Anne sarcastically, 'but I do have some idea.'

'So she brought the child up. She probably spared herself the anguish and upheaval of committing adultery. She has led the life of thousands of other women and she thinks that's something to be proud of, you understand. She found herself in the position of being a young middle-class wife and mother and she did nothing to get out of that situation. She pats herself on the back for *not* having done this or that, rather than for actually having accomplished something.'

'What you're saying doesn't make much sense,' said my father.

'You get lured into it,' I cried. 'Later on you can say to yourself "I've done my duty" but only because you've done nothing at all. If, with her background, she had become a street-walker, then she would have deserved some credit.'

As early as the late 1950s some American female authors had already started to write about post-adolescence, about the woman who has just left college and started work in the big city rather than marrying the boy next door, staying local and becoming a housewife; in some of these books, despite Friedan, the young women are not at all alienated, they are part of a group of similarly educated, working women having The Best of Everything, including sex. The Pill was introduced in America in 1960 and in the UK in 1961, though it was not at first widely available and not officially available at all to unmarried women until 1965 in America, and even then only in twenty-four states. Sexual and social liberation were everywhere: the *Lady Chatterley* trial in England in 1960 had effectively ended censorship in the UK in a triumph for the newly-emerging classlessness of the 1960s: the trial was lost the moment the upper-class barrister asked the all-male jury if this was a book they would want their wife or their servants to read. The trial had only come about because Penguin wanted to republish *Lady Chatterley's Lover* in paperback – it had originally been published in the same year as *The Well of Loneliness*, 1928, but had previously been available mostly in expensive hardbacks which only the upper- and middle-classes could afford and to which the censors often turned a blind eye.

The Best of Everything by Rona Jaffe, 1958, was the first of this new generation of novels about American career girls having it all, followed by Mary McCarthy's *The Group* in 1963 – both were considered shocking in their portrayal of young women enjoying their economic, social and sexual freedom but enough young women recognised themselves, or at least recognised the woman they wanted to be to make them both bestsellers. *The Best of Everything* opens in 1952 with twenty-year-old Caroline Bender coming out of Grand Central Station in New York and heading uptown toward Radio City – an impossibly glamorous and exciting start to the day for most of the adolescents in *Girls in Bloom*, a world away from the suburban housewife they would probably go on to become. Caroline herself might also have become one of those housewives if the wedding had gone ahead.

> Caroline hurried along with the rest of the crowd, hardly noticing anybody, nervous and frightened and slightly elated. It was her first day at the first job she had ever had in her life, and she did not consider herself basically a career girl. Last year, looking ahead to the same day in January, she had thought she would be married. Since she had a fiancé it seemed logical. Now she had no fiancé and no one she was interested in, and the new job was more than an economic convenience, it was an emotional necessity. She wasn't sure that being a secretary in the typing pool could possibly be engrossing, but she was going to have to make it so.

Caroline does make it so, along with a group of other young women in similar situations. Jaffe, like Friedan, had interviewed her friends to see if her life experience was the same as theirs, 'with the men and the jobs and all the things nobody spoke about in polite company.' Her friends talked to her in private but no one was saying these things in public, least of all in literature. Many years later, in the introduction to a reissue of the novel, Jaffe, who kept writing and publishing books on similar themes until 2001, said: 'Back then, people didn't talk about not being a virgin they didn't talk about going out with married men. They didn't talk about abortion. They didn't talk about sexual harassment, which had no name in those days.' Jaffe did.

Scottish author Muriel Spark's *The Prime of Miss Jean Brodie*, which originally appeared in *The New Yorker* and was published as a book in 1961, follows a group of girls in the 1930s as they leave school and start careers. Then in 1963, Spark published *The Girls of Slender Means,* set immediately after the Second World War in a London hostel for the 'Pecuniary Convenience and Social Protection of Ladies of Slender Means below the age of Thirty Years, who are obliged to reside apart from their Families in order to follow an Occupation in London.' During the war, young women had left their families to do jobs that would previously have been done by men and after the war, the shortage of men left a number of young women adrift, not wanting to go back to their families but without much prospect of marriage. On the first floor of the hostel 'lived the very youngest members, girls between the ages of eighteen and twenty who had not long moved out of the cubicles of school dormitories.' Each floor houses a different kind of young woman, and those on the top floor are very modern. These girls are definitely not likely to become like their mothers.

> At the top of the house, on the fourth floor, the most attractive, sophisticated and lively girls had their rooms. They were filled with deeper and deeper social longings of various kinds, as peace-time crept over everyone. Five girls occupied the five top rooms. Three of them had lovers in addition to men-friends with whom they did not sleep but whom they cultivated with a view to marriage.

One of the young women is working in publishing, for a man called George. 'She had achieved some success with the very intellectual author of *The Symbolism of Louisa May Alcott*, which George was now selling very well and fast in certain quarters, since it had a big lesbian theme.' This is a nice piece of irony for us, considering the almost universal worship of *Little Women* and the focus of lesbian coming of age novels in *Girls in Bloom*.

There is no actual sex in Muriel Spark's novels, unlike in *The Group*, which like *Miss Jean Brodie*, follows a group of girls of rather less slender means: educated young women leaving school in the 1930s and refusing to become suburban housewives or emulate their mothers; in the introduction to a much later reissue, Candace Bushnell acknowledged that *The Group* was the inspiration for her newspaper column which was made into the TV series *Sex and the City*. These young Vassar graduates do not let the lack of the Pill stop them enjoying their sexual freedom: one of them is having an affair with a married man; he tells her to get a 'pessary... A female contraceptive, a plug... You get it from a lady doctor.' Nevertheless, then as now, the man has more freedom than the woman, even though she bravely pretends not to be in love with him.

> The happiness in her face caused him to raise an eyebrow and frown. 'I don't love you, you know, Boston,' he said warningly. 'Yes, Dick,' she replied. 'And you must promise me you won't fall in love with me.'

'Yes, Dick, she repeated, more faintly. 'My wife says I'm a bastard, but she still likes me in the hay. You'll have to accept that. If you want that, you can have it.' 'I want it, Dick,' said Dottie in a feeble but staunch voice. Dick shrugged. 'I don't believe you, Boston. But we can give it a try.' A meditative smile appeared on his lips. 'Most women don't take me seriously when I state my terms. Then they get hurt. In the back of their heads, they have a plan to make me fall in love with them. I don't fall in love.'

But not all young working women in big cities were fulfilled by their new-found freedom. Esther Greenwood isn't. She is the woman in the semiautobiographical *The Bell Jar* by Sylvia Plath, published in 1963, the same year as *The Group*, but a completely different kind of novel. Like Caroline Bender, Esther works in New York in publishing, and, like *The Best of Everything* the novel opens with a description of people going to work in the morning in New York, but Caroline is appalled rather than excited by the big city.

New York was bad enough. By nine in the morning the fake, country-wet freshness that somehow seeped in overnight evaporated like the tail end of a sweet dream. Mirage-grey at the bottom of their granite canyons, hot streets wavered in the sun, the car tops sizzled and glittered, and the dry, cindery dust blew into my eyes and down my throat.

Also like Caroline, Esther/Plath has the Best of Everything but does not see it as something to be envied.

I was supposed to be having the time of my life.

I was supposed to be the envy of thousands of other college girls just like me all over America who wanted nothing more than to be tripping about in those same size seven patent leather shoes I'd bought in Bloomingdale's one lunch hour with a black patent leather belt and black patent leather pocket-book to match.

And when my picture came out in the magazine the twelve others were working on – drinking martinis in a skimpy, imitation silver-lamé bodice stuck on to a big, fat cloud of white tulle, on some Star-light Roof, in the company of several anonymous young men with all-

American bone structures hired or loaned for the occasion – everybody would think I must be having a real whirl.

Look what can happen in this country, they say. A girl lives in some out-of-the-way town for nineteen years, so poor she can't afford a magazine, and then she gets a scholarship to college and wins a prize here and a prize there and ends up steering New York like her own private car.

Only I wasn't steering anything, not even myself. I just pumped from my hotel to work and to parties and from parties to my hotel and back to work like a numb trolley-bus. I guess I should have been excited the way most of the other girls were, but I couldn't get myself to react. I felt very still and very empty, the way the eye of a tornado must feel, moving dully along in the middle of the surrounding hullabaloo.

Plath killed herself in 1963, the year *The Bell Jar* was published, at the age of forty-one. Although most of the English novelists we have looked at lived and wrote into a peaceful old age, Shirley Jackson died young in 1965, Carson McCullers died even younger in 1967, Grace Metalious and Flannery O'Connor younger still, both in 1964. The coming of age novel had come of age.

Made in the USA
Las Vegas, NV
19 January 2021

16173161R00164